Regional Sustainability

Contributions to Economics

Christoph M. Schneider
Research and Development Management: From the Soviet Union to Russia
1994. ISBN 3-7908-0757-5

Bernhard Böhm/Lionello F. Punzo (Eds.)
Economic Performance
1994. ISBN 3-7908-0811-3

Lars Olof Persson/Ulf Wiberg
Microregional Fragmentation
1995. ISBN 3-7908-0855-5

Ernesto Felli/Furio C. Rosati/Giovanni Tria (Eds.)
The Service Sector: Productivity and Growth
1995. ISBN 3-7908-0875-X

Giovanni Galizzi/Luciano Venturini (Eds.)
Economics of Innovation: The Case of Food Industry
1996. ISBN 3-7908-0911-X

David T. Johnson
Poverty, Inequality and Social Welfare in Australia
1996. ISBN 3-7908-0942-X

Rongxing Guo
Border-Regional Economics
1996. ISBN 3-7908-0943-8

Oliver Fratzscher
The Political Economy of Trade Integration
1996. ISBN 3-7908-0945-4

Ulrich Landwehr
Industrial Mobility and Public Policy
1996. ISBN 3-7908-0949-7

Arnold Picot/Ekkehard Schlicht (Eds.)
Firms, Markets, and Contracts
1996. Corr. 2nd printing 1997.
ISBN 3-7908-0947-0

Thorsten Wichmann
Agricultural Technical Progress and the Development of a Dual Economy
1997. ISBN 3-7908-0960-8

Ulrich Woitek
Business Cycles
1997. ISBN 3-7908-0997-7

Michael Carlberg
International Economic Growth
1997. ISBN 3-7908-0995-0

Massimo Filippini
Elements of the Swiss Market for Electricity
1997. ISBN 3-7908-0996-9

Frank Hoster/Heinz Welsch/Christoph Böhringer
CO_2 Abatement and Economic Structural Change in the European Internal Market
1997. ISBN 3-7908-1020-7

Christian M. Hafner
Nonlinear Time Series Analysis with Applications to Foreign Exchange Rate Volatility
1997. ISBN 3-7908-1041-X

Sardar M.N. Islam
Mathematical Economics of Multi-Level Optimisation
1998. ISBN 3-7908-1050-9

Sven-Morten Mentzel
Real Exchange Rate Movements
1998. ISBN 3-7908-1081-9

Lei Delsen/Eelke de Jong (Eds.)
The German and Dutch Economies
1998. ISBN 3-7908-1064-9

Mark Weder
Business Cycle Models with Indeterminacy
1998. ISBN 3-7908-1078-9

Tor Rødseth (Ed.)
Models for Multispecies Management
1998. ISBN 3-7908-1001-0

Michael Carlberg
Intertemporal Macroeconomics
1998. ISBN 3-7908-1096-7

Sabine Spangenberg
The Institutionalised Transformation of the East German Economy
1998. ISBN 3-7908-1103-3

continued on page 230

Irene Ring · Bernd Klauer
Frank Wätzold · Bengt Å. Månsson (Eds.)

Regional Sustainability

Applied Ecological Economics Bridging the Gap Between Natural and Social Sciences

With 34 Figures
and 9 Tables

Springer-Verlag Berlin Heidelberg GmbH

Series Editors
Werner A. Müller
Martina Bihn

Editors
Dr. Irene Ring
Dr. Bernd Klauer
Dr. Frank Wätzold

Department of Ecological Economics
and Environmental Sociology
UFZ Centre for Environmental Research Leipzig-Halle
Permoserstr. 15
D-04318 Leipzig, Germany

Dr. Bengt Å. Månsson
Department of Engineering Sciences,
Physics and Mathematics
Karlstad University
S-651 88 Karlstad, Sweden

Cataloging-in-Publication Data applied for
Die Deutsche Bibliothek – CIP-Einheitsaufnahme
Regional sustainability: applied ecological economics bridging the gap between natural and social sciences; with 9 tables / Irene Ring ... (ed.). – Heidelberg; New York: Physica-Verl., 1999
(Contributions to economics)
ISBN 978-3-7908-1233-6 ISBN 978-3-642-58683-5 (eBook)
DOI 10.1007/978-3-642-58683-5

Originally published by Physica-Verlag Heidelberg New York in 1999

Softcover Design: Erich Kirchner, Heidelberg

SPIN 10734758 88/2202-5 4 3 2 1 0 – Printed on acid-free paper

Preface

Founded in 1991, the UFZ Centre for Environmental Research Leipzig-Halle was the first and only research institute in the Hermann von Helmholtz Association of German Research Centres (HGF) to be exclusively dedicated to environmental research. Nowadays environmental research calls for interdisciplinary and applied approaches. At the UFZ, landscape-based research and environmental medicine are combined within interdisciplinary research topics with social sciences and ecological economics.

Economic and sociological environmental research at the UFZ is geared towards the model of sustainable development. Research is currently focused at a local and a regional level. In order to ensure the transferability of regional solutions, work is pursued against the background and in awareness of global ecological interrelations as well as national and international conditions.

In July 1998, the UFZ's Department of Ecological Economics and Environmental Sociology organised an international UFZ Summer School in Leipzig, Germany, dedicated to "Ecological Economics and Regional Sustainability – New Frontiers in Interdisciplinary Research?" Its focus was on the scientific exchange of ideas and experience related to regional sustainable development. The papers concentrated on innovative approaches towards bridging the gap between the natural and the social sciences in applied research projects.

This volume presents the major results of the 1998 UFZ Summer School, its contributions being largely based on interdisciplinary research between the natural and social sciences. Although sadly not all the contributions could be included in this volume, the results reported here reflect the productive environment and the stimulating discussions during the event.

I would like to express my thanks to the Leipzig office of the Friedrich Ebert Foundation and the UFZ for financially supporting the Summer School. The UFZ's Public Relations Department kindly assisted the preparation of the event. I also gratefully acknowledge the support of the Organising Committee of the Summer School, and would like to emphasise the very valuable help of Bernd Klauer and Frank Wätzold in organising the event and supporting the whole publishing process. Core funding for this publication was provided by the UFZ. Kilian Bizer and Bengt Månsson gave constructive advice throughout the editorial process. Birgit Klaus provided valuable assistance to the editorial team in preparing this volume for publication.

Leipzig, April 1999 — Irene Ring

Contents

Introduction

Part 1: Decision making for regional sustainability

Part 2: Modelling as support for policy analysis

Part 3: Evaluating policies for regional sustainability

Outlook

Introduction

Towards regional sustainability: the need for interdisciplinary and applied research

Irene Ring, Bernd Klauer and Frank Wätzold

Department of Ecological Economics and Environmental Sociology,
UFZ Centre for Environmental Research, Permoserstr. 15, D-04318 Leipzig, Germany

1 From global to regional sustainable development

In the face of global and long-term environmental problems, international political organisations such as the World Commission on Environment and Development have put forward the concept of sustainable development (WCED 1987). The origin and political career of this concept as well as debate on how the principles of sustainable development might be defined and put into practice have been the subject of numerous publications[1].

Sustainable development has become a key concept within environmental policy analysis. Compared to the more traditional concept of environmental protection, sustainable development requires new elements and criteria to be considered when environmental policy is formulated and evaluated. A selected number of fundamental characteristics are briefly presented below.

Sustainable development is an intrinsically normative concept addressing the needs of present and future generations. The intention to pursue a sustainable path of development emerges from two essential, ethical decisions: for intergenerational equity between future and present generations and for intragenerational equity with respect to people and localities of the present generation (WCED 1987: 43). Sustainable development calls for an integrative instead of a delimited policy perspective. It represents a goal for overall policy formulation, be it environmental, economic, or social policy. The interrelationship between different policies and the respective institutions needs to be addressed.

Sustainable development also stands for a long-term instead of a short-term policy viewpoint. Sustainability cannot be described as an ideal or fixed state, in terms of a well-defined equilibrium between human beings and nature. Ecological, economic, and social systems constantly change, as do the interrelationships between them, and so there is no definite state of a society which is sustainable at a given point in space and time. Instead, sustainable development represents a co-evolutionary process of change towards a more environmentally sound and socially equitable way of life. Hence the crucial question is: how can we better manage environmental

[1] See Van den Bergh and Van der Straaten (1994) and Klauer (1999) for an overview.

problems while taking both economic and social aspects into account? The aim is to reconcile paths of cultural and economic development with ecological principles of system development, rather than to pursue contemporary societies' path of relying on short-term growth mainly based on the exploitation of non-regenerative resources (Norgaard 1994, Ring 1997).

The integrative character, ideally addressing ethical, ecological, economic, and social questions, makes the concept of sustainable development difficult to grasp. It has given rise to a multitude of studies emanating from a variety of different disciplines and sub-disciplines. As much of this work remains rather abstract, the challenge we face is to express the concept in concrete terms. One important step of implementation consists in reducing its complexity in accordance with the environmental problems to be solved. Here, the spatial or geographical context is an essential parameter.

The concept of sustainable development has developed in the context of global environmental problems. Nevertheless, due to the different cultures, and the varying climatic, physical and biological conditions prevailing on Earth, sustainable development paths too will vary substantially for different regions. Sustainable development involves the proper integration of environmental concerns into policy-making at all levels of decision (Hardy and Lloyd 1994). Therefore, based on the concrete problems in mind, the implementation of the concept has to address all relevant policy levels, ranging from international, national, and regional to local approaches. Problem-solving can require one or more of these levels to be addressed, for there is no clear-cut separation of duties. For example, global issues such as climate change obviously call for activities on a global scale, whereas other action can best be taken at the local and regional level (see *Greiner* in this volume).

Regional sustainable development thus represents an important strategy of operationalising the general concept of sustainable development. Usually, a region's area extends beyond the borders of an individual community or city and stays below the size of a nation state. Although the definition of a particular region often follows political or administrative borders, there are cases where natural or cultural features decide on the region in question. For example, some environmental problems (e.g. transboundary air pollution, water issues requiring catchment area management, or species protection via habitat networks) may transcend administrative borders and therefore can only be reasonably analysed in a transboundary context. Consequently, a region must be defined in the context of the specific problem, and there may be administrative, cultural, ecological or economic reasons for its demarcation.

Regional environmental problems usually require regional strategies and measures to solve them. In these cases, the regional approach is both adequate and obvious. Specifically, all economic activities with a direct spatial link to the environment are relevant to a region's development path. In this context, the primary economic sector is important for it directly interacts with the environment via resource extraction or certain types of land use. The immediate environmental impact of spatially bound activities caused by sectors such as agriculture, forestry and fishery, but also the mining sector, necessitates their consideration in the context of regional sustainable development. In this book, agricultural issues will be intensively discussed (see *Kotchen*, *Kampas* and *White*, *Hellegers*, *Centner* and *Gunter*).

Other sectors relevant for regional sustainable development comprise the utilities and disposal sectors that – like the primary sector – are often spatially connected to a specific region. Water protection in connection with drinking water resources comes under this category, as do sewage treatment and waste disposal. Furthermore, industries and services that meet regular basic needs (e.g. food) can be of special importance for a region's sustainable development path.

2 Sustainability and the challenge of interdisciplinarity

2.1 Improving interdisciplinary environmental research

In the context of sustainable development, the analysis of environmental problems has to take into account ecological, economic and social aspects. This means that no individual discipline can offer a satisfactory solution. Innovative approaches towards bridging the gaps between disciplines are to be developed. The task of integrating knowledge from different disciplines runs counter to the specialisation of science that has occurred in many fields of research. For centuries, the scientific community has increasingly subdivided itself into different disciplines and sub-disciplines, each developing its specific language, theories, methodologies and models. Then again, new disciplines such as biochemistry and biophysics have also emerged as a combination of originally distinct disciplines.

The beginning of environmental research is often associated with the origin and development of ecology as a scientific discipline, founded by Erich Haeckel (1834–1919). Even then it was clear that several fields of knowledge and thus different disciplines must collaborate to develop an adequate understanding of how nature functions (Daschkeit 1998: 51). However, interdisciplinary research into the environment mainly took place within the natural sciences, integrating for example physics, chemistry, biology and the earth sciences.

It is no accident that environmental research is closely connected with a plea for interdisciplinary research. The object of environmental research, i.e. the natural environment of human beings (be it with or without considering human activities) cannot be studied in isolation. Even if environmental research can still be restricted to interdisciplinary research within the natural sciences, sustainability research definitely requires research efforts by both the natural and social sciences. Today, it is widely recognised that:

> "scientific understanding of the physical and biological dimensions of many areas of global change is directly related to an understanding of human activities. Social science data, research, and models will be necessary both to understand the dynamics of natural processes of global environmental change and to deal with the social and economic implications of these changes." (Balstad Miller 1994: 20).

There are several stages of cross-disciplinary co-operation. A first step towards crossing disciplinary limitations consists in choosing research topics that are usually studied by different scientific disciplines. This involves the description and analysis of a new problem to one's own discipline, based on the theories and methodologies with which one is familiar. Innovative results will emerge from the different angle of analysis not previously adopted. The article by *Kneer* (in this volume) belongs to this category by taking a sociological view of the implementation and acceptance of nature conservation policy.

The second, still rather loose form of co-operation represents parallel, multidisciplinary research. Although environmental research of this type already brings researchers from various disciplines together, they work independently, adhering to their traditional theories and methods. 'Integrating' the different results often consists in merely adding them together at the end of the project. This type of research may frequently be dominated by the concerns of one set of scientific disciplines despite drawing on the findings of other fields (Balstad Miller 1994).

A more advanced and third model of cross-disciplinary co-operation is collaborative interdisciplinary research. This involves scientists from distinct scientific traditions starting their co-operation by reconceptualising and jointly defining the research problem. Interdisciplinary research often leads to reconsidering the nature of the problem in order to reach a commonly accepted problem description as a basis for the subsequent project work. Finally, the results of interdisciplinary projects are viewed in the context of results from other disciplines, thus becoming subject to modification (Becker et al. 1997: 42). Therefore, collaborative interdisciplinary research leads to different insights that could not possibly have been reached by individual or disciplinary research efforts. The integrative, discipline-transcending approach of interdisciplinary projects considerably enhances our capacity of understanding the research problem under review, and opens up new perspectives for finding innovative solutions. Many articles in parts 1 and 2 of this book belong to this category. Decisions in the context of sustainable development require a multitude of criteria to be considered that involve intense analysis integrating different disciplinary perspectives.

Furthermore, multi-criteria analysis, an economic tool of decision-making, has to be reconsidered with respect to its ethical foundations if discursive and participative implementation strategies are to be realised (c.f. *Rauschmayer* in this volume). The models that are developed as support for policy analysis draw on both ecological and economic knowledge (c.f. *Frank* and *Ring*, *Schmieman* and *Van Ierland*, *Kotchen*), and come up with conclusions that could not have been found by relying on an individual discipline.

2.2 The economic approach to environmental problems

The natural and engineering sciences as well as law have a long tradition of dealing with at least spatially and locally restricted environmental problems roughly dating back to the 19th century. Contrary to these disciplines, economics got off to a rather late start in addressing environmental problems. It was Arthur Cecil Pigou who laid important foundations for economic research into environmental problems by formulating the theory of externalities (Pigou 1920). At the focus of economic research lies the problem of relative scarcity. Therefore, environmental economics only developed during the 1950s and 1960s when the perception and knowledge of natural resource problems and environmental pollution became more widespread among economists. However, even then, environmental economics adhered to monodisciplinary approaches to environmental problems, trusting in the power of right price signals and markets that would encourage others – engineers, technicians, politicians, etc. – to find adequate solutions. This optimistic attitude among economists is based on their belief in the fundamental substitutability of all non-renewable resources, the regenerative capacity of natural systems, and the success of scientific and technological progress (Faber et al. 1994).

This economic approach to environmental problems underestimates the problem of absolute scarcity, including the risk of contemporary consumers' and producers' choices having a negative effect on future life quality. However, the absolute scarcity of essential goods can only be seriously studied by departing from the actual field of economics. Economists must learn from other scientists about how natural systems function and the limitations of technical solutions, and thus develop a differentiated and more realistic view of environmental problems and how they can be solved.

A pioneer of integrating knowledge of the natural sciences into economic analysis was Nicholas Georgescu-Roegen (1971), his work on energy and resource flow analysis being fundamental to subsequent related economic research. Starting from the entropy law and thermodynamic analysis he drew important lessons for economic processes. One is that the production process necessarily results in an entropy deficit, a reduction of "wealth" in terms of available energy and resources (Harris 1995). Therefore, strict limits concerning resource recycling exist.

In 1989, a new scientific school of thought called ecological economics emerged that systematically considers both economic and ecological knowledge. Realising that economic activities depend on ecological systems, and most ecological processes are affected by economic activities, ecological economics addresses the relationships between ecosystems and economic systems in the broadest sense. Encouraging new ways of thinking about their linkages, ecological economics implies a substantive change in the method of analysis. It includes both traditional economic analysis and ecological studies, and also calls for methodological pluralism as a prerequisite for understanding complex systems behaviour (Norgaard 1989).

Ecological economics implies a new perception of environmental problems: economic research must be based on the properties of the underlying physical and biological systems. Based on the interdependence of ecological and economic systems, the spatial and temporal structure of the joint system evolution, and the relationship between the scale of economic activity and the nature of change in ecological systems are important areas of research (Perrings et al. 1995). The dynamics of the jointly determined systems are characterised by discontinuous change around critical threshold values both for biotic and abiotic resources, and for ecosystem functions. Important characteristics of the non-linearity of system behaviour include path dependency, irreversible processes, far-from-equilibrium behaviour, and uncertainty. At the focus of ecological economic research lie not the properties of a equilibrium state of a system, but the persistence or sustainability of system functions under varying environmental conditions. In other words, ecological economics has been described as the science and management of sustainability (Costanza 1991). It is from this perspective of ecological economics that this book tries to contribute new insights based on the integrated ecological and economic analysis of environmental problems.

3 Implementing regional sustainable strategies

The practical implementation of the sustainability concept has to be seen as the permanent process of rendering a region's development more environmentally friendly and socially equitable. Sustainable development only happens if relevant insights and new findings are translated into concrete actions. A concrete regional context is usually a prerequisite for operationalising the concept of regional sustainability. Therefore, most of the following articles are based on regional case studies and thus represent applied ecological economic research. Furthermore, they predominantly draw on the results of interdisciplinary research projects, thus realising the new approach inherent in ecological economic research that lies in social research considering the underlying physical and biological properties of systems.

The book's structure follows three main research themes: decision-making, modelling as support for policy analysis, and evaluating policies for regional sustainability. Bearing in mind the manifold theoretical and practical approaches to sustainable development, our choice of themes does not claim to be complete. However, we believe that each of them represents an important step towards the realisation of regional sustainability. In the following, the various research themes and contributing articles are briefly presented to give an overview of the book's contents.

3.1 Decision-making for regional sustainability

What should we do in order to attain regional sustainability? At the very centre of this question lies a problem of decision-making: Which alternative is most useful for realising the aim of sustainability? How should we decide on the alternatives?

Conventional economic analysis usually assumes (explicitly or implicitly) a very simple procedure of decision-making. Let us consider an example (c.f. Faber, Jöst, Manstetten 1995: 235-236): How should the "optimal" use of the regional renewable resource groundwater be determined? Answering this question requires knowledge of all the essential factors concerning nature and society which are relevant to both the present and future:

1. Geologists and hydrologists ascertain the amount of groundwater newly formed and what pollutants threaten its quality. Soil scientists investigate the transport of the pollutants from the surface to the groundwater, while both ecologists and medical researchers determine the critical loads and levels for groundwater pollution.
2. Engineers point out what techniques are available for agriculture and other land uses, and what technologies are able to reduce negative impacts on the groundwater in the future.
3. This will enable scientists and economists to evaluate the impacts of different land use options on the groundwater.
4. On the basis of this information, politicians and administrators decide on the groundwater protection targets and on the instruments to enforce them (e.g. groundwater protection zones, emission limits, or certification). They perform a rational decision calculus, during the course of which it is assumed that all alternative actions and all possible impacts of the decisions are known, and that they are able to assign probabilities to each possible outcome. Using the decision calculus they can determine the limits for the emissions of pollutants and the restrictions of land uses.
5. Within both these limits and the corresponding regulative framework, the economic agents can decide on their individual plans – a step which involves taking responsibility for future generations.

It is very likely that the path to sustainability outlined here will fail since it ignores several important aspects, e.g.:

- The complexity of ecological and economic systems is only partly known. We do not know for instance all the services groundwater renders us, nor how to value them.
- The politicians' and administrators' decisions must be accepted by society. It is not enough for certain laws to be passed; they must also be obeyed by individuals.

The examples demonstrate that conventional economic analysis does not satisfactorily cope with the problem of uncertainty and social acceptance. The papers in the first part of the book tackle the crucial question: How can we improve decision-making under uncertainty? They take into account that multiple criteria are necessary to assess the non-commensurability of alternative outcomes and that there are different interest groups which influence political decisions and acceptance in society. The acceptance of decisions can be increased if the stakeholders are integrated into the decision-making process. The integration of stakeholders and the struggle for a decision acceptable to all leads to an understanding of decision-making as a process.

The first article by *Rauschmayer* focuses on the ethical foundations of decision making. The central concern of ethics is to do good and to leave aside the bad. Rauschmayer addresses the crucial ethical question of how to achieve good decisions in an environmental context where uncertainty is ubiquitous. Yet this seemingly simple question aims right at the core of the environmental problem. In his answer he suggests multi-criteria analysis, which includes a participatory process, as a tool for ethically based decision-making. However, in his study of the various ethical foundations of multi-criteria decision-making he reveals the weaknesses of utilitarism and discursive ethics which are usually used. As a way out, he proposes a pluralistic approach as an ethical foundation of multi-criteria decision-making methods. Finally, he checks existing proposals for consensual participatory decision-making in terms of their ethical foundations and discusses whether an explicitly normative discussion can be fruitfully incorporated into such decision-making procedures.

Decisions about sustainability which focus on long-run developments imply intertemporal evaluation. There is a considerable lack in the conceptual foundation of intertemporal evaluation (Lind 1982, Brennan 1995, Kula 1997). *Månsson* initiates in his article a necessary further development of the theory of intertemporal evaluation under uncertainty. He states the proposition that there should be quite different approaches to discounting depending on the context. Before determining a discount rate, it should be asked who the stakeholders are and who actually holds the power to decide. His considerations give an authoritative overview of the problems of discounting. Månsson contributes to a basis which later on should form the foundation of an ecological economic theory of intertemporal evaluation.

Applying the general objectives of sustainable development to the practical management of a region is certainly a demanding task. *Turner* investigates the potential of integrated coastal management as a tool for providing sustainability in coastal zones. Integrated coastal management aims at providing a socially desirable mix of coastal zone products and services in the long run. It covers both biogeochemical and socioeconomic modelling and particularly the participation of stakeholders in the decision-making process. Turner points out that integrated coastal management must exceed an assessment of the benefit-cost residuum and the internalisation of externalities; it must take into consideration the complexity, dynamics and the open system nature of coastal zones. Turner shows where the theoretical foundation of integrated coastal management needs to be strengthened and how practical application needs to be improved.

Sustainable development decisions require information about the economic and social impacts of human activities. *O'Hara*, *Shandas* and *Vazquez* take up an issue that is systematically neglected in conventional decision-making theory. They deliberate the possibilities of scientists to communicate the complex information to the decision-makers. Since they are convinced that decisions should not be made solely by experts, they discuss how local expertise and stakeholders can be integrated into the decision process. This integration requires tools that are able to give a structured and clear picture of the situation. O'Hara, Shandas and Vazquez suggest that the two available communication tools, i.e. Geographic Information Systems and dynamic simulation models, should be integrated within an interactive modelling framework. The authors base their discussion on a regional case study at the Lake George in upstate New York, United States, a rural area where the economic benefits and ecological hazards of further tourism development are the subject of controversial discussion.

3.2 Modelling as support for policy analysis

Analysing options for sustainable development with formal models can be helpful for the integration of economic and ecological aspects in a single framework of analysis. The strength of modelling lies in offering a simplified, comprehensible depiction of a problem with a formal or numerical solution. Its greatest difficulty is to select simplifications, aggregations and assumptions in such a way that predictions, implications and policy recommendations are acceptable (Van den Bergh 1996). A precondition for successful modelling in the context of sustainability is that both the economic and the ecological foundations of the problem are understood and adequately modelled. This requires the inclusion of knowledge from the natural sciences in economic models. All the articles presented in part 2 of this book have integrated insights from ecology, biophysics, hydrology or chemistry in their analysis. As a result they gain new insights compared to a purely economic approach, and therefore provide a better basis for policy recommendations[2].

Frank and *Ring* develop a scheme to evaluate incentive programmes in the realm of nature conservation. They focus on the assessment of the ecological effectiveness of programmes which according to their definition is achieved when the available resources for the programme yield the highest ecological benefit. In a regional case study they apply their evaluation scheme to incentive programmes for nature conservation in Saxony. Using a metapopulation model from the natural sciences, they derive guidelines for the optimal allocation of resources and analyse the Saxon directive on nature protection and landscape maintenance. The paper illustrates that a typical problem in the field of economics — the optimal allocation of a given budget — can only be insufficiently solved with economic theory alone if the benefit function needs an ecological foundation.

Schmieman and *Van Ierland* deal with the problem of soil acidification and tropospheric ozone. They perform a dynamic optimisation of cost effective abatement strategies for a combined reduction of the major acidifying compounds SO_2 and NO_x. They draw on knowledge from the natural sciences by incorporating dynamic aspects of soil acidification in their model. The results from their numerical model indicate that an analysis of acidification in a dynamic setting gives useful additional insights compared to the currently used critical loads approach. Including the problem of ozone in their analysis, they show that additional policy measures with respect to VOCs are needed if the increased risk of damage from ozone is to be reduced.

The starting point of the article by *Kotchen* is the problem of insects' resistance to pesticides. Kotchen develops a conceptual, regional model of how pesticide management strategies can incorporate resistance costs. In his paper, he first discusses threshold models, which have been traditionally used to derive guidelines for pesticide treatment. They are, however, unable to include the aspect of resistance build-up. Therefore, Kotchen develops a dynamic optimisation model which allows him to integrate the future costs of increased pest resistance. He includes in the model insights from biological theory on the functional relationship between pesticide use rate and crop yield as well as resistance.

Kampas and *White* address nitrate pollution from agriculture. They develop an economic model in order to assess a range of feasible nitrate reduction policies for the River Kennet in south-east England. Using this

---

[2] For further discussion on models for sustainable development we refer to Van den Bergh (1996: 103-112) and the literature given there.

model it is possible to assess the first-best solution for a given reduction in the level of nitrogen emissions and then use this as a benchmark against which feasible second-best instruments are compared. Kampas and White include the natural sciences in their analysis by using a biophysical model to measure nitrogen losses under arable crops. Furthermore, a hydrological model is used to convert estimates of soil nitrate losses into the ambient concentration of nitrates in the drain flow.

3.3 Evaluating policies for regional sustainability

The last part of our book deals with the evaluation of existing policy instruments for sustainable development in a regional context. The interdisciplinary perspective comes into play as policy instruments are evaluated from the viewpoint of various disciplines.

From an economic perspective, policy instruments can be distinguished by the way decisions of environmentally relevant actors can be influenced. Turner and Opschoor (1994) propose three different routes:

1. Alteration of the set of options open to actors;
2. Alteration of the cost and/or benefits relevant to actors;
3. Alteration of the priorities and significance actors attach to environmental change (i.e. altering the structure of agents' costs and benefits).

Providing new alternatives or forbidding old ones is central to route (1). This approach has been used by all industrialised countries and is the so-called "command and control approach". Instruments used in this approach have included standards, bans and zoning. Route (2) leads to the application of economic incentives or market stimuli. The idea is that if environmentally more appropriate conduct is made more rewarding in the eyes of the actors involved, the actors' behaviour will shift towards this socially more desirable conduct. Examples of instruments used in the context of economic incentives include subsidies, charges and taxes. The aim of route (3) is to change the preferences of the relevant actors. Instruments include education and information, as well as social pressure.

In the past all countries' environmental policies have heavily relied on the command and control approach (Opschoor and Vos 1989). Since the late 1980s more emphasis has been given to economic and persuasive instruments. Reasons for this shift include among others an increasing awareness that economic instruments have efficiency advantages under certain circumstances. In addition, environmental problems such as the greenhouse effect have emerged where the use of economic instruments has been considered most suitable (Ikwue and Skea 1994). Furthermore, a rise in public concern over environmental pollution has led to an increase in social pressure on companies to voluntarily reduce their negative environmental impacts.

Nowadays we can observe a wide variety of existing policy instruments, which is reflected in the contributions to this book.

Hellegers' background is agricultural economics and her article deals with agricultural subsidies from the EU. She assesses the impact of present and alternative agricultural policies in the EU on High Nature Value farming systems in selected regions. High Nature Value farming systems play an important role in the maintenance of biodiversity and landscapes. Their economic viability depends to a great extent on the EU's Common Agricultural Policy. Hellegers' results show that payments for Less Favoured Areas and changes in the Common Agricultural Policy of the 1992 reform do not significantly increase the viability of farms. However, an increase in agri-environmental payments could significantly contribute to the viability of farms. Her analysis reminds us that in order to achieve an ecological improvement, it is often not necessary to create a new instrument but is sufficient to introduce an ecological bias into existing instruments.

Centner and *Gunter*'s background is law. Their contribution tackles the problem of unwanted pesticides in the United States. Agricultural producers often possess pesticides for which they no longer have a use or which they are not allowed to use anymore. These pesticides create a risk for human beings. Human error or a natural disaster discharging pesticides into the environment might create health hazards for humans or the environment. Therefore, several state governments have introduced pesticide collection programmes in the United States, and these are analysed by Centner and Gunter. They evaluate them in terms of organisational features, funding, efficiency, equity and goal attainment. Their research shows that existing programmes are a good starting point but have to be developed further in order to significantly reduce the risk from unwanted pesticides. Their main proposal is to co-ordinate pesticide collection with the collection of other household hazardous waste, which might reduce collection costs significantly. The pesticide collection programmes entail elements from all categories of the classification made above. There are some instructions on what owners of unwanted pesticides ought to do, the costs and benefits of the actors are influenced by the various ways of funding the collection programmes, and the programmes must take into account that the agricultural producers attach significance to the problem of unwanted pesticides. Their voluntary participation is necessary as the authorities have little information on who possesses unwanted pesticides.

Kneer analyses implementation and acceptance issues with regard to nature conservation in urban landscapes from a sociological point of view. He develops a theoretical framework which integrates questions of implementation and acceptance. This framework is applied to analyse the regulation of impact and compensation (*Eingriffs- und Ausgleichsregel*) in Germany which is directed towards nature and landscape protection. It states that avoidable impairment of nature and the landscape is forbidden while unavoidable impairment must be compensated. If impairment cannot be compensated it must be forbidden or substitution measures such as landscape greening have to be carried out. The regulation can be classified as a mixture of a command and control instrument and an economic instrument. In the context of the implementation of this regulation, an enforcement deficit can be observed. The main conclusion of Kneer's analysis is that the reduction of the enforcement deficit can be achieved by giving conservation groups more rights to take legal action if they feel that the decisions of the administration do not comply with legal requirements.

Greiner shows in her article that actions against global environmental problems such as the greenhouse effect can successfully be taken at a local level. This is surprising as traditional economic theory suggests just the opposite. Given the public-good characteristic of environmental improvements at a local level, it seems likely that everybody would adopt a free-rider position. However, reality has proven this position wrong. As a counterexample, Greiner presents the "fifty-fifty project" designed to reduce water and energy consumption in Hamburg's schools. Financial savings from the reduced use of resources are shared equally between the respective school and the local administration. The project has been so successful that it has received worldwide attention in the framework of Local Agenda 21 and has been copied many times. In economic terms the idea behind the project was to partly privatise a former public good. While not disputing that the global level is important for taking action against global environmental problems, Greiner concludes from the analysis of the project that the increased assignment of responsibility to local communities is desirable.

The book closes with an outlook by *Bizer* on perspectives for economic research into sustainable policies. Based on the insight that sustainability is associated with a different meaning for different disciplines as well as for different cultures, methodological pluralism serves as a sensitivity analysis for the personal and institutional setting of the researcher. The standard behavioural model of economics is based on the assumption that individuals behave rationally. Modern economics, by contrast, is inspired by institutional, psychological and sociological analysis and takes the various aspects of human behaviour dependent on cognitive limits, ethical motives, and institutions into account. Therefore, advanced economic research into sustainability should integrate both ecological and social sciences, moving from ecological economic research to socio-ecological economics.

References

Balstad Miller, R. (1994): Interactions and collaboration in global change across the social and natural sciences. Ambio 23(1), 19-24

Becker, E., Jahn, T., Stiess, I., Wehling, P. (1997): Sustainability: A Cross-Disciplinary Concept for Social Transformation. MOST Policy Papers 6, UNESCO, Paris

Bergh, J.C.J.M. van den, Straaten, J. van der (Eds.) (1994): Toward Sustainable Development. Concepts, Methods, and Policy. Island Press, Washington DC

Bergh, J.C.J.M. van den (1996): Ecological Economics and Sustainable Development: Theory, Methods and Applications. Edward Elgar, Cheltenham, UK and Brookfield, US

Brennan, T.J. (1995): Discounting the Future: Economics and Ethics. Resources, Summer 1995, No. 120, Resources for the Future: 3-6

Costanza, R. (Ed.) (1991): Ecological Economics. The Science and Management of Sustainability. Columbia University Press, New York

Daschkeit, A. (1998): Umweltforschung interdisziplinär — notwendig, aber unmöglich? In: Daschkeit, A., Schröder, W. (Eds.): Umweltforschung quergedacht. Perspektiven integrativer Umweltforschung und -lehre. Springer, Berlin Heidelberg, 51-73

Faber, M., Jöst, F., Manstetten, R. (1995): Limits and perspectives of the concept of sustainable development. Economie Appliquée 48, 231-249

Faber, M., Manstetten, R., Müller, G. (1994): Interdisziplinäre Umweltforschung aus ökonomischer Sicht. Naturwissenschaften 81, 193-199

Georgescu-Roegen, N. (1971): The Entropy Law and the Economic Process. Harvard University Press, Cambridge, Mass.

Hardy, S., Lloyd, G. (1994): An impossible dream? Sustainable regional economic and environmental development. Regional Studies 28(8), 773-780

Harris, J.M. (1995): Energy and resource flow analysis. In: Krishnan, R., Harris, J.M, Goodwin, N.R. (Eds.): A Survey of Ecological Economics. Island Press, Washington DC, 169-176

Ikwue, A., Skea, J. (1994): Business and the Genesis of the European Community Carbon Tax Proposal. Business Strategy and the Environment 3(2), 1-10

Lind, R.C. (Ed.) (1982): Discounting for Time and Risk in Energy Policy. Johns Hopkins University Press, Baltimore

Klauer, B. (1999): Defining and achieving sustainable development. The International Journal of Sustainable Development and World Ecology (forthcoming)

Kula, E. (1997): Time Discounting and Future Generations. Quorum Books, London

Norgaard, R.B. (1994): Development Betrayed. The End of Progress and a Coevolutionary Revisioning of the Future. Routledge, London, New York

Norgaard, R.B. (1989): The case for methodological pluralism. Ecological Economics 1, 37-57

Opschoor, J.B., Vos, H.B. (1989): Economic Instruments for Environmental Protection. OECD, Paris

Perrings, C., Turner, R.K., Folke, C. (1995): Ecological Economics: The Study of Interdependent Economic and Ecological Systems. EEEM Discussion Papers No. 9501, University of York, York

Pigou, A.C. (1920): The Economics of Welfare. Macmillan, London

Ring, I. (1997): Evolutionary Strategies in Environmental Policy. Ecological Economics 23, 237-249

Turner, R.K., Opschoor, J.B. (1994): Environmental Economics and Environmental Policy Instruments: Introduction and Overview. In: Opschoor, J.B., Turner, K. (Eds.): Economic Incentives and Environmental Policies: Principles and Practice. Kluwer Academic Publishers, Dordrecht, Boston, London, 1-38

World Commission on Environment and Development (WCED) (1987): Our Common Future. Oxford University Press, Oxford

Part 1

Decision making for regional sustainability

Decisions in the context of sustainable development: ethics and implementation of multi-criteria analysis

Felix Rauschmayer

Department of Agricultural Economics, University of Göttingen,
Platz der Göttinger Sieben 5, D-37073 Göttingen, Germany

1 Introduction

Decisions in the context of sustainable development entail simultaneously meeting obligations in three domains: economic development, ecological stability and social fairness. Any instrument of decision analysis which is to help us make decisions needs to be accessible for all aspects of decision-making in the three domains. These decision-analysis tools have to incorporate multiple criteria from different fields which generally are not reducible to merely one criterion, as will be substantiated below. The group of multi-criteria analyses (MCA) is commonly divided into MC decision-*making* and MC decision-*aid* tools (see Roy 1990b). While the former is meant to select an action in a well-stated decision context with multiple criteria, the latter should help the decision-maker either to group or select possible actions, or to clarify the relevant criteria and their respective importance.

Before using the decision-analytical tools, we have to answer one question: Why do we judge a decision good? What are the criteria which enable us to favour one decision over another? In democracies, a dictatorial decision cannot be called a good decision as it does not respect the fundamental value of personal autonomy within society. The first and most basic condition for good decisions in democracies is respect for individual values and convictions. The decision-analytical tool of multiple criteria analysis must fulfil this basic condition, otherwise it cannot aid democratic decision-making. This condition can be operationalised in the context of sustainable development by the foundation of the criteria on values and convictions of all three domains. In this article, I argue that the fulfilment of this condition has implications for the appropriate methods of MCA as well as for their implementation.

In section 2, I describe some arguments in environmental ethics as the new branch of ethics in the sustainability debate, and I present the ethical concepts that integrate these arguments. These concepts represent the framework for arguing which decisions are ethically right or wrong. If this framework can integrate all individual values and convictions, it might provide a good basis for a democratically justifiable MCA. The third section of the chapter shows that an explicit foundation of MCA on individual values and convictions in environmental contexts needs modifications in its structure and methods. In section 4, I show how such a MCA could be implemented in participatory models, and in section 5, I give an example of this.

2 Arguments in environmental ethics and ethical frameworks

Why should we protect nature or our environment? What arguments exist, and how can they be classified?

Arguments can be classified within a range which can be characterised by its two extremes. At one end we find narrow anthropocentric arguments with no consideration for future human generations, non-humans, etc. Even from this angle, some natural components are to be protected to fulfil the basic requirements for life (food, shelter, water, air), as well to permit the joy of walking in the countryside, recognising one's home landscape, etc. At the other end we find holistic arguments which demand, for example, the preservation of whole ecosystems, and of the systemic rules of the planet Earth. In between these two extremes, arguments for the further preservation of nature are based on the fate of future human generations, on a theological viewpoint, on respect for other sentient animals (pathocentrism), on respect for other living beings (biocentrism), or even on respect for non-living parts of nature such as rivers etc. (physiocentrism). This whole range of arguments has been widely discussed in ethical literature (see for example: Krebs 1999, v.d. Pfordten 1996, Pierce and VanDeVeer 1994, Sylvan and Bennett 1994, and in general the journals "Environmental Ethics" and "Environmental Values"), as well as in contingent valuation studies of the willingness to pay for nature conservation programmes (Spash and Hanley 1995, Stevens et al. 1991) and analyses of political debates (Booth 1994: 173-201). Participants in the debate about normative ethics fiercely discuss the relevance of some of these arguments. Decision analysts should be aware of this debate. In democratic decisions, though, all arguments have to be permitted *a priori*. It is the decision-making body in its deliberation process which may judge the relevance of the arguments in each specific case, and not a circle of ethicists. The ethicists' role is to help the decision-making body in the deliberation process.

Ethicists do not only debate specific arguments for or against acting in a particular way. In order to judge the rightness of an action, they assess the validity and weight of arguments within certain frameworks. Which ethical framework could be of assistance in the deliberation process within the context of sustainable development? Here I will describe only briefly three possible groups of frameworks which might be able to integrate all the arguments of environmental ethics. The first group is utilitarianism,[1] which is

[1] Consequentialism ought to be the real group name (see e.g. Trapp 1989), but it is utilitarianism (originally part of consequentialism) which has caught on in a *pars pro toto* process (Nida-Rümelin 1996: 13).

used as a basis for cost-benefit analysis or some multi-criteria analyses. The second is deontologism, which integrates ethical frameworks such as Kantianism or discourse ethics. The third can be called pluralism. It will be argued that this third group can substantiate why a democratically and explicitly normative decision-making process results in a decision which may be judged ethically correct.

1. Utilitarianism judges actions by their consequences on humans or at most on sentient beings. In the original concept of utilitarianism, judgements of actions themselves cannot be integrated into the deliberation process. Killing is not wrong *a priori*; its judgement depends on the consequences. If the utility gain of the murderer is higher than the utility loss for the victim (other utilities being equal), than the murder was ethically correct. Apart from this fundamental argument (which has been debated over and over), utilitarianism cannot incorporate arguments from environmental ethics other than anthropocentric and pathocentric arguments. There is no rational way of defining an individual utility of non-sentient beings. This limitation (among other things) must lead to its rejection as a basis for democratic deliberation processes aimed at decision-making.
2. Deontological ethics judges actions directly. Decisions about the correctness of an action are made following one single rule (or just a few rules, albeit a very restricted number). Examples include the Ten Commandments, the Kantian rule(s), and discourse ethics, which is debated more intensely in environmental ethics. "For discourse ethics, it is ... the *consensus* of all in a symmetrical and argumentative discourse which constitutes the morally right" (Krebs 1997: 271). Here, we have to distinguish between the normative claim of discourse ethics, i.e. its claim to define in discourse what is morally right, and a descriptive version which "does not aim at establishing ethical norms or at seeking to identify conditions for ethical judgement, but simply acknowledges that people are ethically motivated, just as they are socially, culturally, economically, or ecologically motivated" (O'Hara 1996: 97f.). The normative version is tied, as in all deontological ethics, to reasonable beings as moral subjects. Only reasonable beings may participate in the discourse, and only their consensual judgement decides about the rightness of actions. The validity and the weight of anthropocentric and, to a higher degree, non-anthropocentric arguments depend on the convictions of the discussion participants and their consensus. The descriptive version, though, has no normative claims. It places the deliberation focus on ethical issues, thereby facilitating the integration of lay-people and marginalised perspectives.

3. Descriptive discourse ethics investigates the ethical arguments of the people concerned by the action examined. Pluralistic ethics do the same[2]. But, and here is the main difference between the two, pluralistic ethics maintains a normative claim on resulting judgements. This branch of ethics bases its judgements heavily on actual people's convictions. It deviates from central and apparently convincing elements of our convictive systems and tries to arrange the different elements of individual ethical life systematically and coherently. Pluralistic ethics rejects the idea of a master-principle being able to order the different arguments and to decide their respective validity and weight. They do not seek a single axiom in the sense of immediately evident assumptions, from which the individual theorems and criteria can be deduced. The pluralist theories do not want to base their normative content on a speculative foundation of a theory of objective and intrinsic values (Nida-Rümelin 1997: 181). This ethical debate can be seen in analogy to the discussion of a "second-best world" in economic theory: In economics, there is a trend (new institutional economics, ecological economics, etc.) to come closer to the 'real' world with all its distortions, inefficiencies and irrationalities. Following this trend, economic decisions must be based on the existing preferences, prices and institutions which might not be rational and efficient, rather than on a speculative theory of rational and efficient people and institutions. It is nevertheless the role of economists to make institutions more efficient, just as it is the role of ethicists to make people's convictions more coherent.

3 Implications for multi-criteria analysis

Before analysing a decision process, an analyst does not know the convictions or values of the decision-makers. In new areas (such as sustainable development with its integrative tasks), decision-makers do not know the convictions and values either beforehand. The (partly emerging) convictions will not be reducible to one *numéraire*. If the analyst respects the actual convictions (which might change in the process) as the basis of his decision analysis, he cannot use monodimensional methods based on utility. Yet, these methods of multi-criteria decision-*making* based on the multi-attribute utility theory (Keeney and Raiffa 1976) are mainly used in the American school of MCA (Roy and Vanderpooten 1996). Instead, the analyst should use methods which allow for incommensurabilities of values, ignorance and uncertainties, and which consider the fuzziness of the set of feasible alternatives. The results of these (European school) methods are obviously

[2] Without claiming completeness, examples of pluralistic ethics include moderate pluralism (Wenz 1993), expressive rationalism (Anderson 1993) and practical coherentism (Nida-Rümelin 1997).

softer: No precise numbers indicate what should be done. According to Roy (1990b: 28), these methods of MC decision *aid* "should help an actor taking part in the decision process:

- either to shape, and/or to argue, and/or to transform his preferences,
- or to make a decision in conformity with his goals."

All parts of multi-criteria analysis (MCA) change by the adoption of a pluralistic[3] point of view:

1. the understanding and aim of MCA: in complex fields as environmental decision-making, MCA can only be understood as an aid to the decision-maker; it cannot provide the decisions by itself;
2. the criteria: they should respect the differences of ethical arguments rather than those of accustomed sciences;
3. the calculating method: it has to allow for incommensurabilities of the different ethical criteria, i.e. it has to be possible that, due to their different juxtaposed ethical foundations, weights of different criteria cannot be assessed.

While the last point can be treated by the choice of an appropriate method (see e.g. Munda 1995), it is the second point which remains unsolved. How are the criteria to be built?

The classical point of view is formulated by Bouyssou (1990: 59): "In a multiple criteria approach, the analyst seeks to build several criteria using several points of view. These points of view represent the different axes along which the various actors of the decision process justify, transform and argue their preferences." They "should be understood and accepted by all the actors of the decision process, even if they disagree on the relative importance that they would like each of them to have" (ibid.: 61). Bouyssou demands in the same "general guidelines for constructing a criterion" that "the method allowing to arrive at the evaluation on the criterion for each alternative (...) should be as free as possible from elements deeply linked to a particular value system" (ibid.). For him, as for other MC analysts, the points of view are not ethical points of view but criteria such as 'impact on the environment', 'social impacts', 'economic impacts' etc. Does a criterion such as 'impact on the environment' really fulfil his basic guidelines, i.e., is it "a point of view along which it seems adequate to establish comparisons" (ibid.: 62)? Is it feasible to collect data on 'economic impacts' without a close link to the efficiency paradigm and to utilitarianism? I believe not. Is the building of explicitly normatively founded criteria feasible, and could their use be fruitful for the decision-making process?

---

[3] In my article, I always use the word "pluralistic" to refer to the ethical foundation of an MCA, not to the understanding of administrations as pluralist vs. rationalist (cf. Fiorino 1995: 223-237).

In order to build these criteria, we should take central elements of the ethical foundations of the people concerned and structure them interactively so that every participant in the discourse can structure his own arguments in a coherent way. In the ensuing normative discussions in the group preparing or making the decision, several ecological subcriteria, for example, could be integrated into criteria such as intergenerational fairness, respect for non-human living beings, intragenerational fairness, self-appreciation etc.

What would change? Firstly, scientific advisors would have to think of the ethical values involved by proposed measures in their respective fields. Secondly, argumentation in the decision-making process would be more about the values that matter and not about the concrete facts which are only made meaningful by a whole range of ethical values. These two points would implicate an open, truthful and credible style of exchanging arguments which would be most uncommon. The discourse could be organised along the lines of O'Hara's (1996) descriptive discourse ethics as a way of explicating normative judgements.

4 Implementation

What would the implementation of an "ethical MCA" look like? In our present political systems, generally one or more democratically or bureaucratically legitimised persons make public decisions. Implementing MCA in the existing decision structures would imply that these people make decisions after having received adequate information about the consequences of some possible actions and after discussion with an aiding decision analyst about their personal ethical values. There would be no need for interpersonal ethical discourse with people who are foreign to the decision-making body. However, this process is not adequate for three reasons: (1) it does not meet the necessary democratic conditions of sustainable development; (2) it is dubious whether the elected or bureaucratic representative could represent the ethical criteria of the persons concerned; (3) a non-participatory process does not use the fertility of the ethical MCA to generate better solutions.

ad 1. Sustainable development implies at least respect for the needs of future generations. Assuming a standard of living above mere survival, there exists no ethical argument which could substantiate favouring current generations over future ones. Consequently, the principle of intergenerational fairness, which is inherent to the concept of sustainable development, does include the equal distribution of possible welfare between human generations. This consideration implies a profound change in the way of life, at least for currently wealthy societies. If actions are to be oriented to sustainability, they need to be socially acceptable. This acceptance of a fundamental insight should not be assumed by indirect approval via the elected decision-maker and/or by the supposed approval of the existing bureaucratic system.

Acceptance could be verified or even achieved by a participatory process whose aim is "to form a collective understanding and to construct a coherent basis for choice" (Vatn and Bromley 1994: 143). Such a process has to be organised by encouraging values that go along with sustainable development.

ad 2. Furthermore, a pluralistically based MCA enhances the need for participation. While a decision-maker could take into account material consequences for concerned persons, it would be very difficult for her to decide on the foundation of ethical values which are foreign to her. The point is increasingly valid as, in new contexts, pluralistic values emerge in a process of deliberation. This process has to take place and its results would not be of great use if the deliberation was only hypothetical. Nevertheless, in most cases, it is surely not practical for all the persons concerned to participate in the process. There are different models of participation which allow for different degrees of integration of the persons involved. Some of them are described below.

ad 3. It is this process of deliberation which creates the fertility of the pluralistically founded MCA. The information transmitted and generated in a public discussion helps individuals to clarify their respective ethical convictions and to state commensurabilities and incommensurabilities (Bohnet and Frey 1994: 345). Only after the individual ethical values have been clarified can new or unconventional solutions which have emerged be accepted or rejected on rational grounds. The view of pluralistic ethics as a process accords with the view of sustainable development as a process rather than an end state (Achterberg 1996: 158).

What form of participation could be useful? This primarily depends on the conflict itself. Renn et al. (1995) classify environmental conflicts into three groups: (1) Some can be understood as conflicts defined by incommensurable values. While these tend to be the conflicts with the highest degree of complexity and/or conflict intensity, two other types of debates are relevant: (2) debates about factual arguments and (3) debates about public confidence in institutions that deal with environmental hazards. This classification is not always apparent, as there is a strong tendency to reframe the conflicts: business and government tend to present value-based conflicts as factual or confidence conflicts. "This is an attempt to focus the discussion on technical evidence, in which the agency is fluent. Citizens who participate are thus forced to use first level (factual) arguments to rationalize their value concerns. Unfortunately, this is often understood by experts as 'irrationality' on the part of the public." (Renn et al. 1995: 357, referring to Dietz et al. 1989). Consequently, the attempt to find a value-based decision aid which can be implemented in participatory structures can be understood as an aid to the competence of agencies in the value basis.

Another criterion for the choice of an appropriate participation model is its ability to be used as a framework for a pluralistically based MCA. Before actually choosing a model, I will describe the main properties of different models. Here I ignore some of the approaches described in the volume of Renn et al. (1995), which are either not easily repeatable (Dutch study groups), sharply contrast with the pluralistic approach (compensation/benefit sharing), are too specific (citizen initiatives), or are too similar to other models (citizen juries). The following list considers only (formalised) models which meet a sufficient number of criteria guaranteeing a fair, competent and value-open participation process (see Webler 1995 for the criteria which are developed from a discourse ethical approach):

- Citizen Advisory Committees;
- Planning Cells (Citizen Panels);
- Negotiated Rule Making;
- Mediation.

Regarding these models, I purposely ignore the possibilities of only gradually enlarging the traditional representative and administrative decision system. The political system increasingly uses these possibilities, such as public hearings or enquiries, social surveys, scientific advisory groups and referenda. These possibilities mainly enlarge the factual and democratic foundations of the decisions, but do not meet the basic conditions of a discursive and value-pluralistic process. I will explain this point by the (rarely used) possibility of referenda.

Even with preceding public debate, referenda, as usually understood and practised, are orientated to neither consensus nor genuine participation. Furthermore, they are not adequate to clarify individual ethical convictions and still less as a way to discuss these concerns with others. While a sufficiently high quorum could guarantee consensus orientation, participation and ethical revelation need small, confidential groups.

I will describe the essential elements of the above-listed models before examining the Planning Cell more closely by means of an example. In practice, the models do not appear as pure forms, but as mixtures of different elements. Often, a combination of at least two models is recommended (e.g. Hadden 1995: 250, Vari 1995: 113).

Citizen Advisory Committees (CAC)

In this participatory technique, the hand-picked members should include a representative sample of the major interest positions. The brief, agenda and focus of the committee are prearranged by the sponsor (which could be a local, regional or national government, their respective agencies or industry). The sponsors expect the committee to "formulate a more or less consensual position with regard to certain issues with the help of a moderator" (Vari 1995: 106). The members may raise explicative, factual, normative, or expressive issues, but they in doing so risk being ignored by the sponsor. The practical impact of Citizen Advisory Committees "is contingent on the intentions of the institutions being advised" (Lynn and Kartez 1995: 98). The committees have all the time they need, but limited resources. "Decision analytical models, including multi-attribute utility models or other multi-criteria structures, are frequently used to provide a framework for the iterative development of a coherent representation of the problem" (Vari 1995: 108). The process is consensus-oriented. The concept of CACs is very broad, and has been applied from early forms in the 1950s to new currently used procedures which are more open in their agenda and less determined by the sponsor. Normally, the chosen members are members of the same class of elite as the sponsors of the process. This leads to a lack of representation in cases where a large public and/or a large number of affected groups are involved. "As a consequence, in many cases, the recommendations of the CAC are rejected by the decision-makers of the general public" (ibid.: 109).

Planning Cells

Planning Cells gather a representative set of citizens, bring them together in a structure conducive to dialogue and reflection, and educate them about the problem at hand. Randomly chosen citizens, divided into groups of 8-10 persons, study the problem with the help of prepared literature, expert hearings or discussions with stakeholders. Planning Cells are supposed to recommend specific policy or decision problems. "They are highly competent in explicative, theoretical, and practical discourse" (Renn et al. 1995: 343). Planning Cells try to bring technical knowledge, political and stakeholders' interests, and citizen preferences to a coherent outcome. They require a large investment of time and money and are not suitable for all types of problems and contexts. Due to the lack of cultural tradition compared to for example CACs, the democratic legitimacy of Planning Cells is often disputed.

Regulatory Negotiation

This decision-making process is strongly moulded by the regulatory agency that has convened the event. "In a regulatory negotiation, administrative agencies bring together the representatives of the interests that are affected by proposed rule before the agency makes decisions on the content of the rule" (Fiorino 1995: 225). Interests that are unorganised will lack access to the negotiations. The purpose of Regulatory Negotiation is not so much to resolve specific disputes as to reach agreement on the substance and the language of a proposed rule. In the negotiation process, the agency is one of the members. The committee "has substantial control over its mode of operation, its composition, its use of resources, and the terms and timing of its dissolution" (ibid.: 228). All decisions are made consensually. Regulatory Negotiation has no explicit intention to address normative issues outside of a technical context in which cost-benefit analysis is the dominant mode of reasoning. Its appeal is that a satisfactory solution is usually found within a reasonable amount of time and that legal challenges are reduced or eliminated. As Regulatory Negotiation is oriented towards a compromise upon a cost–benefit basis, inviting a radical group that prides itself on the politics of non-compromise would be fatal to the process. Regulatory Negotiation "should not be used to make decisions about the acceptability of risks or the distribution of costs and benefits across groups or among generations" (Fiorino 1995: 235). It is embedded in a cultural and political context of the complete representation of interests by organisations. This context affects the likelihood of its success.

Mediation
Mediation is a voluntary and consensus-aimed process undertaken by disputing partners with the help of an intermediary. Its focus is more upon collective rather than individual interests. The selection of partners in Mediation is based on the disputing-power principal. Partaking in Mediation is useful in cases that involve an uncertain outcome of a legal debate and an unattractive 'loose' situation regarding an envisaged compromise situation after a Mediation. Partaking groups must nominate their spokespeople, who jointly define the agenda and the body of information needed to settle the conflict. The negotiations take place partly at a round table and partly in separate closed-door discussions between the mediator and the representatives. It is incumbent upon the parties to develop links between informal agreements and binding contracts, something which is difficult when it comes to conflicts with an agency or any other public body. Evaluating mediation is a difficult process as "it is essential for mediation to take place behind closed doors" (Nothdurft 1995: 268). The strength of Mediation lies in explicative discourse. Normally, the technical competence of a Mediation discourse is worse than that of Regulatory Negotiation. Practical discourse in Mediation is also unlikely to be highly competent on normative issues, and there is no intention to focus the discourse on normative argumentation.

In Figure 1 below, Renn et al. located the participatory models on a two dimensional taxonomy. As noted above, conflicts may be classified into three groups: (1) Conflicts about worldviews and values; (2) conflicts about factual arguments arising from knowledge and expertise, and (3) conflicts arising because of different perceptions of the experience and the trustworthiness of institutions dealing with environmental hazards. It is shown that by choosing the right model, the decision-maker can cope with different degrees of "intensity of conflict" and "complexity".

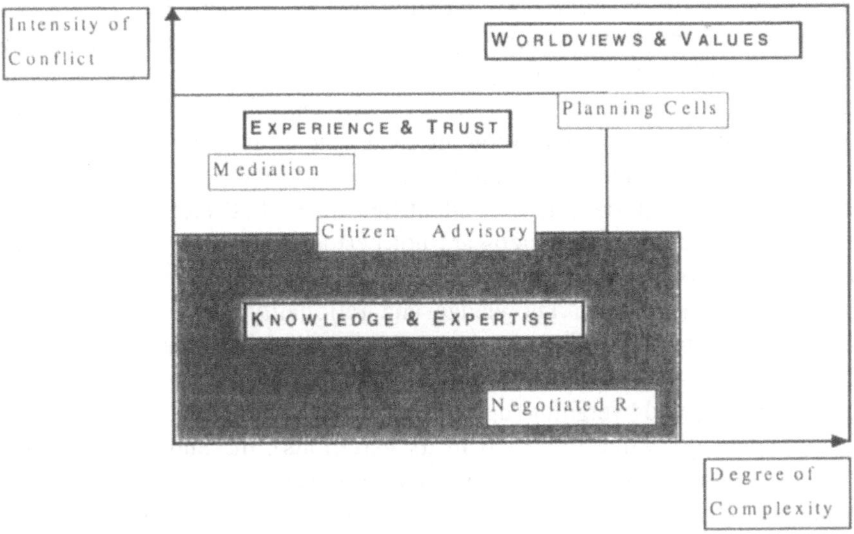

Source: adapted from Renn et al. (1995: 360).

Figure 1. Locating the four participatory models in a two-dimensional taxonomy.

Although it is possible to include explicitly normative decision analysis in all models, it does not seem necessary in conflicts which primarily address questions of knowledge and expertise. An ethically based MCA whose outlines I sketched in the third section is urgently required in cases of conflicts based upon different worldviews and values. Having seen the attempts to downsize the conflicts from stage (1) to (2) and from stage (2) to (3), an explicit openness to normative questions can be very useful in conflicts that are seen as conflicts over experience and trust in institutions. This said, I will pick from the literature one example of participatory decision-making which is based on the Planning Cell (Renn et al. 1993). The Planning Cell, with its openness to value and trust conflicts, seems to be a useful model for showing the changes in participatory decision-making which occur due to the use of an ethically based MCA. I will try to include in this example an ethical MCA instead of the multi-attribute-utility based decision-making which has been used. Here I do not want to discuss the major advantages or disadvantages of Planning Cells, but merely use it as a fair example.

5 The four-step model

Renn et al. (1993: 189) start from the premise that a "model is needed that combines technical expertise and rational decision making with public values and preferences". In the first step, their model includes stakeholders in order to identify and select concerns and evaluative criteria. The stakeholders build value-trees, i.e. they hierarchically structure the relevant decision criteria and sub-criteria and place weights on each of them, but they do not assess any options. In the second step, experts identify and measure the impacts of the different decision options. "The desired outcome is a performance profile for each option" (ibid.: 191). In the third step, randomly selected citizens aggregate and weigh up the expected impacts in order to prioritise the options and to give recommendations to the political actor. They may change the criteria that were identified in the first step as well as the weights of the criteria. The steps are not hermetically separated from each other. All actors involved "play a role in each step, but their influence is channeled to the type of knowledge and rationality they can offer best" (ibid.: 193). Experts use the concerns and criteria of the stakeholders; These might comment later on the work done by the experts. By assigning the task of aggregating and weighing up to the citizens who use the information condensed in the value tree (and in its variations), the authors also avoid strategic bargaining by stakeholders as well as scientific recommendations, which are often far removed from lay judgements. The numerical results in the value tree "are *not* used as an expression of the final judgment of the participant, but as a structuring aid to improve the participants holistic, intuitive judgment. By pointing out potential discrepancies between the numerical model and the holistic judgments, the research team encourages the participants to reflect upon their opinions and search for potential hidden motives or values that might explain the discrepancy. The final recommendations are always based on a holistic judgment by individuals or groups" (ibid.: 198).

This approach of the planning cell, which includes stakeholders, responds to the criticisms concerning the democratic legitimacy of planning cells.

As an example of their procedure, Renn et al. (ibid.: 201ff.) cite a participatory process intended to define the 'best' energy policy out of four preformulated options for Germany. This process is also described by Keeney et al. (1990), who concentrate on the weighing-up process in order to elaborate a multi-attribute utility function which I will describe shortly. Stakeholder representatives identified eight independent criteria: financial, technical, and material requirements; the security of energy supplies; national economic impacts; impacts on the natural environment; health and safety; social impacts; political impacts; and international impacts. The staff of the study aggregated the criteria in only one value tree. Experts added the relevant sub-criteria which, in some cases, were reformulated by the citizens. The citizens intuitively evaluated the four different energy futures on a scale from 0 to 100 (worst to best). After eliciting the trade-offs between the various criteria, and having normalised the weights, the staff were able to calculate a multi-attribute utility evaluation of the four energy futures for each of the participants. In the following discussion, participants were asked to resolve the inconsistencies between the model and their initial evaluation. Most subjects achieved ordinal consistency between the two evaluations. "Apparently, the value forum and the multiattribute utility modeling had a significant influence on their thinking ... they felt that these two sets of evaluations should agree, refused overwhelmingly the 'easy solution' to reject the objectives or the model, and worked hard, up to three hours, to achieve ordinal consistency. In this reconciliation phase the primary changes were in weights and in intuitive evaluations" (Keeney et al. 1990: 1028f.).

The example questions the above-cited statement of Renn et al. (1993: 198): the numerical results in the value tree "are *not* used as an expression of the final judgment of the participant, but as a structuring aid to improve the participants holistic, intuitive judgment." Their interpretation of 'holistic' and 'intuitive' is rather unusual. Having analysed and compartmentalised an object, an intuitive and holistic judgement has become impossible. The new judgement might be more adequate in some respects, but it cannot be holistic and intuitive.

Based upon the three-step model of Renn et al. (1993), I developed a four-step model which implements an ethical MCA. Table 1 shows the basic concept and the elements of the four-step model. The figure shows that although all the actors involved (the experts, the interest groups, the citizens, the sponsor, and the research team) play a role in each step, the citizens' opinion guides the whole process. The other actors cooperate with the citizens' group (the most important activities of each step are emphasised in bold face in Figure 2). In my first step, stakeholders build group-specific value trees in a conventional approach, i.e. without an explicit ethical discourse. Experts and the sponsor augment the concern list and generate option examples in order to help the citizen panel discussion. The discussion is supported by the research team in order to facilitate an explicit ethical discourse which should enlighten the links between the traditional criteria and ethical criteria. The aim of the first step is a preliminary and consensual model for an MCA. The second step concentrates on the option generation: option generation is only useful in the light of the chosen criteria. Here, the sponsor and citizen panel have to closely collaborate with the help of experts and interest groups. The research team has to translate between the mostly unused ethical criteria and the more materially based concepts of the other groups. In the third step, the various options are assessed quantitatively or qualitatively on the basis of the operationable subcriteria without aggregating the assessments into an overall evaluation of the options. The expert judgements will have to be adapted to the criteria of the citizen panels, and the criteria might eventually need to be changed. The fourth step serves to evaluate the options (with or without weighing up the criteria, depending on the MC method) and to build priority-rankings which might contain incomparable options. MC methods used in this step have to allow

Table 1. Basic concept and elements of a four-step model.

	Step 1	Step 2	Step 3	Step 4
	Concerns and criteria	Option generation	Non-aggregated assessment of options	Evaluation of options
Actors:				
Interest groups	Elicitation of group-specific value trees	Input to option generation	Group-specific assessments	Witnesses to citizen panels
Experts	Addition to concern list (generation of option examples)	Input to option generation	Collections of expert judgements	Participation as discussants or videotaped presenters
Citizens	Elicitation of different consensual value trees	Option generation and option choice	Adaptation of expert judgements	Option evaluation and recommendation
Sponsor	Input to concern list (generation of option examples)	Option generation	Incorporation of institutional knowledge	Witness to citizen panels
Research team	Discursive moderation centred on ethics	Interpretation aid between sponsor and panel	Verification of expert judgements	Compilation of citizen report
Products	Separate value trees	List of options	Performance profile for each option	Priority of options and policy recommendations

Source: adapted from Renn et al. (1993: 192).

for incommensurabilities of criteria (appropriate methods could be ELECTRE IV (Roy 1990a, Maystre et al. 1994) or NAIADE (Munda 1995)). This final step is the only step completed under the sole authority of the citizen panel.

The main differences between the four-step-model and the concept of Renn et al. are:

- The introduction of the second step. In the three-step model, option generation is a first-step task of the sponsor. Option generation (2nd step) can be carried out more appropriately once the decision criteria are known (1st step).
- The chosen MCA method: the aim of the procedure is to aid legitimised decision-making, to generate new options, and to influence the final deci-

sion to the effect that citizen judgements are respected to a greater extent. Therefore, a decision-aiding method respecting incommensurabilities is more appropriate than the multi-attribute utility model aimed at decision-making used in the three-step model.

- The enhanced role of the citizen panel. In the three-step model, the citizen panels' sole major task is option evaluation and recommendation. In our model, the panel has a co-decisive role in each step. This important role is founded in the task-guiding function of the ethical criteria integrated into the citizens' discursive process in the first step.
- The major difference will probably not be found in the formal description of the process, but only after having performed some experiments. The four-step model will lead the decision process to debates about normative questions. This orientation will be strongest in the citizens' group, but neither experts nor stakeholders or sponsors will be left untouched. It is my conviction, albeit without any practical evidence, that this framework could give more space to values promoting sustainability, and in this way, that the "paradox of democratic sustainability" (Jacobs 1997: 228), i.e. a potentially unsustainable outcome resulting from a sustainability-intended procedure, could be weakened.

6 Conclusion

In this article, I advance a method of decision aid which ought to bring about better decisions and I propose its participatory implementation. Furthermore, I argue that participation is necessary in order to have democratically justifiable and competent decisions. Why is participation so important in my concept?

Firstly, I base judgement of whether a decision is a good decision more on the values of the persons concerned and less on the scientific data. Empirical data may be soft or judged irrelevant. Additionally, rationality is, in my approach, not so much an external affair of cost-benefit analysis as an internal process; internal to each participant and internal to the decision-making group.

Secondly, by basing competence on ethical and discursive processes, the adoption of a consensual perspective should normally enhance competence. I do not place strong emphasis on the legitimacy of the decision. A decision prepared by a participatory ethical MCA will exert pressure on the elected or bureaucratically chosen decision-maker and will empower citizens. This will lead to a change in further decision-making structures.

A decision process which can integrate all the arguments of the people concerned fulfils a necessary condition for democratic processes. Pluralistic ethics offers a normative foundation for decision analysis which has not yet been sufficiently explored. Decision analysis which must be multicriterial in sustainability contexts changes its significance and its methods. Participation will expand the potentiality of MCA, and is a necessary condition for its normative foundation. My example showed how this could work.

I am optimistic that explicitly normative and participatory decision-making combined with a method of assistance will result in better decisions. I hope that the decisions taken are also good decisions for future human generations and other sentient animals. Although my proposal does not automatically avoid the paradox of democratic sustainability, it fundamentally helps citizens to achieve sustainable decisions.

References

Achterberg, W. (1996): Sustainability and associative democracy. In: Lafferty, W.M., Meadowcroft, J. (Eds.): Democracy and the environment: problems and prospects. Edward Elgar, Aldershot, 157-174

Anderson, E. (1993: Value in Ethics and Economics. Harvard University Press, Cambridge

Bohnet, I., Frey, B.S. (1994): Direct-Democratic Rules: The Role of Discussion. Kyklos 47, 341-354

Booth, D.E. (1994: Valuing Nature – The Decline and Preservation of Old-Growth Forests. Rowman and Littlefield, London

Bouyssou, D. (1990): Building Criteria: A Prerequisite for MCDA. In: Bana e Costa, C.A. (Ed.): Readings in Multiple Criteria Decision Aid. Springer, Berlin, 58-80

Dietz, T., Stern, P., Ryecroft, R. (1989): Definitions of Conflict and the Legitimation of Resources: The Case of Environmental Risk. Sociological Forum 4, nach Renn et al. 1995, 47-70

Fiorino, D. (1995): Regulatory Negotiation as a Form of Public Participation., In: Renn, O., Webler, T., Wiedemann, P. (Eds.): Fairness and Competence in Citizen Participation. Kluwer, Dordrecht, 223-237

Hadden, S.G. (1995): Regulatory Negotiation as Citizen Participation: A Critique. In: Renn, O., Webler, T., Wiedemann, P. (Eds.): Fairness and Competence in Citizen Participation. Kluwer, Dordrecht, 239-252

Jacobs, M. (1997): Environmental valuation, deliberative democracy and public decision-making institutions. In: Foster, J. (Ed): Valuing nature? Economics, Ethics and Environment. London, Routledge, 211-231

Keeney, R.L., Raiffa, H. (1976): Decision with Multiple Objectives: Preferences and Value Trade-offs. Wiley and Sons, New York

Keeney, R.L., Winterfeldt, D.V., Eppel, T. (1990): Eliciting Public Values for Complex Policy Decisions. Management Science 36(9), 1011-1030

Krebs, A. (1997): Naturethik: Grundtexte der gegenwärtigen tier- und ökoethischen Diskussion. Suhrkamp, Frankfurt

Krebs, A. (1999): Ethics of Nature – A Map. St. Martin's Press, New York

Lynn, F.M., Kartez, J.D. (1995): The Redemption of Citizen Advisory Committees: A Perspective from Critical Theory. In: Renn, O., Webler, T., Wiedemann, P. (Eds.): Fairness and Competence in Citizen Participation. Kluwer, Dordrecht, 87-102

Mayestre, L.Y., Pictet, J., Simos, J. (1994): Méthodes multicritères ELECTRE. Presses polytechniques, Lausanne

Munda, G. (1995): Multicriteria Evaluation in a Fuzzy Environment. Physica, Heidelberg

Nida-Rümelin, J. (1996): Theoretische und angewandte Ethik: Paradigmen, Begründungen, Bereiche. In: Nida-Rümelin, J. (Ed.): Angewandte Ethik: Die Bereichsethiken und ihre theoretische Fundierung. Kröner, Stuttgart, 2-85

Nida-Rümelin, J. (1997): Praktische Kohärenz. Zeitschrift für philosophische Forschung 51(2), 175-192

Nothdurft, W. (1995): Environmental Mediation: Insights into the Microcosm and Outlooks for Political Implications. In: Renn, O., Webler, T., Wiedemann, P. (Eds.): Fairness and Competence in Citizen Participation. Kluwer, Dordrecht, 267-282

O'Hara, S.U. (1996): Discursive ethics in ecosystems valuation and environmental policy. Ecological Economics 16, 95-107

Pfordten, D. v.d. (1996): Ökologische Ethik: Zur Rechtfertigung menschlichen Verhaltens gegenüber der Natur. Rowohlt, Reinbek

Pierce, C., Vandeveer, D. (Eds.) (1994): People, Penguins, and Plastic Trees. Wadsworth, Belmont

Renn, O., Webler, T., Wiedemann, P. (Eds.) (1995): Fairness and Competence in Citizen Participation. Kluwer, Dordrecht

Renn, O., Webler, T., Rakel, H., Dienel, P., Johnson, B. (1993): Public participation in decision making: A three-step procedure. Policy Sciences 26, 189-214

Roy, B. (1990a): The Outranking Approach and the Foundations of Electre Methods. In: Bana e Costa, C.A. (Ed.): Readings in Multiple Criteria Decision Aid. Springer, Berlin, 155-183

Roy, B. (1990b): Decision-Aid and Decision-Making. In: Bana e Costa, C.A. (Ed.): Readings in Multiple Criteria Decision Aid. Springer, Berlin, 17-35

Roy, B., Vanderpooten, D. (1996): The European School of MCDA: Emergence, basic features and current works. Journal of Multi Criteria Decision Aid 5, 22-38

Spash, C.L., Hanley, N. (1995): Preferences, Information and Biodiversity Preservation. Ecological Economics 12, 191-208

Stevens, T.H., Echeverria, J., Glass, R.J., Hager, T., More, T.A. (1991): Measuring the Existence Value of Wildlife: What Do CVM Estimates Really Show? Land Economics 67(4), 390-400

Sylvan, R., Bennett, D. (1994): The Greening of Ethics. White Horse Press, Knapwell

Trapp, R.W. (1989): Systematische Klassifikation und vergleichende Betrachtung der wichtigsten Ethiktypen unter dem Gesichtspunkt ihrer Eignung als allgemein akzeptable Handlungsrichtlinien. Grazer Philosophische Studien 35, 123-151

Vari, A. (1995): Citizens' Advisory Committee as a Model for Public Participation. In: Renn, O., Webler, T., Wiedemann, P. (Eds.): Fairness and Competence in Citizen Participation. Kluwer, Dordrecht, 103-116

Vatn, A., Bromley, D.W. (1994): Choices without Prices without Apologies. Journal of Environmental Economics and Management 26, 129-148

Webler, T. (1995): "Right" Discourse in Citizen Participation: An Evaluative Yardstick. In: Renn, O., Webler, T., Wiedemann, P. (Eds.): Fairness and Competence in Citizen Participation. Kluwer, Dordrecht, 35-86

Wenz, P. (1993): Minimal, Moderate and Extreme Moral Pluralism. Environmental Ethics 15(1), 61-74

Stakeholder approaches to intertemporal valuation

Bengt Å. Månsson

Department of Engineering Sciences, Physics and Mathematics,
Karlstad University, S-651 88 KARLSTAD, Sweden

1 Introduction

The two most widely discussed subjects concerning the economics of the environment are sustainable development and climate change. The frequently cited definition of the first ("Sustainable development is development that meets the needs of the present without compromising the ability of future generations to meet their own needs... [It] must not endanger the natural systems that support life on Earth...", WCED 1987: 42, 44-45) explicitly stresses the needs of future generations and acknowledges that the decisions we take today may have effects far into the future. The second involves processes that may have very long delays between action (cause) and effect and where the ecological and economic effects may be large. In both cases, valuation of benefits, costs, and effects at different points in time is of primary importance for decision-making. It is therefore surprising that the approaches to intertemporal valuation used in these areas are crude and undifferentiated.

Of course, intertemporal valuation is a pervasive feature of decision-making, not only in environmental economics. All decisions involve processes or outcomes occuring at different points in time; thus, ethical issues are at stake and valuation problems appear. The scientific analysis of such ethical issues is of surprisingly recent date in the economic literature. For a long time they were either wholly ignored or only dealt with in the form of normative postulates. There is therefore yet much to do before the intertemporal valuation issues are satisfactorily integrated in economic theory. I will here attempt to move the discussion a small step forward in the direction of integration of stakeholder perspectives in intertemporal valuation theory.

In the orthodox (neoclassical) economic theory, a single, constant discount rate applying generally is used. In continuous time, the discount factor has the form $\exp(-\delta t)$, where t is time and δ is the discount rate. Thus, for a non-zero positive discount rate, the value of future events declines rapidly towards zero. (The same applies to the corresponding discount factor in discrete time.) There are many well-known problems with this form of intertemporal valuation, some of which will be mentioned below.

As pointed out by Faber (1998, personal communication), there are two steps, which should always be carefully distinguished, to determining a procedure for intertemporal valuation. The first step deals with the question whether the object of the valuation (a process, good, service, unit of consumption, amount of capital etc.) may at all be given different values at different points in time. This may, for ethical or other reasons to be determined and specified, not be the case. Then, the conventional exponential discounting obviously cannot be applied (or it may be applied with discount rate zero). The second step consists in determining an intertemporal valuation rule or method appropriate for the particular *context*.

The rule or method of the second step may be the conventional exponential discounting, but for many reasons, some of which are discussed below, this will rarely be the case.

Already here, we see a clear breach with tradition, since the traditional approaches do not include the possibility of excluding some entities from valuation, nor do they allow differentiation according to context. It is worth noting here that, as discussed by Goodin (1982) and others, some of the derivations underlying the conventional discounting procedures should, if consistently made, lead to different discount rates applied to different goods. The discussions in the recent literature have made it clear that there are many more examples of context-dependence. The key components of the context is a combination of

1. a certain decision or set of *decisions to be made* (typically an investment decision or a decision on distribution between consumption/investment possibilities);
2. a set of *rules and procedures* by which the decision(s) are taken (e.g., a certain political process);
3. a *setting* or the circumstances determined by the state, structure and dynamics of both the natural and social environment;
4. a single or a group of *decision-makers* (social agents making the decision), and
5. the social agents (persons or groups of persons) or non-human *entities that are influenced by the decision.*

In this paper, the latter two components constitute what is called the stakeholders. Note that there will typically be a certain, possibly large overlap of the two sets of social agents. In most cases, and in particular for the purposes of this paper, the set of stakeholders may be restricted to social agents, excluding non-human entities such as animals. The social agents of 5. may include unborn future and potential persons.

In addition to the five components listed above, there are the *objects to be decided upon*, the objects for which a valuation must be done to provide a basis for the decision.

The setting, 3., can make a large difference for the possible procedures. The context is, e.g., significantly different if growth is assumed to be exponential in perpetuity or if it abates and eventually approaches zero. It is only in the first case that a traditional discounting procedure can be applied. Note that this case must involve a rather peculiar meaning of 'growth' to be compatible with our physically finite world – it must be assumed that economic growth is decoupled from growth in material and energy use.

The setting is never completely known, i.e., there are also fundamentally *incomplete sets of knowledge* about both the social agents and the physical environment in which they live. The incompleteness brings in uncertainty, risk and unpredictability as intrinsic features of the valuation problematique.

The differentiation according to contexts implies that any theory of intertemporal valuation must be able to take into account that there may be conflicts between stakeholders. Furthermore, it must recognise that there may be quite different kinds of values (for a pertinent taxonomy of different kinds of environmental values, see Rolston 1988) involved and that categories of value derived from different premises may not be compatible, see Prior (1998).

In environmental economics, there are two opposing arguments concerning the traditional discount rate. The most common one says that the discount rate should be zero, basically because it should not matter when environmental damage occurs. Another, quite different argument is put forward by Pearce and Turner (1990). They point out that a high discount rate leads to low investments, which in turn results in less environmental deterioration. The main problem with their argument is that it ignores the environmental effects of consumption, which will increase if the investments decrease (assuming sum of consumption and investments constant). Anyhow, with the more differentiated approach towards intertemporal valuation promoted here, this debate may well turn out to be largely irrelevant.

Orthodox economics largely avoids problems of intragenerational as well as intergenerational equity or justice. This is no longer possible with a stakeholder approach. In addition, there may be incompatibilities or conflicts between these two categories of equity, as indicated by the difficulties experienced when attempting to apply the framework of Rawls (1972) to intergenerational justice (see, e.g., Phelps and Riley 1978 and Becker 1982).

2 Stakeholders

Some thought shows that there can be many different kinds of stakeholders. A few of these have already been given a place in the economic literature, cf. the JEL category D9: "Intertemporal Choice and Growth", which has subcategories oriented towards "Consumer Choice" and "Firm Choice".

The *individual* stakeholders have so far dominated the economic theory. There are then three kinds of individuals being regarded. First, there is the now living person, a member of the current generation, which is also the group of people containing the actual decision-makers. Second, there is the yet unborn person, who will come into being at a certain future date. Third, there is the potential person, who might or might not come into being at a future date. For intertemporal valuation, the most important feature of individual persons is their finite life-time.

Dasgupta (1998) points out that approaches to social ethics that are based on the notion of impartiality, such as the ones of Harsanyi (1955) (impartial preferences) and Rawls (1972) (veil of ignorance), can deal only with the first two kinds of individuals and not the third.

The value systems of the individual stakeholders are multifaceted. In terms of the neoclassical utility concept, it is well known that the utilities of different individuals may be interdependent. In addition, 'utility' is not the only kind of value. This causes a number of problems, e.g., with aggregation. Furthermore, the preferences of individuals, which are used to determine utility, may be inconsistent. Attitudes towards risk and uncertainty have been observed to vary greatly. It remains to be explored to what extent such phenomena can be included in the theory or alternatively postulated away. Here, economists must make use of theories and observations from disciplines such as psychology.

The dominant *group* stakeholders in the literature are families at the micro level and the entire humanity at the macro level. Sometimes the entire humanity, including all future generations, is treated as one individual with infinite, or sometimes finite, lifetime.

In addition, however, there are certain group stakeholders that dominate the actual intertemporal decision-making being done at present. The intertemporal valuation principles and activities of these stakeholders are seldom discussed in economic theory. There are first of all the stakeholders belonging to the political system (public sector), e.g., communities, regional authorities and the national governments. Then there are different kinds of special interest groups and actors belonging to the private sector, e.g., companies.

When acquiring the necessary information on the value systems and attitudes towards intertemporal valuation of group stakeholders, theories and observations from political science and sociology will play a crucial role.

For the public sector stakeholders, intertemporal valuation principles and procedures are determined mostly by the political systems at the national level. As pointed out by Kula (1997) and others, the policies differ widely between different contexts. There are even large differences in the policies of a single public authority. Such differences are unaccounted for and not explicable within the framework of current economic theory.

The private sector stakeholders form a more coherent group in which intertemporal valuation is dominated by market interest rates (real) and profit rates. Nevertheless, there are differing investment strategies between both different industry sectors and between firms in the same sector.

3 Traditional arguments drawn upon in the economic literature

In order to illustrate some of the shortcomings of traditional theory from a stakeholder point of view, a brief review of the dominant lines of argument and modelling assumptions is called for.

As described above, the conventional approach to intertemporal valuation is discounting with a general, constant discount rate. As shown by Kula (1997), Price (1993), Lumley (1997), Lumley (1998), and others, the theoretical (both conceptual and philosophical) as well as the empirical foundations for this approach are very weak. Within economics, it is already well recognized that there are many difficulties with the traditional way of discounting in its implementations in public policy. Lind (1982) is a collection of papers that give a very good introduction to the field. Parfit (1984) discusses several key philosophical and ethical aspects. Norgaard and Howarth (1991) discuss the relation between sustainability and discounting. Goodin (1982) gives an excellent introduction to a number of the fundamental problems of discounting.

In particular, in the conventional approaches the decision-maker is assumed to be either

- an individual with finite lifetime – causing problems when aggregating to find a social discount rate; or
- the whole society treated as a single individual with infinite life-time – an assumption that is both far from reality and involves a number of problems with aggregation of individual utilities or values.

The early discussions on discounting were focused on saving and rates of interest (Ramsey 1928; Fisher 1930). This still directs the discussions, e.g., so that in order to find the discount rate, derivations based on market equilibrium concepts are often used. Such approaches are unsatisfactory for ecological economics on at least two grounds: an equilibrium is just as unlikely in economics as it is in ecology; and the market is anyhow unable to take proper account of the environment so that any market equilibrium is bound to be environmentally inefficient. Furthermore, as shown by Price (1993), there are numerous obstacles to empirically determining growth rates, rates of return on investment as well as real interest rates, which are the three main alternatives as inputs to a procedure for determining a social discount rate.

3.1 The growth argument

This argument is based on two assumptions. First, there will be growth in the economy, so that future generations are better off. Secondly, there is a diminishing marginal utility/welfare of consumption, so that a unit of the increased consumption that the future generations enjoy is of less value than a unit of consumption in the present.

Typically, the stakeholders are here generations, i.e., the collective of all persons living at a point in time. The possibly uneven distribution of consumption within a generation is then mostly disregarded. Note that, as indicated above, there may easily be inconsistencies between the principles of intergenerational and intragenerational equity.

To get the traditional form of the discount factor, it has to be assumed that the growth is exponential for all future or at least to a certain, finite planning horizon. As pointed out by Solow (1987) and others, the use of a finite horizon is connected with a number of complex problems concerning the final state. Furthermore, the exponential growth implies that per capita consumption tends towards infinity – a meaningless concept. A more realistic growth assumption might be, e.g., logistic growth (Sterner 1994; Azar and Sterner 1996).

Growth is associated with productive capital, which brings in the opportunity cost of capital argument. It starts out with the assumption that capital is productive, in the sense that one unit today will generate more than one unit in the future. This assumption leads to a positive discount rate, since acquiring one unit today is equivalent (of equal value) to an assured promise to acquire something more than one unit at a certain future time.

A basic problem with this kind of argument is that growth is explicitly or implicitly presumed to exist, regardless of which decisions are taken. Even for the models that are used to determine optimal savings (investment) rates in different circumstances, this assumption can be a cause for inconsistencies.

In economic modelling, a proper treatment of this kind of argument would mean that not only the growth rate but also the discount rate would be an endogeneous variable in any model. Then, even in the framework of the conventional approaches, a consistent treatment would mean that it should be taken into account that the discount rate may be varying with time. This would be an advantage in those models where discounting is mainly introduced for reasons of mathematical convenience, e.g., to ensure existence of an integral over utility or welfare. As an example of time-varying discount rates, see Sterner (1994). However, the consequences for intertemporal decision-making consistency may be severe. One possible effect is that the resulting programme may be what Dasgupta (1998) denotes 'intergenerationally incoherent,' meaning that an intertemporal investment-consumption distribution programme set in motion by one generation would be revoked by a later. This is one example of the problem of time invariance, but it should be noted that in a stakeholder approach, time invariance might not be necessary or desirable. As an example, stakeholders with access to fossil fuels may be treated differently from the ones without.

Another problem in this context is that as soon as the growth rate is made dependent on the investment/consumption distribution decisions, the 'optimal' outcome may well be that no investments are made.

3.2 The uncertainty arguments

As noted above, the knowledge about the physical environment in which we live is always incomplete. In addition to the incompleteness of knowledge about the state of the environment, there is the incompleteness related to the environmental dynamics. Ecology tells us that all biological systems, from individual and parts of individuals to the largest collective systems extant, are dynamic non-equilibrium entities characterized by complex mixtures of regular and irregular behavior. This is also the case for many abiotic parts of nature. Quite often, the reactions of ecological systems to the impact of human activities occur as shocks and surprises. Taken together, this means that unpredictability is one of the primary facets of nature. In ecology, unpredictability is closely tied to instability, randomness or evolutionary emergence of radically new entities and features. This also means that ecological systems have irreversible dynamics – it is impossible to retrieve a previous state (and it is just as impossible to preserve a particular state). Consequently, there can be no truly ecological economic theory without including uncertainty and unpredictability.

That the choice of discount rate can have important consequences for ecological systems (overexploitation causing extinction) is well known (Clark 1973). In some cases, notably forestry, this has had the effect that governments, having declared extinction as unacceptable, have put sufficiently low discount rates into law. This procedure has effects on economic efficiency, see below. For an early discussion on the significance of uncertainty and irreversibility for environmental economics, see Arrow and Fisher (1974).

In environmental economics, it is well known that the risk or uncertainty of an outcome varies with time and that this has implications for discounting procedures (e.g., Brown 1983; Prince 1985). In these discussions, three kinds of uncertainty play key roles:

1. The 'risk of death', i.e., the uncertainty about the presence of the economic agent at some future date.
2. Uncertainty about the value system of the economic agent even when his existence can be regarded as certain.
3. Uncertainty about the magnitude of the benefit or cost.

In addition, there is the uncertainty concerning the existence of a future economic agent, see, e.g. Dasgupta (1998).

The first kind of uncertainty is usually regarded as relevant only on an individual level; society is treated as an 'immortal' economic agent. For other kinds of stakeholders, this kind of uncertainty needs a different treatment, which however is largely lacking in the literature.

As pointed out by Drepper and Månsson (1993), given the possibility of total collapse of the environmental life-support systems, the assumption of immortality ought to be surrounded with some caveats. Nevertheless, if the aim is to develop a theoretical framework to be used to investigate different possibilities for realising a society that can be sustained forever, introducing a finite societal lifetime as a *basic* assumption is counter-productive.

In the economics literature, the second kind of uncertainty is mostly noted to exist but rarely analysed and included in the modelling. Note here that one part of the (time-dependent) value system includes the individual's attitude towards risk and uncertainty! The intricate interplay of decisions, probabilities and values (utility) is discussed in, e.g., Gärdenfors and Sahlin (1988). In particular, one should be wary of the use of expected values (e.g., expected utility, see discussion on the third kind of uncertainty below, in models of individual decision-making: empirical research speaks against it Kula 1997; Price 1993). This means that agents (stakeholders) may not be 'rational' (cf. the discussion of "rational" economic behaviour and discounting of Ainslie 1991), since rationality is often defined with the help of expected utility. In this area, sociology probably has a better theoretical and empirical basis for modelling than economics.

Welfare functions are typically not only risk-averse functions of their arguments in the traditional sense, i.e., that the value gain arising from an improvement of a certain magnitude is smaller than the value loss resulting from an equally large decrement, but they are also assumed to be time-invariant. In a stakeholder perspective, it is important that there are several distinct aspects in the societal value system. This may lead to conflicts between stakeholders or involve incompatibilities between different aspects. Furthermore, the relative weights of these aspects may, and most likely do, change with time (cf. the discussion on the evolution of time preference of Rogers 1994). The basic question is then if and how it is possible to predict or at least model such changes. In this, a stakeholder-based analysis may turn out to be particularly fruitful, since it reduces the possibility set of value aspects coming into play.

The third kind of uncertainty is treated extensively in the economics literature. In this case, the rationale for a discount rate is an idea with deep roots. The idea is that a benefit or cost is valued less the more uncertain it is. This declining value is formally expressible in the form of a discount factor. However, this rationale is likely to be in conflict with other valuation principles for some stakeholders, e.g., if it matters whether the uncertainty is an intrinsic natural feature. In cases with catastrophic collapse of the life-support systems, uncertainty as to the exact magnitude of the collapse (provided it exceeds the human extinction level) or to the exact path of the catastrophe (e.g., different pathways of climate change) does not constitute grounds for discounting the costs involved.

The conventional approaches to handling this kind of uncertainty operate with different kinds of expected values. For example, if the social welfare is a function of a stochastic variable, the central notion involved in conventional economic decision-making procedures is the *expected* social welfare; cf. Perrings (1987, 1989, 1991). A fundamental limitation is that the expected value approaches can only deal with uncertainty for which certain probability distributions are known. In environmental economics, it is often assumed that the natural sciences possess knowledge of the environmental probability distributions. This is fairly seldom the case, at least with the precision necessary. Here, it is well worth noting that the individual as well as groups of scientists are also stakeholders pursuing their own interests.

3.3 The finite lifetime arguments

For the rational, utility-maximising 'economic man' so popular in the economics literature, the fact of a finite lifetime is of overwhelming importance. After death, no utility can be got. The question is how far this idealized social construct is from real human beings. A study of various empirical results, e.g., the ones discussed by Price (1993), reveals that real human beings are neither rational (in a narrow individualistic economic sense) nor utility-maximising when it comes to intertemporal valuation. In a stakeholder approach, such empirical results must of course form a basis for development of theory.

The problems do not end with the properties of the individual person. An individual person is not only a stakeholder by itself, it is also a member of several group stakeholders. It is realistic to assume that there will be conflicts between the interests of such stakeholders. A complete treatment of such conflict situations needs going outside the realm of economics, although such parts of economics as game theory provide important insights. Again, sociology has an important role to play.

One approach that could be generalized with gain is the one proposed by Kula (1997). At the bottom of his idea lies the fact that just as utility is no longer derived after death, it is also not derived before birth and neither is disutility. This fact should be taken into account also in the framework where the finite individual lifetime argument is accepted as a basis for discounting. The basic idea is therefore that the discounting clock should not start ticking before the birth of a person. This leads to a discounting procedure that differs significantly from the conventional one for long time spans.

4 A note on negative discount rates

Once outside the traditional arguments for discounting, one finds that there are no a priori arguments for always putting a lesser value to the future. In terms of the exponential discount factor, this would involve negative discount rates, a phenomenon to be treated with extreme care. The appearance of a negative discount rate is not new to economics, there are in fact several cases were it appears (e.g., Stokey and Zeckhauser 1978: 175; Mitra 1981; Daly and Cobb 1989: 155; Loewenstein and Prelec 1991; see also Goodin 1982).

One of the main results of Drepper and Månsson (1993) is that the combination of risk aversion expressing the concern for sustainability and the unavoidable increase in unpredictability of the states of nature leads to a form of negative discount rate.

The arguments based on the opportunity cost of capital do not always imply a positive discount rate, e.g., in the case with natural capital with decreasing productivity. Furthermore, some other common arguments for discounting may lead to zero or even negative discount rates in the case of nature as capital, e.g., the argument of diminishing marginal utility. In a situation of expected growth, this says that the more one has in the future, the less one is willing to sacrifice today to obtain even more in the future. The environmental dynamics may undermine the premise that future generations are going to be wealthier than the present ones.

In the economics literature, there are very few empirical observations of economic agents applying negative discount rates. Nevertheless, it does happen in reality, e.g., in situations with negative real interest rates there are still people saving for an investment at a later time.

Here, a note should be made of an important objection to negative discount rates, namely that they imply perpetual subsistence level consumption; see, e.g., Pearce and Turner (1990: 223). In certain contexts, it may be the case that the equivalent of negative discount rates could be used for a limited period of time. Again, the difference between generations with and without access to abundant fossil fuels comes to mind.

5 Stakeholder approaches and economic efficiency

Dubourg and Pearce (1996) discuss conflicts between sustainability and optimality in the sense of economic efficiency. Generally, it is worth noting that there may be fundamental conflicts between the intertemporal valuation principles and procedures of different stakeholders (e.g., equitable temporal distribution of consumption) and the principle of economic efficiency (the most productive use of resources). The economically efficient is in fact likely to be inequitable if the traditional discounting procedures are used.

This problem is related to the general problem with the economic efficiency concept in the presence of externalities that cannot be internalised. Since such externalities are not efficiently allocated, the outcome of a market efficiency maximisation process is suboptimal.

Economic efficiency presupposes a one-dimensional value measure. Thus also from this point of view the incommensurability of values mentioned above is a major difficulty for the choice of intertemporal valuation procedures. Unfortunately, the economic theory for multiple values is undeveloped, in particular so in the context of intertemporal valuation. Note that it is not far from the idea mentioned above – that different discount rates apply to different goods – to the idea that different intertemporal valuation procedures should apply to different kinds of values. Multidimensional value systems and representations of the environment will necessarily involve complicated intertemporal valuation procedures. Then, economic efficiency may become an intractable concept.

6 Stakeholder approaches: concluding remarks

Taking up the threads of the previous sections, I suggest that stakeholder approaches to intertemporal valuation should explicitly take into account that

- stakeholders can only do valuation during their lifetime, which of course can differ significantly from the lifetime of individuals;
- there are irreducible sources of uncertainty and unpredictability, which for risk-averse stakeholders might lead to precautionary principles or similar policies being put into effect;
- growth (and decay) will have different effects on different stakeholders;
- dynamic ecological-economic modelling with discounting should be done so that the discount rates are endogeneous, i.e., arising from *within* the framework of the model;
- the most important stakeholders, in the sense that they are the ones actually taking the decisions, are neither individuals nor the whole of humanity, but primarily families, communities and national governments;
- there might be some contexts in which a future potential gain or loss may be given a larger value than in the present;
- value systems may be multidimensional and also that they will differ between different stakeholders.

Of course, many components of such an economic theory already exist, in particular within the framework of institutional economics, but also in, e.g., game theory.

I have repeatedly pointed to potential gains in a closer interaction between economics and sociology. There are also a number of other disciplines that must be brought into the development of new, stakeholder-oriented approaches to intertemporal valuation. Among these, ethics and axiology are prominent.

Although it has only been possible to touch superficially on the subject of intertemporal valuation in this paper, the indications are that the use of the traditional discount factors for intertemporal valuation should be abandoned except in certain special cases.

References

Ainslie, G. (1991): Derivation of "rational" economic behavior from hyperbolic discount curves. American Economic Review 81, 334-340

Arrow, K.J., Fisher, A.C. (1974): Environmental preservation, uncertainty, and irreversibility. Quarterly Journal of Economics 87, 312-319

Azar, C., Sterner, T. (1996): Discounting and distributional considerations in the context of global warming. Ecological Economics 19, 169-184

Becker, R.A. (1982): Intergenerational Equity: The Capital-Environment Trade-Off. Journal of Environmental Economics and Management 9, 165-185

Brown, S.P.A. (1983): A Note on Environmental Risk and the Rate of Discount. Journal of Environmental Economics and Management 10, 282-286

Clark, C.W. (1973): The Economics of Overexploitation. Science 181, 630-634

Daly, H.E., Cobb, J.B., Jr. (1989): For the Common Good. Beacon Press, Boston

Dasgupta, P. (1998): Population, consumption and resources: Ethical issues. Ecological Economics 24, 139-152

Drepper, F.R., Månsson, B.Å. (1993): Intertemporal Valuation in an Unpredictable Environment. Ecological Economics 7, 43-67

Dubourg, R., Pearce, D. (1996): Paradigms for Environmental Choice: Sustainability versus Optimality. In: Faucheux, S., Pearce, D., Proops, J. (Eds.): Models of Sustainable Development. Edward Elgar, Cheltenham

Fisher, I. (1930): The Theory of Interest. McMillan, New York

Gärdenfors, P., Sahlin, N.-E. (1988): Decision, Probability, and Utility. Cambridge University Press, New York

Goodin, R.E. (1982): Discounting discounting. Journal of Public Policy 2, 53-71

Harsanyi, J.C. (1955): Cardinal welfare, individualistic ethics and interpersonal comparisons of utility. Journal of Political Economics 63, 309-321

Kula, E. (1997): Time Discounting and Future Generations. Quorum Books, London

Lind, R.C. (Ed.) (1982): Discounting for Time and Risk in Energy Policy. John Hopkins University Press, Baltimore

Loewenstein, G., Prelec, D. (1991): Negative Time Preference. American Economic Review 81, 347-352

Lumley, S. (1997): The environment and the ethics of discounting: An empirical analysis. Ecological Economics 20, 77-82

Lumley, S. (1998): The theory and application of cost-benefit analysis. Ecological Economics 24, 121-123

Mitra, T. (1981): Some Results on the Optimal Depletion of Exhaustible Resources Under Negative Discounting. Review of Economic Studies 48, 521-532

Norgaard, R.B., Howarth, R.B. (1991): Sustainability and Discounting the Future. In: Costanza, R. (Ed.): Ecological Economics – The Science and Management of Sustainability, Columbia University Press, New York

Parfit, D. (1984): Reasons and Persons. Oxford University Press, Oxford

Pearce, D.W., Turner, R.K. (1990): Economics of natural resources and the environment. Harvester Wheatsheaf, London

Perrings, C. (1987): Economy and Environment. Cambridge University Press, Cambridge

Perrings, C. (1989): Environmental bonds and environmental research in innovative activities. Ecological Economics 1, 95-110

Perrings, C. (1991): Reserved Rationality and the Precautionary Principle: Technological Change, Time and Uncertainty in Environmental Decision Making. In: Costanza, R. (Ed.): Ecological Economics – The Science and Management of Sustainability, Columbia University Press, New York

Phelps, E.S., Riley, J.G. (1978): Rawlsian Growth: Dynamic Programming of Capital and Wealth for Intergeneration "Maximin" Justice. Review of Economic Studies 35, 103-120

Price, C. (1993): Time, Discounting and Value. Blackwell, Oxford

Prince, R. (1985): A Note on Environmental Risk and the Rate of Discount: Comment. Journal of Environmental Economics and Management 12, 179-180

Prior, M. (1998): Economic Valuation and Environmental Values. Environmental Values 7, 423-441

Ramsey, F. (1928): A mathematical theory of saving. Economic Journal 38, 543-559

Rawls, J. (1972): A Theory of Justice. Oxford University Press, Oxford

Rogers, A.R. (1994): Evolution of time preference by natural selection. American Economic Review 84, 460-481

Rolston, H., III. (1988): Environmental Ethics. Temple University Press, Philadelphia

Solow, R.M. (1987): Growth Theory: An exposition. Oxford University Press, Oxford

Sterner, T. (1994): Discounting in a world of limited growth. Environmental and Resource Economics 4, 527-534

Stokey, E., Zeckhauser, R. (1978): A Primer for Policy Analysis. W.W. Norton & Company, New York

WCED, World Commission on Environment and Development (1987): Our Common Future (Brundtland Report). Oxford University Press, Oxford

Sustainable development of society, economy and environment: consequences for integrated coastal management

R. Kerry Turner

Director, Centre for Social and Economic Research on the Global Environment (CSERGE), University of East Anglia, Norwich, Norfolk, NR4 7TJ, UK

1 Introduction: sustainability perspectives

The intensification of the process of global environmental change and its manifestation across a range of temporal and spatial scales has served to highlight the importance of the contemporary sustainability debate. It is tempting to characterise the wider debate in terms of two polar viewpoints which contrast economic growth-orientated technological optimism with steady-state-oriented technological pessimism. The latter position also implies that there is a need for some new environmental ethic to guide individual and collective action and public policy.

Pushing this caricature further it may be argued that growth optimists contend that over the long run, economic growth, trade expansion and environmental protection are not just mutually consistent, but are highly correlated. Some empirical work using Kuznets curve models seems to support this optimism by positing an inverted U-shaped relationship between 'flow' pollutants with local to regional scale impacts over time. The inference that has been drawn is that increasing income per capita will, over the long term, reduce an individual's environmental damage impact. Existing and new technologies, if properly deployed and encouraged, can achieve significant eco-efficiency savings. Capitalism and technological innovation can in the future be directed to produce resource productivity gains (four to ten-fold increases), just as in the past when economic growth was stimulated by labour productivity improvements (Weizsäcker et al. 1997).

Growth pessimists counter that the Kuznets curve evidence is far from sufficient to prove that economic growth will induce generalised environmental improvement, or that an indefinite process of economic growth is feasible. The U-shaped curve finding does not apply to bioaccumulating 'stock' pollutants, or to global scale emissions such as carbon dioxide, or to the maintenance of resource stocks. From this viewpoint, continuous economic growth is neither feasible nor a socially desirable option. Taking an evolutionary perspective, the direction of technical progress and economic activity is not seen as an autonomous phenomenon, but as an endogenous process conditioned by the structure of economic incentives, technological opportunities and prevailing institutions. Many contemporary institutions are not well adapted to environmental system variability and change. They lack the necessary flexibility to ensure continuing resilience in environmental and socio-economic systems. Future outcomes are therefore relatively unpredictable because of the complex interaction taking place between different actors who are endogenous to the process of change. Coastal situations exemplify these risk and uncertainty considerations.

The continued sustainable utilisation of coastal resources will require new applications of multidisciplinary scientific findings in order to reorientate coastal protection and sea defence strategies away from hard engineering works towards softer approaches which work with nature. A policy of managed coastal realignment will play an increasingly important role in the future, together with new institutions to mitigate risk (inundation and erosion problems) by preventing new development and/or phasing out of existing inappropriate development, and by implementing compensation schemes. Technological progress can also help to reduce risk by containment, by improving natural defences or by realignment to provide more space.

Technical innovations are the outcome of learning processes inside firms, but progress can be hindered by inertia in the firms' organisational routines and by path dependency, with the attendant risk of becoming locked into an unsustainable technological trajectory. So the pessimists hold that technological innovation is less important than the capacity of ecological processes to adapt, and that the focus of policy should be technological and institutional measures to reduce the 'throughput' of matter and energy from the environment into the economy and back out into the environment (a thermodynamic imperative). If such switches are not made then they argue that nature itself will force such changes via an under-supply of food, energy or materials, or waste assimilation and an increasingly unstable set of environmental conditions.

The polar viewpoint caricature rapidly loses both natural and social science credibility as soon as the details of the sustainability debate are addressed and practical policy prescriptions are required. Table 1 portrays the debate differently in terms of a spectrum of overlapping sustainability positions. It is meant to indicate that there is a new substantive multidisciplinary research agenda, straddling a range of disciplines and requiring a plurality of valuations, waiting to be tackled and with findings that could be meaningfully and constructively debated. Networked multidisciplinary research teams and findings may lead to significant future interdisciplinary insights (Turner 1999).

From an economics perspective weak and strong sustainability positions can be most readily distinguished by their assumption about the substitutability of the different forms of capital – reproducable capital, human capital

Table 1. Spectrum of overlapping sustainability positions.

very weak sustainability / weak sustainability	weak sustainability / strong sustainability	strong sustainability / very strong sustainability
economic efficiency criteria	efficiency and equity criteria	bioethical criteria and constraints
neo-classical economics paradigm	ecological system functional diversity	non-anthropocentric intrinsic value; rights-based approach, environmental 'trump' cards
individualism: rational self-interested consumer	systems perspective: ecosystem "health" and "integrity", total system value > total economic value (TEV)	preferences not appropriate basis for valuation
fixed preferences/values	individualism and collectivism: consumer and citizen motivations	citizen motivations as a distinct and separate category
market-based resource allocation and valuation	endogenous preferences: psychosocial and cultural theory variables	keep 'markets' out of the environment
anthropocentric instrumental value in nature	expressed and revealed preferences: focus group testing of contingent valuation surveys	'expert' opinion
marginal/discrete environmental change and its valuation	anthropocentric intrinsic value	contingent valuation surveys as opinion polls
revealed preferences via markets; household production functions; travel costs, hedonic pricing	benefits transfer: validity/reliability testing protocols	deliberative processes: citizen juries, consensus conferences etc.
positive rates of time discount	multiple policy goals; trade-off analysis: multi-criteria analysis, risk analysis, lifecycle assessments	
total economic value (TEV) concept (private values)	standards/regulations; "critical" natural capital; uncertainty and irriversibilities; precautionary principle conditioned by cost-effectiveness	
near infinite economic capital substitution possibilities via technical progress	integrated assessment process	
economic welfare significant component of social welfare		

and environmental (natural) capital. Weak sustainability requires only that an aggregate capital stock is maintained, or enhanced, over generational time, because there are virtually unlimited substitution possibilities between the different capital components, generated by technical progress. Strong sustainability, on the other hand, requires the maintenance of the natural capital stock overtime, because of the non-substitution of many environmental systems (critical natural capital) necessary for life-support or an enhanced quality of life, and irreducible uncertainty over the functioning of complex environmental systems. Table 1 illustrates the overlapping weak and strong sustainability viewpoints and the value systems and ethical/belief systems which also underpin them. As one moves along the spectrum from weak towards strong positions, individualism, economic efficiency, consumer sovereignty and market-based allocation mechanisms and axioms are supplemented or replaced by notions of collective citizen-type values, equity concerns and non-market deliberative processes for some resource allocations. In reality these positions are much less distinct than the diagram implies, but the general change of emphasis in terms of belief and value systems is clear. What will be argued in the case-study section of this chapter is that these fundamental ethical and value changes must play an important part, along with other environmental, technical and economic factors, in the debate over future formulation and implementation of a more sustainable and integrated approach to the management of increasingly vulnerable human coastal communities and their supporting ecosystems.

The research agenda therefore includes, questions about sustainability and the substitutability of different forms of capital, including natural capital; macroenvironmental scale and thermodynamic limits in 'source' and 'sink' terms; future technological and other changes together with the problems of novelty and 'surprise', ecosystem resilience, thresholds and chaos; value systems, social policy, philosophy and ethics (Turner, Perrings and Folke 1997). But while sustainable development has been accepted as a general policy goal, a practicable implementation strategy has yet to be devised.

Assuming that both national and international economic processes will continue to operate via markets, albeit regulated markets, it is possible to distinguish a number of generic sustainability rules. But this set of guidelines still falls short of a blueprint. The steering of a socio-economic systems towards a more sustainable development path will first of all require that existing market and policy intervention failures related to resource pricing and property rights should be corrected (Pearce and Warford 1993). Steps should be taken to ensure that the regenerative capacity of renewable natural capital is maintained i.e. harvesting rates should not exceed regeneration rates; and that cumulative pollution which could threaten waste assimilation capacities and life-support systems should be, wherever feasible, avoided (Clayton and Radcliffe 1996; Jansson et al. 1994). The endogenous nature of technical progress should be recognised and technological innovation and application should be steered via an indicative planning system, such that switches from non-renewable natural capital to renewable natural capital are fostered, and eco-efficient technical progress should dominate throughput-increasing technology (Common 1995; Faucheux, Pearce and Proops 1996; Van den Bergh 1999). Overall resource utilisation rates should be constrained by the rate of feasible substitution, including recycling, and the macroenvironmental 'scale' of economic activity should be limited so that it remains within the carrying capacity of the existing and augmented natural capital (Daly and Cobb 1990). Given the inevitable scientific and social uncertainties surrounding the feedback mechanisms between the coevolving socio-economic and environmental systems, a precautionary approach should be adopted with a built-in margin of safety (Faber, Manstetten and Proops 1996).

Taken together the general sustainability rules should be sufficient to 'kick start' the transition of the contemporary socio-economic systems towards a situation in which the components of sustainable development – a more secure wealth creation process, guided by principles of environmental stewardship provision of more scope for citizen empowerment and the production of a set of common futures and values, can be realised (O'Riordan and Voisey 1998), see Figure 1.

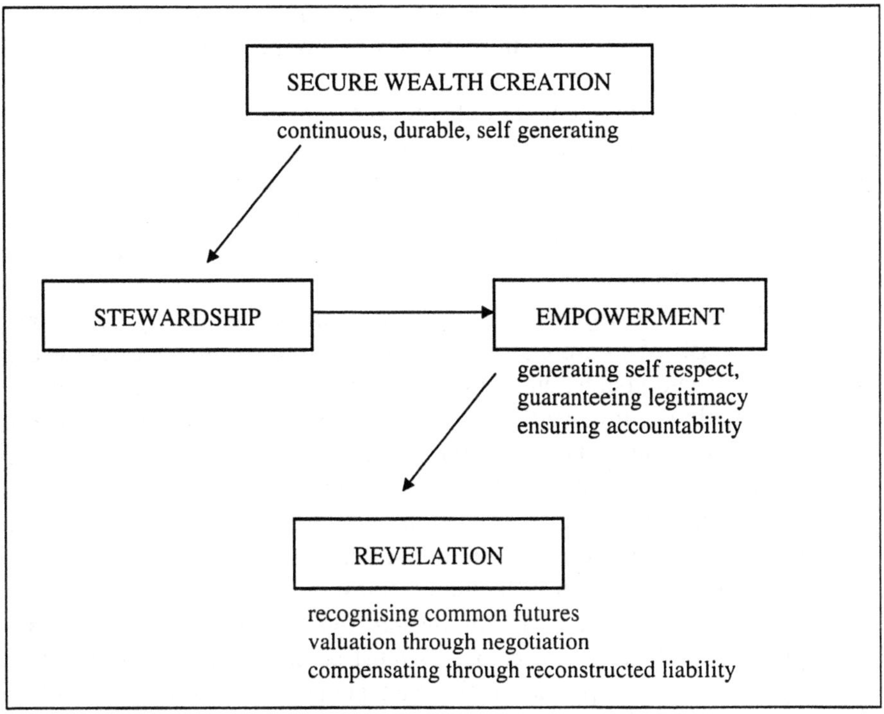

Source: O'Riordan and Voisey (1998: 25).

Figure 1. Four components of sustainable development.

2 Delivering sustainability

The sustainability transition process will require mechanisms for delivery of change to improve the natural environment and foster economic development. The aspiration to integrate environmental concerns into all aspects of social and economic life brings unprecedented cultural and political challenges. The causes of unsustainable human activities lie in lifestyle choice and patterns of consumption as well as in production activities. The context is one of shifting perceptions of environmental risk, changes in demography and household formation, cultural pluralism and changing relationships between individuals and governance institutions at all levels.

A sustainable economic system also requires that the environmental and social impacts of economic activity are more fully internalised in production and consumption decisions. The pursuit of sustainability within a more liberalised globalised economy is another challenge. Over the medium-term technological change can help to reduce the environmental impacts of human activity. Innovation in the service sector and transport as well as industry is important. 'Factor 4' eco-efficiency thereby holds much promise in this context. Figure 2 indicates how formidable the sustainability challenge is because of its comprehensive requirements, encompassing socio-cultural, legal and institutional as well as techno-economic factors and their coordination.

Sustainable development may therefore be interpreted as discourse – a process through which knowledge is constituted through communication. It is shorthand for a set of ideas that become universally acknowledged, even if ill-defined, and that are not necessarily coherent. It is also an active agent in interpreting events which, unconnected, have fragmented meaning (O'Riordan and Voisey 1998).

To summarise the argument so far, because the sustainability transition is beset by a clash of interpretatives and reactions regarding the purpose of sustainable developments, enabling the transition to a more sustainable development path will involve the devising of new ways to encourage the provision of sustainable goods and services. These should meet people's needs (rather than wants) while simultaneously requiring the use of less natural resources (including waste assimilation services) i.e. securing the wealth creation process. It will also require the building of sustainable communities and supporting infrastructure (including transport modes) for people to live and work in, as well as feeling empowered by. At the macro-level the sustainable utilisation of natural resources must be constrained by stewardship and a precautionary approach to the management and conservation of the environment and its life supporting processes.

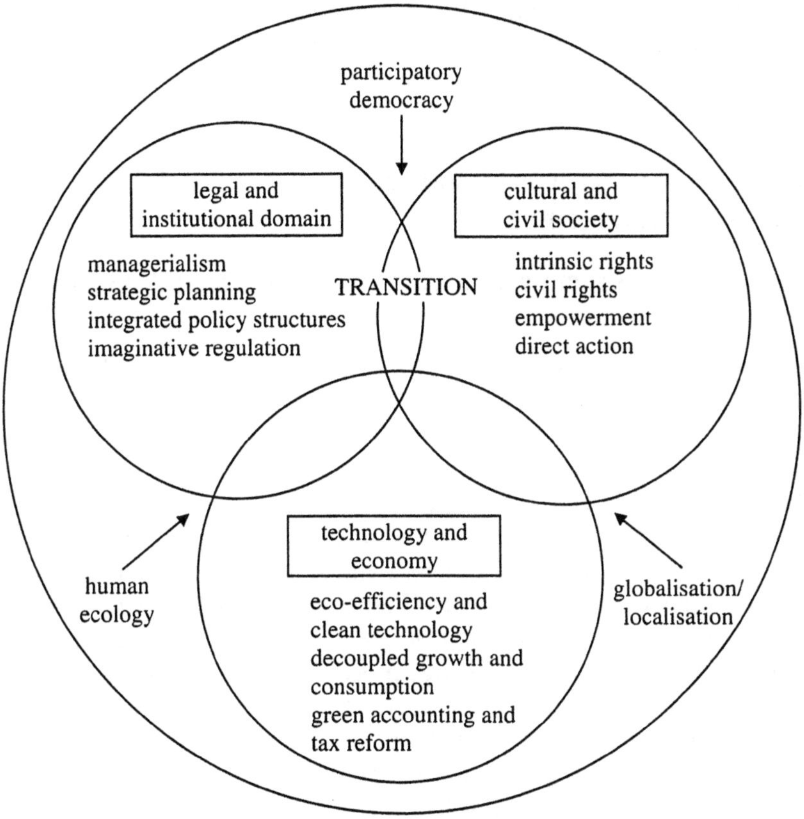

Source: based on Pezzoli (1997: 555); quoted from O'Riordan and Voisey (1998: 5).

Figure 2. The domains of sustainability.

These general rules are a necessary but not sufficient foundation for the achievement of the strong sustainability goal. The rules together with enabling policy instruments and institutions should be buttressed by an ethical re-evaluation which addresses the role and rights of present individual humans in relation to the environmental system's survival and therefore the welfare of future human generations and present and future non-human species. The re-appraisal of the welfare of the current generation will include existing poverty and income inequalities and the institutions that perpetuate such conditions. An increased role for international co-operation and development, including real resource transfers from rich to poor will need strong and effective promotion.

In the light of this ethical re-evaluation, it is likely that socio-economic systems dominated by market principles will need to be modified by more participatory political systems. The concept of community and collective values should be fostered, alongside greater investment in social capital, in order to counter the loss of trust in society and related declines in norms of reciprocity and co-operative networks that fast growth market economies seem to suffer from (Lutz and Lux 1988).

3 Sustainability at the regional scale: coastal zone management

3.1 Coevolution of socio-economic and environmental systems in coastal areas

All countries with a coastline have an interest in the sustainable management of the coastal resource systems. The task of sustainable management, defined here as sustainable utilisation of the multiple goods and services provision generated by coastal resources (processes, functions and their interrelationships), is likely to be made more difficult because of the consequences of global environmental change (including climate change). Coastal zones are currently experiencing intense and sustained environmental pressures from a range of driving forces (Turner, Subak and Adger 1996). Responsible agencies are seeking ways of better managing the causes and consequences of the environmental change process in coastal areas. A particular characteristic of environmental change is that it has led to, among other things, the progressive opening of biogenic nutrient cycles e.g. much increased mobility of nitrogen and phosphorus. This increased mobility of nutrients has meant increased exchanges between land and surface water and consequent impacts on the ecological functioning of aquatic systems. Other process changes have also added to the cumulative changes experienced in coastal systems. This is the scale problem as multiple resource use demands pressurise the carrying capacity of coastal environmental systems.

Understanding the interactions between the coastal zone and global changes cannot be achieved by observational studies alone. Modelling of key environmental processes is a vital tool that must be used if coastal management is to achieve its overall goals and objectives, particularly in view of the fact that many of the uncertainties in global carbon flow models may represent unquantified processes occurring within the coastal zone. For any group of researchers wishing to investigate and model a particular local coastal system (or aspects of that system) for subsequent up-scaling into larger models or wider regional estimates, there are initially two types of information required:

- estimations of biogeochemical fluxes in the system as it is now, for eventual incorporation into global estimates of flux through the coastal zone; and

- dynamic simulations of processes in the coastal system which can be used to explore the consequences of environmental change, and produce forecasts of future fluxes.

The second type of information set will require the integration of socio-economic and natural science data and models in two basic analytical contexts:

- to provide an understanding of the external forcing effects of socio-economic changes such as, for example, population growth, urbanisation, and other land use changes on fluxes of C, N, P and sediment; and
- to assess the human welfare impacts of flux changes because of consequent processes and function changes in coastal resource systems. Such assessments of the social costs and benefits involved will provide essential coastal management intelligence based on social science and possible resource and value trade-offs.

The second analytical context poses a more formidable research task, not just because of the data requirements and the integration problem involving data which differs in form and in spatial and temporal scale, but because the long term goal is the development of an integrated prognostic assessment capability (Turner, Adger and Lorenzoni 1999).

The assessment of the impact of changes in the coastal zone on human use of resources (wealth creation) and habitation (quality of life aspects) requires the application of socio-economic research methods and techniques in the context of coastal resource assessment and management. A particular contribution of socio-economic research is the incorporation of evaluation methods and techniques which can be applied to specific resource damage and utilisation situations. These situations can involve projects, policies or courses of action which change land use/cover, alter or modify residuals from point and non-point sources etc. because of C, N and P flux changes, with related consequences, including loss of functions and even habitats, see Table 2. Most of the valuation studies will be at a local and/or regional level and the same scaling-up problem presents itself. However, the transfer of economic valuation estimates (known as benefits transfer) across time and geographical and cultural space is controversial (Turner, Adger and Brouwer 1998; Costanza et al. 1997). The valuation analysis highlights the resource use efficiency principle and its relationship with potentially conflicting principles of equity in the distribution of resource gains and losses.

3.2 Integrated coastal management (ICM)

The last 20 to 30 years have seen the gradual evolution of a strategy aimed at an integrated assessment of environmental science, technology and policy problems. A multi-disciplinary tool kit has been presented which, for example, global climatic change researchers have tapped into (Schneider 1997).

Table 2. Coastal zone impacts and valuation methods.

Effects categories	*Valuation method options**
Productivity	
E.g. Fisheries, agriculture, tourism, water resources, industrial production, marine transport, storm buttering and coastal protection	Market valuation via prices or surrogates Preventive expenditure Replacement cost/shadow projects/ cost-effectiveness analysis Defensive expenditure
Health	
	Human capital or cost of illness Contingent valuation Preventive expenditure (avertive behaviour) Defensive expenditure
Amenity	
Coastal ecosystems, wetlands, dunes, beaches, etc., and some landscapes, including cultural assets and structures	Contingent valuation/ranking Travel cost Hedonic property "value" method
Existence values	
Ecosystems; cultural assets	Contingent valuation

Source: Bower and Turner (1998).

*Valuation methods:
Market orientated benefit valuation – benefit valuation using actual market prices of productive goods and services based on changes in the value of output, or loss of earnings. Examples include loss of fisheries output due to pollution, or value of productive services or recreational benefits loss, through increased illness caused by coastal waters pollution.
Surrogate markets benefit valuation – environmental surrogates may include marketed goods, property values, other land values, travel costs of recreation, wage differentials, compensation payments. Examples of such proxies are entrance fees to national parks as a proxy for value of visits to protected areas, changes in commercial property values as a result of water pollution, or compensation for damage to fisheries.
Cost valuation using actual market prices of environmental protection inputs – preventive expenditures, replacement costs, shadow projects, cost-effectiveness analysis. For example the cost of environmental safeguards in project design, cost of replacing resource damage by pollution or conversion, cost of supplying alternative facilities destroyed by development activities, or cost of alternative means of sewage sludge disposal in marine waters can be used as cost indicators.
Survey orientated (hypothetical valuation) – contingent valuation or contingent ranking questionnaire-based surveys of individuals to elicit willingness-to-pay or to-be-compensated valuations.

The integrated assessment framework must include coupled or integrated models (biogeochemical and socio-economic) but it is not limited to just this. According to Rotmans and Van Asselt (1996) integrated assessment is "an interdisciplinary and participatory process of combining, interpreting and communicating knowledge from diverse scientific disciplines to achieve a better understanding of complex phenomena". The critical importance of making value-laden assumptions highly transparent in both natural and social scientific components of integrated assessment models (IAMs) needs to be highlighted, practitioners now argue that incorporating decision-makers and other stakeholders into the early design of IAMs greatly facilitates this process. Valuation in this process is more than the assignment of monetary values and includes multi-criteria assessment methods and techniques in order to identify practicable trade-offs.

The objective of coastal zone management is to produce over time a "socially-desirable" mix of coastal zone products and services. This mix is likely to change over time with changing demands, changing knowledge and changing pressures. Fulfilment of this objective, under the general goal of sustainable development, will require the mitigation of current market and intervention failures; continuous monitoring of performance and of coastal zone conditions; and application of research findings over time. The desired social mix can be most effectively and efficiently provided by an integrated approach to coastal zone management. The analysis required for ICM performs an overall resource management auditing role; it forces decision makers to ask relevant questions relating to coastal ecosystems and processes, coastal zone pressure trends, trade-offs, environmental impacts and various aspects of response strategies, including sources of finance and human/institutional capital resource potential. In macro-policy terms, ICM can be seen as a component of sustainable resource management within a regional/national economic development strategy (Bower and Turner 1998).

Because the resources of a coastal zone can generate a range of different products and services, not all of which are naturally compatible, conflicts are likely and trade-offs are necessary. This situation is exacerbated by the variety of different stakeholders that are usually present in any given coastal zone. Moreover, the coastal zone resource base is now under severe pressure from the sheer "scale" of the resource demands that are being generated. Parts of the coastal zone have become increasingly susceptible (more vulnerable) to stress and shock and consequent environmental/economic damage by climate and other natural geophysical factors, together with population, urbanisation, waste generation and disposal pressures. The management process deployed in order to maintain an acceptable mix of 'outputs' from the coastal zone into the future must therefore be both a dynamic and adaptable process. It will have to combine least cost provision of 'outputs' with an equitable distribution of the ensuing risk and social benefits.

Finding a consensus position will also require more participatory decision making procedures than those which have operated in the past, in order to legitimise the inevitable trade-offs that will arise.

3.3 ICM practice

In the context of regional or area-economic development, the objective of the ICM can be expressed as follows:

Maximise the present value of

$GRP - C_p - C_{cm} - D + B - C_a,$

where

GRP = gross regional product;
C_p = normal production costs;
C_{cm} = net coastal management costs, e.g. discharge reduction cost, beach replenishment cost, coastal protection costs;
D = remaining damages;
B = benefits from improved environmental quality; and
C_a = administrative costs of ICM.

But to manage practicably requires proper resource assessment, involving the evaluation of (including costs of, and, wherever feasible, monetary evaluation of the benefits) multiple resources exploitation in the coastal zone and the interactions between and among the competing resource uses. A fundamental management problem is that of deciding among the possible sets of outputs of goods and services which can be produced. Various combinations of outputs are possible, involving marine transport, waste disposal, fisheries yield, recreation, national defence, amenity, and preservation of unique coastal ecosystems. The different combinations will reflect different trade-offs among the feasible outputs, and will also be distributed differently across a range of stakeholders.

The economic efficiency criterion underpinning the *GRP* maximisation objective outlined above is therefore too narrow to serve as the only measure for coastal management evaluation. Coastal situations will involve some resource values which are difficult to translate into monetary terms and equity concerns to do with the distribution of costs and benefits from management actions or inaction. Operational trade-offs will need to be developed by the imposition of constraints such as ambient environmental quality standards, regional employment and/or income targets, designation of priority conservation areas etc., on net economic benefit estimation.

Further complexity in the management task occurs because of the dynamic and "open system" nature of coastal zones. Analysis for planning and management must consider at least three areas (multiple foci for ICM). These are:

- *The politically designated management area:* the political process in any given country, or in an international setting, will designate the boundaries of the management area, and will assign the management responsibilities to one or more public and private agencies.
- *Ecological areas:* a designated coastal management area may be within the boundaries of an identified ecosystem. More likely, the area will encompass, or be encompassed by, several ecosystems or catchment areas.
- *Demand areas:* demand areas are those from which demands are exerted on the resources of the designated coastal area. These demands comprise: demands from within the designated management area; demands from outside the designated management area but within the catchment area; demands from outside the catchment area, with respect to, e.g. waste disposal of pollutants transported into the area via atmospheric transport, demands for coastal recreation, including visits to unique marine resources area; and internationally determined demands, such as for global shipment of crude oil and oil products.

Thus, ICM involves *multiple* regions, the boundaries of which rarely – if ever – coincide. For example, governmental boundaries for countries, states and provinces are rarely contiguous with watershed or ecosystem boundaries. In analysis, explicit consideration must be given to cross-boundary flows via drainage basins connected to the coastal area and through atmospheric deposition. However, the management structure established for a designated coastal area is not likely to have jurisdiction over activities beyond its area.

Because the coastal zone is the most biodiverse zone, it may be prudent, under a strong sustainability policy, to impose a "zero net loss" principle or constraint on resource utilisation (affecting habitats, biodiversity and the operation of natural processes) in the zone, at least at the start of the analysis. Such a set of constraints, influenced by the precautionary principle, will probably conflict with some other human needs. A typical multiple objective and value conflict problem is posed, for example, by: the need of local fisheries to increase fisheries yield in a given zone; the increasing use of the same or nearby waters for waste disposal; improving conditions for marine transport; and increasing need to raise the quality of bathing waters/beaches; and a political desire to increase the stringency of pollution controls on dischargers to coastal waters. A difficult sustainability balance will need to be struck depending on the real and full economic value of the various resource management options, the extent to which sustainable human livelihoods can be fostered with alternative income sources substituting for unsustainable current usages, and the actual resilience of various natural systems and processes.

Advocates of integrated coastal management believe that there is a positive correlation between the degree of integration and the probability of achieving an acceptable and sustainable mix of coastal products and services. To achieve such an ambitious goal will take time and often a radical departure from existing national coastal policies which tend to be implemented in an uncoordinated way by a variety of institutions. The future integration goal should at a minimum include, the integration of economic development plans with environmental quality management; the coordination of sectoral plans for energy, water resources management, waste disposal and tourism and their linkages with natural hazard management strategies; integration of responsibilities for various tasks of ICM among levels of government and between the public and private sectors; effective engagement of all stakeholders in all aspects of the management process. ICM itself must also encompass all the elements of management from planning and design through financing and implementation and requires an interdisciplinary analytical and operational approach.

4 Conclusions

Adapting the general aims and objectives of sustainable development into a practicable strategy for regional coastal management is clearly a formidable task and one which will take time to evolve. At the level of sustainability principles, ICM at its core should support environmental sustainability decision making through the principles of economic efficiency, optimal scale, distributional fairness and justice, participation and legitimacy and precaution. In the face of an increasing degree of environmental risk, uncertainty and ignorance, the distributional incidence of the risks, costs and benefits becomes a key issue. Public consultation and consequent acceptance of the inevitable trade-offs involved will be an important requirement in any legitimisation process.

There is therefore a need for a future more active and conciliatory approach to consultation across and between stakeholders in any given resource allocation and environmental decision-making situation if ICM is to be progressed. It can be argued that there are strong social, political and economic arguments for widening the consultative arrangements and ensuring a more face-to-face participatory role for representatives interests. O'Riordan and Ward (1997), for example, have explored the theory of legitimation and legitimacy in negotiative participatory processes in the context of shoreline management planning in the UK. They have sought to justify the development of empowerment through respect, authenticity and trust in the conduct of mediating exercises.

The shoreline management case studies they investigated all posed the policy dilemma of how to provide compensatory equivalents for land and internationally important wildlife resources threatened with inundation because of sea-level rise and/or best-practice shoreline management. It was found that local networks can play an essential role. In many cases incipient networks based on personally co-operative individuals exist and can be mobilised and extended. Such networks are vital for sharing information, formulating positions and for mutual education. This is the basis of empowerment. However, the implementation of the management plans has made only slow progress. Existing institutional arrangements which have failed in almost all respects to deliver the required sustainable shoreline and coastal zone management in the UK remain largely intact. This inertia is reinforced by a planning system which still does not do enough to discourage settlement and economic activity in risk prone areas. The consequent enhancement in the economic value of the sites only encourages demands for increased protection. Breaking this economic/political cycle is the primary obstacle which a more integrated coastal management strategy most overcome.

References

Bergh, J.C.J.M. van den (Ed.) (1999): Handbook of Environmental and Resource Economics. Edward Elgar, Cheltenham, forthcoming

Bower, B.T., Turner, R.K. (1998): Characterising and analysing benefits from integrated coastal management. Ocean and Coastal Management 38, 41-66

Clayton, A.M.H., Radcliffe, N.J. (1996): Sustainability A Systems Approach. Earthscan, London

Common, M. (1995): Sustainability and Policy. Cambridge University Press, Cambridge

Costanza R., d'Arge, R., Groot, R. de, Farber, S., Grasso, M., Hannon, B., Limburg, K., Naeem, S., O'Neil, R.V., Paruelo, J., Raskin, R.G., Sutton, P. and Belt, M. van den (1997): The value of the world's ecosystem services and natural capital. Nature 387, 253-260

Daly, H., Cobb, J. (1990): For the Common Good. Green Print, London

Faber, M., Manstetten, R., Proops, J. (Eds.) (1996): Ecological Economics: Concepts and Methods. Edward Elgar, Cheltenham

Faucheux, S., Pearce, D., Proops, J. (Eds.) (1996): Models of Sustainable Development. Edward Elgar, Cheltenham

Jansson, A.-M., Hammer, M., Folke, C., Costanza, R. (Eds.) (1994): Investing in Natural Capital. Island Press, Washington DC

Lutz, M.A., Lux, K. (1988): Humanistic Economics: The New Challenge. The Bootstrap Press, New York

O'Riordan, T., Voisey, H. (Eds.) (1998): The Transition to Sustainability: The Politics of Agenda 21 in Europe. Earthscan, London

O'Riordan, T., Ward, R. (1997): Building trust in shoreline management. Land Use Policy 4, 257-276

Pearce, D.W., Warford, J. (1993): World without End. Oxford University Press, Oxford

Pezzoli, K. (1997): Sustainable development: a transdisciplinary overview of the literature. Journal of Environmental Planning and Management 40, 507-575

Rotmans, J., Asselt, M. van (1996): Integrated assessment: a growing child on its way to maturity. Climate Change 34, 327-336

Schneider, S.H. (1997): Integrated assessment modelling of global climate change: transparent rational tool for policy making or opaque screen hiding value-laden assumptions? Environmental Modelling and Assessment 2, 229-249

Turner, R.K. (1999): Environmental and Ecological Economics Perspectives. In: Bergh, J.C.J.M. van den (Ed.): Handbook of Environmental and Resource Economics, ch. 67, Edward Elgar, Cheltenham, forthcoming

Turner, R.K., Adger, N., Brouwer, R. (1998): Ecosystem services value, research needs and policy relevance: a commentary. Ecological Economics 25, 61-65

Turner, R.K., Subak, S., Adger, N. (1996): Pressures, trends and impacts in coastal zones: interactions between socio-economic and natural systems. Environmental Management 20, 159-173

Turner, R.K., Perrings, C., Folke, C. (1997): Ecological economics: paradigm or perspective. In: Bergh, J.C.J.M. van den, Straaten, J. van der (Eds.): Economy and Ecosystems in Change: Analytical and Historical Approaches. Edward Elgar, Cheltenham, 25-49

Turner, R.K., Adger, N., Lorenzoni, I. (1999): Towards Integrated Modelling and Analysis in Coastal Zones: Principles and Practice. IGBPK/LOICZ Reports and Studies, Texel, Netherlands

Weizsäcker, E.U. von, Lovins, A.B., Lovins, L.H. (1997): Factor Four: Doubling Wealth, Halving Resource Use. Earthscan, London

Communicating sustainable development options – who evaluates the trade-offs?

Sabine O'Hara, Vivek Shandas and Jose Vazquez

Department of Economics, Rensselaer Polytechnic Institute, Troy, New York 12180, USA

1 Introduction

The search for models of sustainable development has not been easy. Some concepts and definitions have taken their cue from the Brundtland report's temporal understanding of sustainability as maintaining the welfare of present generations without endangering the welfare of future generations (WCED 1987); others see sustainability as a spatial concept which implies that sustainable communities or regions stay within their ecological carrying capacity (Wallner et al. 1996); yet others view sustainability as a concept of development that promotes a balance between three interrelated systems – the economy, social systems and ecological systems (Robinson and Tinker 1995, O'Hara 1998).

Given these conceptual ambiguities among theoreticians (Eichler 1996) it is not surprising that there are many questions about what sustainable development might mean for practitioners, or how the concept can best be communicated to those at the forefront of implementing more sustainable development practices. An essential factor in overcoming the ambiguities surrounding sustainable development is improved clarity and communication about what sustainability means to different disciplines and particularly to the core disciplines involved in the sustainability debate – economics and ecology (Norton and Toman 1997, O'Hara 1996). Moreover, improved clarity and communication are also at the center of advancing practitioners' ability to develop and evaluate sustainable development options.

The following article explores the role new information technologies can play in providing local communities and decision makers with the information necessary to evaluate the sustainability of alternative development options. The concept of sustainability underlying this exploration draws on both the notion of maintaining ecological capacity constraints and of recognising the interrelatedness of economic, social and ecological systems. Robinson and Tinker (1995: 19) write:

"Addressing any one of the three imperatives in isolation, without also satisfying the other two, virtually guarantees failure, first because each is independently crucial, second because the satisfaction of each is urgently necessary to remove elements of gross unsustainability from human society, and third because the three imperatives ... are intimately connected".

Given the complex information necessary to evaluate the economic, social and ecological systems' interactions relevant to assessing sustainable development issues, much of the needed information cannot be readily captured by using one discipline's notion of sustainability or by one commensurate measure of sustainability. Instead, multiple measures may be necessary to assess the environmental, economic, and social effects of various development options and to evaluate their respective trade-offs. In fact, the selection of measures itself raises the question where information ends and evaluation starts, and what criteria selection and evaluation processes might be considered to assess viable development options (O'Hara forthcoming a).

To place this discussion of concepts and implementation of sustainable development into a concrete context, the following discussion is based on a regional example of sustainable development options in the Lake George region of upstate New York. This rural area in the Northeast of the United States has experienced both the economic benefits and the ecological dangers of tourism development. The article starts with a brief historical overview of the Lake George region's development challenges followed by a discussion of the information needs for sustainable development and the implicit and explicit valuation processes that affect selection and assessment of alternative development options.

2 Sustainable development – past gains and future limits

Communicating the need for balanced development that protects a region's ecosystems health as well as its economic and social well-being is often a challenging task. This is true even in regions where residents are well aware of the fact that economic well-being depends on the integrity of the region's environment. One of the problems lies in the different time frames according to which different systems operate. Economic effects tend to be visible in the short run while the effects of pollution on a region's environmental assets may not be visible until twenty-five or thirty years later. Another difficulty lies in linking economic and social systems functions to the quality of a region's environmental assets. Pollutants travel, are absorbed, altered and diluted so that it is often difficult to link pollution impacts to the anthropogenic sources that cause them. A third set of challenges lies in the fact that economic, social and ecological systems follow different spatial boundaries. To analyze a lake's water quality impacts, its watershed or basin may be the relevant spatial dimension. To analyze a region's economic and social factors, political boundaries like counties or towns are the most common dimensions. These political boundaries are generally not consistent with ecologically relevant space.

The lake George region is no exception. Located in upstate New York on the eastern edge of the Adirondack Park, Lake George's natural beauty and pristine water quality are legendary. The Lake is approximately 1.5 miles wide and 31 miles long, nestled within a spectacular setting of forest covered mountains. The watershed consists of approximately 100 square miles of state owned "forever wild" forest preserve and 155 square miles of privately owned land (plus 45 square miles of water surface). Three counties share the shoreline and watershed of Lake George. All three counties combined extend over an area almost three times the size of the watershed. Despite these spatial incompatibilities an analysis of the social and economic changes in the counties surrounding Lake George can provide a significant amount of information about potential sources of observed environmental quality changes.

2.1 Economic development

Most of the economic activity within the three county area surrounding Lake George is limited to Warren County on the southwestern shore of the lake. This is also where Interstate 89 extends in north-south direction as close as 1 mile from the lake. The completion of I 89 in 1967 provided access to Lake George for millions of tourists from the Albany, Boston, New York and Montreal metropolitan areas and Lake George became a major tourist attraction. Essex and Washington county which border the northern and eastern shore of Lake George are largely undeveloped with large tracts of 'forever wild' protected land stretching particularly along the eastern shore of the lake.

Balancing the interests of economic development and environmental protection is imperative to maintaining the Lake George region's future. A decline in the lake's water quality due to increased population pressures and shoreline development would seriously endanger the area's main economic base. Yet overly stringent protection may deny local residents access to and enjoyment of a local resource that affects their economic and non-economic well being.[1]

An analysis of Warren County's tourism related sectors shows just how strong the region's economic dependence on tourism is. Retail trade and services increased from $55 mill. in 1970 to $448 mill. in 1995. This increase of $393 mill. is higher than the growth of all other sectors combined. The county's service sector employment grew a staggering 25% per year between 1960 to 1995 compared to an annual growth rate of less than 1% in the manufacturing sector. The share of the region's total employment in services and retail increased by 32% between 1960 and 1995, compared to a 24% decrease in the percentage share of manufacturing sector employment,

[1] For a discussion of the dilemma facing many tourism dependent rural areas see Tisdell (1991), Cater (1995).

and a 4% decline in the percentage share of employment in all other sectors (other than retail and services) combined (see Figure 1).

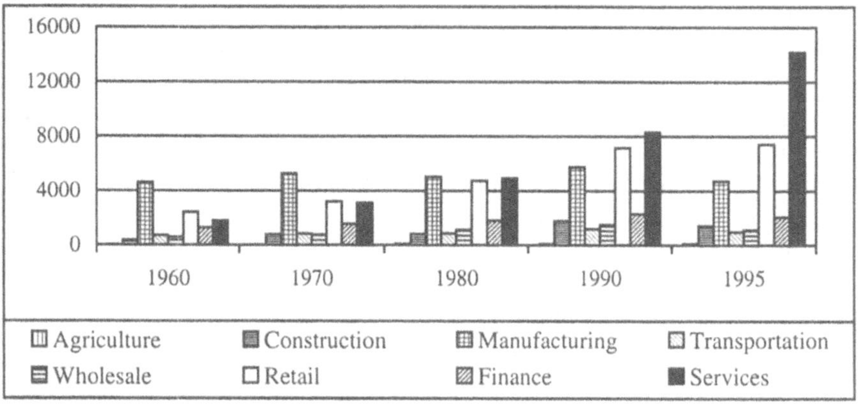

Figure 1. Employees per sector in Warren County 1960-1995.

The income effects of the employment growth in tourism related sectors are more ambiguous. Total payroll paid by the retail and service sectors in Warren County were the highest of all sectors. Yet wages in retail and services are low. The difference in total wages received in services and manufacturing was therefore small, despite considerable differences in the size of the workforce. In 1995 wages for the service sector were still almost 60% below manufacturing wages. Figure 2 shows the deviation of sector specific wage rates from the mean wage for Warren County from 1960 to 1995. The Figure shows that retail and service wages were consistently well below the mean wage for the county.

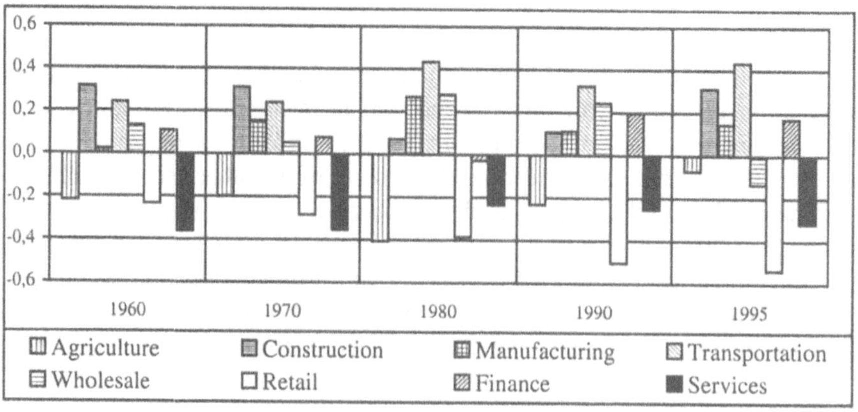

Figure 2. Deviation of sector specific wages from the mean wage for Warren County 1960 to 1995.

2.2 Demographic change

One of the most obvious results of the region's increased tourism development is the dramatic change in the region's permanent and seasonal populations. Between 1930 and 1960 the permanent population of Warren County increased by 28% (or 0.96% per year) just below New York State average of 34%. Between 1960 and 1996 Warren county's population increased by 35%, well above the 7% increase observed in New York State on average. This trend is not unique to Lake George. Other studies confirm above average population growth rates in rural areas that are in close proximity to recreation centers (Rudzitis 1989, Keith et al. 1996). Even more dramatic than the observed changes in permanent population were the changes in seasonal population. Lake George's summer population is as much as ten times above the number of winter residents. A 1975 study by the Lake Champlain/Lake George Planning Board showed that the population of several Warren County municipalities on the southern shore of Lake George increased by 80% on average summer days and by 130% on peak summer days. By 1996 Warren County's 61,544 year round residents grew to an estimated 228,217 during May and 886,196 during July. Towns within the watershed also experienced a dramatic increase in seasonal housing units of an average 85% between 1970 and 1990.

Most towns welcomed the second home development. Additional residential housing increases a town's tax base and provides income for improvements in infrastructure and public services. Yet despite the perception that tourism is less environmentally damaging than manufacturing related point sources, concerns about the long-term effects of the increased tourism development, particularly on the southern end of the Lake close to the regions most highly developed tourism centers, have grown steadily.

2.3 Environmental consequences

In the early 1970s the Darrin Freshwater Institute of Rensselaer Polytechnic Institute, which is located on the south western shore of Lake George, initiated a number of monitoring and recording studies (Aulenbach et al. 1972a, 1972b, 1973). Research results indicate a slow but steady decline in water quality particularly along the Lake's shore line due to rising chloride, nitrate, and phosphorous levels, all indicators of advancing eutrophication, and all indicators of so called non-point pollution sources (Boylen 1985, Boylen et al. 1991a and 1991b).[2] Chloride concentrations, for example, increased from an average of 5.89 mg/l in 1980 to a lake-wide average of 8.71 mg/l in 1990, or a 32% increase in chloride concentrations over ten years

[2] Eutrophication is the process by which a lake, stream, or estuary experiences increased productivity through increased nutrient enrichment. The result is a continuous decline in water clarity and, in the extreme, a complete oxygen loss in the water body.

(Boylen et al. 1991b). Nitrate levels increased an average 15% over the same time period, and increasing algae and plankton growth are further evidence of the growing nutrient levels threatening the lake's meso- to oligotrophic water quality. Figure 3 shows the rate of change, both actual and expected, for total phosphorous and chlorophyll.

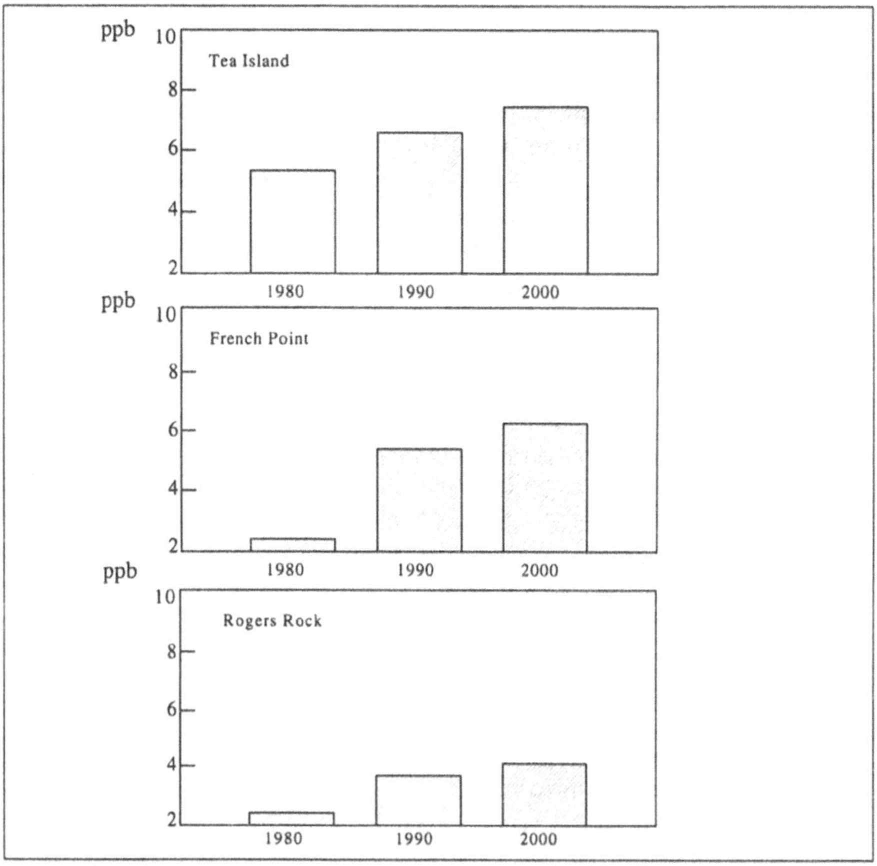

Source: RPI Darrin Freshwater Institute (1984).

Figure 3. Phosphorus concentrations in three locations in Lake George.

So far, the observed water quality changes appear to fluctuate considerably and seem to be largely restricted to the southern end of the lake as Figure 3 illustrates. While changes in phosphorus concentration (as well as other development related substances like nitrates and chlorides) increased throughout the lake, the largest changes were observed in French Point located in the south, followed by Tea Island. The lowest levels were measured in Rogers Rock located in the northeastern part of the lake.

Despite the overall increases nutrient levels in the lake remain low, particularly when measured in comparison to human health standards, the most commonly used guidelines for pollution prevention. Oligotrophic lakes like Lake George have nutrient levels far below acceptable drinking water standards (for example, 9 ppm of nitrates compared to the World Health Organization's recommended drinking water standard of 40 ppm). Meeting human health based water quality standards would, therefore, exceed the ecological standards necessary to preserve the nutrient poor ecosystem of Lake George. So far, human use standards and concern for the Lake's water clarity have dominated the debate. These are not necessarily reliable indicators of ecosystems' health. The slow, almost invisible decline of the lake's water quality and the fact that pollution impacts stem mainly from non-point sources, make it difficult to communicate the need for stringent water quality controls and for developing more sustainable development alternatives.

3 Sustainability: structuring complex information

The above discussion of economic, demographic and water quality changes in the Lake George area shows that sustainable development decisions require information about linked, but distinctly different systems. While information about economic and demographic changes is available, information about the links between economic and environmental systems is often sparse, fraught with uncertainty and poorly understood. The same applies to changes within the watershed which impact the severity of anthropogenic pollution on the water body itself. What natural processes occur within the watershed and between the pollution source and the lake? What human economic activities support rather than undermine natural processes in the ecosystem? What are the economic and social effects of less polluting and more environmentally sustainable economic activities? To communicate the complex information necessary to address these questions to local decision makers it is essential that information about complex, uncertain and often unperceived factors be structured and made visible.

3.1 GIS and systems modeling: a historic outlook

Two tools that can serve to communicate the effects of changes in a region's economic activities and their resulting ecological effects are dynamic simulation models and geographic information systems. Geographic Information Systems (GIS) can capture, manipulate, process, and visually display spatially referenced data. This ability to visually display changes can be a powerful advantage in processing information about changing characteristics within a region. In GIS, the basic concept is one of location, of spatial distribution and relationship, and basic elements are spatial objects. This can include GIS data that reflect the spatial distribution of economic uses as part of its spatial or land use description.

In dynamic simulation or environmental modeling, as it is often called, the basic concept is one of 'states', expressed in terms of numbers, mass, or energy, of interaction and dynamics. Its basic elements are 'species', which may be economic or ecological data describing such media as air, water or land use. The overlap between these two modeling tools is apparent, as is the ability to generate useful added information by integrating both. Merging different analytical tools, or adding new applications to an established and mature field of inquiry, often leads to new and exciting developments. Both environmental modeling and GIS are well-established research methods. Their integration, however, seems at best an emerging field. The integration of GIS and dynamic modeling can come in many forms. One model, for example, may read some of its input data from the other. In this way, the dynamic model can, for example, produce some of its output in a format that allows processing and display with the GIS (Figure 4).

This kind of model interaction seems to be a rather common approach, since it requires little if any software modifications. Only the respective formats and corresponding input and output routines, have to be adapted.

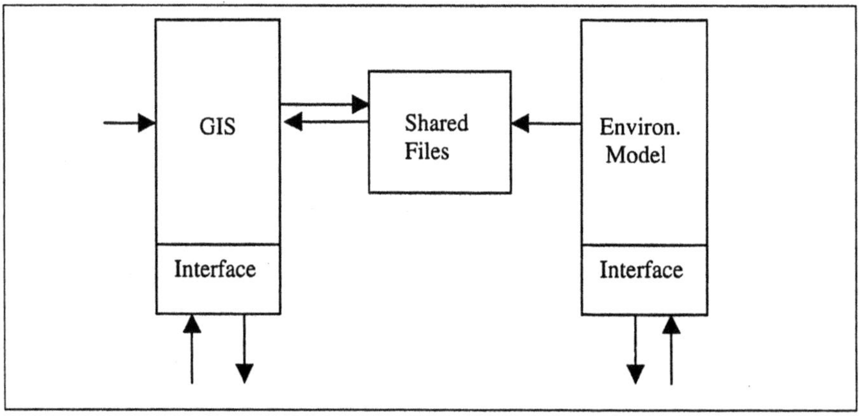

Figure 4. Linkage of separate programs through common files (Fedra 1993).

At a deeper level of integration, which links and displays anthropogenic and natural processes, however, the models will need to account for dynamic changes and integrate them into the analytical functions of the GIS. At this stage of model integration the GIS becomes an alternative option for generating additional state and output variables and for providing additional display options. This requires tools that are sufficiently modular, so that the coupling of software components within one single application with shared memory rather than files and common interface becomes possible (Fig. 5).

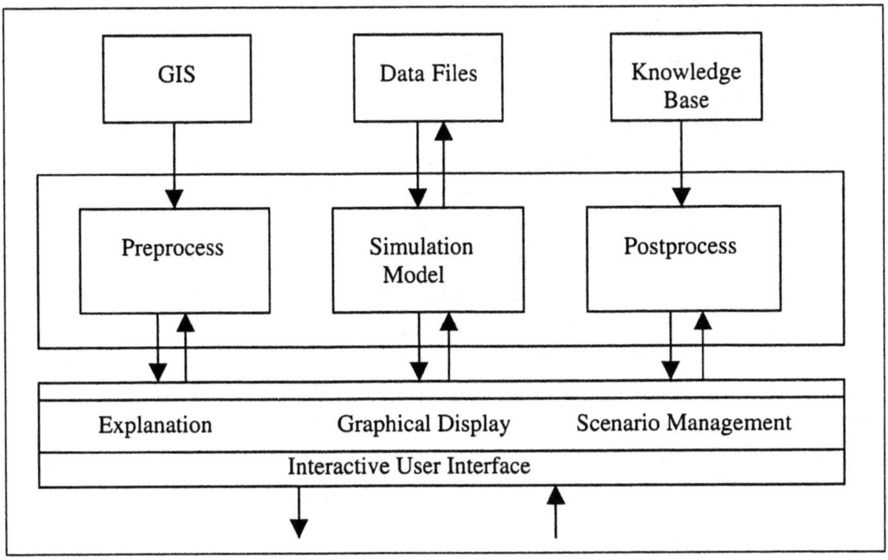

Figure 5. Interactive modeling in an integrated framework (Fedra 1993).

For environmental applications, including land use management, there is a considerable tradition with geographical information systems. Major initiatives have been under way to build and integrate geographical and environmental databases in many countries, including most of the European countries (e.g. Van Est and de Vroege 1985, Jackson et al. 1988), the European Community as a whole (Wiggins et al. 1986), and countries within the framework of the United Nations (Kessell 1990, Witt 1989). Yet while many of these systems have explicit environmental components and functions, they are not usually integrated with modeling capabilities that simulate transport or processes of environmentally relevant substances or population developments. Throughout the literature, the idea of integration is obvious and discussed frequently (Granger 1989, Tikunov 1989, Fedra 1993, Lam and Swayne 1991). Spatial patterns also have a history in plant sociology, forestry, and plankton studies. Until recently, any consideration of patterns or spatial distribution, however, was statistical in nature rather than explicit, that is connected to absolute location with an X,Y coordinate system. An earlier spatially distributed ecological model is the famous spruce budworm exercise (Holling 1978). According to Laurenroth et al. (1993), few examples of spatially distributed models, mainly in the river and lake modeling areas exist.

Hunsaker's et al. (1993) review of a rich literature with numerous examples of studies that include GIS methods in the various applications demonstrates a movement from a point or spatially lumped models towards distributed models. A development that, in part, seems to be made possible, if not motivated by increasingly affordable computer resources. The trend is clearly towards more spatial resolution and linkage of dynamic modeling with GIS as a ready-made technology to handle spatial information. Problems, however, identified by Hunsaker et al. (1993), include the software engineering problems of tight linkage and data requirements; related to the need for large volumes of data are problems of their effective storage. Problems of scale and uncertainty, of course, come up consistently.

Environmental modeling has itself a considerable history. A number of analytical approaches applied to biological and ecological problems date back to Lotka (1925), and fields like hydrology can look to more than a hundred years of modeling history. With the advent of digital computers numerical simulation models became feasible. Early linear models (Patten 1971), applications of systems dynamics of ecological problems (Forrester 1982), and ever more complex multi-compartment models like CLEANER and MS. CLEANER (Park et al. 1974, 1979) or CREAMS (for an application see O'Hara 1983) were developed. None of these approaches had explicit spatial dimensions. In limnology, oceanography, and plant sociology concepts such as patchiness were discussed, however, not in relation to a fixed coordinate system as used in GIS.

If the ultimate goal is not only to develop a better research tool, but also to aid local decision makers in making more informed decisions about their region's long-term sustainability, GIS tools will have to integrate model components that can successfully communicate environmental, economic and social systems dimensions. More powerful computers, inevitably, allow more complex models to be developed. Spatial distribution and increased dimensionality and resolution is one straightforward way of "improving" models. Such spatially distributed models can interact with GIS to visually display complex systems changes.

The availability of information, however, continues to be a severely limiting factor. Tax parcel information from government agencies is the primary source of land use data for GIS models and is currently only available for Washington and Essex counties. No level of significant information is available for Warren county, the region's most economically important and most populated county. While plans are under way to remedy this situation other alternatives will need to be developed in the short term until the necessary information base for developing a region wide GIS model is available.

3.2 Modeling applications to the Lake George region

To bridge the current lack of information while still achieving meaningful results a third modeling option will be pursued in the Lake George region. This option employs a regional input-output model to simulate a variety of alternative development scenarios. The concept of scenario analysis underlying this approach follows Schwartz's definition of scenarios as "... stories about the way the world might turn out tomorrow... and finding your appropriate movement down each of those possible paths" (Schwartz 1991: 3-4). By introducing sector specific water use and water discharge information as well as emission coefficients into the regional Input-Output model, the model can be used to simulate the different water use levels, emission discharges, employment effects, and income effects of alternative development scenarios within the region.

Three development alternatives will be analyzed in the context of the Lake George region. One scenario will examine the impacts of a further expansion of tourism. A second scenario will examine the effects of a more diversified economic development strategy of expanding a high value-added forest products sector rather than tourism. The selection of this economic alternative is based on the historical analysis of the region, which had a strong history in paper and pulp production and forest products processing. Using new, low emission technologies a re-focusing on forest products would allow the region to reconsider economic alternatives associated with its past, and thus with a regional 'collective memory' of successful past development alternatives. A third alternative will examine the effects of expanding new information technology intensive sectors associated with so called 'smart-communities'. This term refers to communities which support low pollution sectors and market their high quality of life which, in the case of Lake George, relates particularly to the area's natural beauty.

Preliminary analysis of the region's main economic sectors shows that the largest emission generators for the organic emissions that pose the biggest threat to the lake's water quality are human waste and waste water emissions. These are primarily related to demographic changes, lodging, and recreational land uses with high run-offs such as golf courses and amusement parks. Chloride emissions appear to be related to increased road salting activities and the larger expanse of paved roads and driveways surrounding the lake. The slow changes in water quality despite significantly increased human uses, however, also indicate that natural processes affect the lake's water quality beyond the identified anthropogenic sources.

In the case of Lake George, the watershed area is small compared to the lake's water surface area. A main source of water quality impacts thus stems from atmospheric sources. Giddens (1974) calculated, for example, a nitrogen budget for Lake George in 1974 of 271,000 kg. Assuming a constant growth rate of 3% from increased population growth and lake-shore development this would indicate current levels of 542,000 kg of nitrogen from human development, and nitrogen emissions from precipitation of 238,000 kg (see also Hubacek et al. 1997). Such preliminary results, however, lack the detailed data to account for minute, yet significant changes in emission impacts occurring within the oligotrophic ecosystem as well as ecosystems activities between the pollution source and the lake itself.

Moreover, before incorporating significant atmospheric impacts, water quality changes from anthropogenic sources must be isolated. This poses added challenges to further improving simulation results as well as efforts to effectively reduce water pollution impacts.

4 Modeling and decision-making: information or evaluation?

At this point the question might be raised whether the kinds of models discussed here are not 'social science' models rather than the 'scientific' models of physical or chemical processes in the environment that usually form the basis for environmental simulation models or GIS type information systems about spatial change. The development scenarios discussed here have different impacts on economic, land use, and social factors, not just on environmental ones. A further expansion of tourism, for example, may generate a significant number of employment opportunities, albeit at relatively low income, add to the region's diversity in summer versus year-round populations, and cause a further increase in non-point pollution affecting the lake's water quality. An expansion of the forest products sector might generate fewer jobs but at higher wages, offer more year-round employment, reduce seasonal population fluctuations and may generate less organic intake, but possibly add other non-organic pollutants.

4.1 Information and decision making

It might be argued that the modeling of physical phenomena prevalent in environmental simulation and GIS models can be done with greater efficacy and precision than the modeling of social or economic phenomena. Finite element analytical simulations, for example, predict almost exactly how a structure behaves under particular conditions. In contrast, regional economic or macro-economic simulations seldom predict anything exactly and even the particulars of the conditions under which economic or social changes occur are difficult to capture. One might, therefore, conclude that 'scientific' models represent the 'truth' more accurately, as demonstrated by their predictive power, and they will therefore be more readily accepted as a basis for decision making, whether regional planning or policy decisions. Yet things are not that simple. Trust in scientific certainty and reliance on scientific models that are 'right' and relevant for decision making has become increasingly moot. To the extent that anything can be predicted with precision, as for example the structural behavior of a particular bridge design, the effect of such precision is to move predictive models out of the planning or policy decision realm altogether and into the realm of engineering expertise. Few decision-makers will tangle with the risks associated with bridge design, because failures are noticeable and disastrous. Engineers stand ready to build bridges and they use models to do so. But their models lose their utility when one steps back from the structural design decision and into the question of whether a bridge should be built at all, where it should be built, how large it should be, or even how it should be financed.

These questions force modelers back into the social realm of decision making where the word 'science' is often considered somewhat of a euphemism. Not surprisingly, dynamic simulation and GIS models are generally built for the purpose of scientific research, or at best information support. Modeling for decision support for solving environmental problems or conflicts have been discussed and advocated for some time (Bell and Senge 1980; Forrester and Senge 1980; Sklar and Costanza 1991). Yet success stories of actual application of simulation models as decision-making tools are rare. King (1983) cites a rather unappealing view of models as "datawars of public policy-making", and Hall et al. (1989) report the successful use of a stream ecology model to aid various users in regulating water management decisions.

Any kind of decision making which steps back from an engineering approach to modeling and places the engineering (or science) question within a context of socio-economic effects requires that the context specific knowledge of the life world of those most affected by the decision be linked to the knowledge of the scientific community. Models are useful when fundamental questions of what might happen are at stake, but are insufficient in deciding how the 'what might happen' is to be evaluated overall (Renn et al. 1993). What value do those most affected by changing economic, social and environmental conditions, assign to effects like reduced income levels, increased employment, and deteriorating water quality associated with the simulated development alternatives?

Despite the ability to use various modeling approaches to identify multiple factors associated with different development options, it is still necessary to evaluate the relative importance of these factors. In this way, model results can be viewed as input for evaluating well informed scenarios of sustainable development which seek to balance a region's competing needs for economic development, social stability and environmental protection. This then raises the fundamental question of who evaluates the trade-offs associated with different development alternatives and their varying economic, social and environmental effects? The expert community, those affected, or both?

4.2 Stakeholder participation and decision making

Generally it has been the expert community that has evaluated trade-offs between different systems effects, albeit this valuation process is rarely made explicit but is generally hidden in model assumptions or implicit valuation methods. Economists, for example have generally sought to evaluate trade-offs between the economic, social and environmental effects of alternative development options by assigning them the common denominator of monetary value. A variety of methodologies have been developed to assign monetary value to environmental effects, for example,[3] or to assess the option-, existence- and future value of environmental resources (Tietenberg 1988, Pearce and Turner 1990, Tisdell 1991). In this way, economic models have all too often acted like engineering or 'science' models in which relevant states and behaviors are well identified. Alternative approaches have used various physical indicators like energy or material units to evaluate the environmental impacts of economic production and consumption processes.[4] As much as these measures may differ in their chosen unit of measurement, they have in common that they assign a common measure to incommensurable systems impacts (O'Hara and Mesner 1998, O'Neill 1996). As a result valuable information may be lost and assumptions about the relative value assigned to different impact categories remains veiled behind far-reaching assumptions that are hidden from public scrutiny, since they are not openly communicated to local decision makers and those affected by development decisions.[5] A variety of community based indicators of development and sustainable development have been devised to make social, economic and environmental impacts *explicit*. While they may differ in detail, all use a wide variety of indicator categories reflecting physical/chemical environmental, monetary and non-monetary economic, and qualitative social impacts (Cities International 1996).

In order to serve as a tool for making information explicit rather than further obfuscating complex information and systems uncertainties, a model's ability to present information visually and in an easily comprehensible way cannot be a sufficient criteria. What is decisive instead is whether the information presented is made transparent and communicable, including model assumptions based on which visual changes appear on a screen or

---

[3] Commonly used assessment methods include hedonic pricing (Murdoch and Thayer 1988, Brookshire et al. 1993), various types of Contingent Valuation (Eberle and Hayden 1991, Harris et al. 1989), and travel cost methods (Smith and Desvousges 1993).

[4] See for example H. Odum's Energy Return on Energy Input (EROI) (Hall et al. 1986), Pimentel's energy requirements of agriculture (Pimentel 1973), Vitousek's measure of the human appropriation of Net Primary Production (HANPP) (Vitousek et al. 1986), or Wackernagel and Rees's ecological footprint (1995) or the Wuppertal Institute's MIPS index which measures all directly and indirectly used materials of a product or service (Schmidt-Bleek 1994).

[5] Methods to assess the social impacts of changing economic, social and environmental conditions tend to be more explicit, since they tend to rely on a variety of objective indicators, which document changes in such quality of life related categories like public health, education, and income distribution (Shyns 1998, United Nations Development Programme 1996, Easterlin 1974, 1995); subjective quality of life research tries to avoid indirect assessments altogether by surveying individual respondents' perceptions of changes in their quality of life.

map. The above described GIS and simulation based model of alternative development scenarios can thus be considered a valuable, but limited tool to assess the overall effects of the selected development options, unless its design is flexible enough to record *explicit* measures by which individual systems' effects can be assessed. These selected economic, social and environmental valuation categories can then be used to compare the effects of different redevelopment scenarios and evaluate potential trade-offs. In this way the model can serve to make relevant trade-offs visible and to present them in a communicable form to local decision-makers or the public at large.

Such a modeling approach, however, does not eliminate the painstaking work of selecting relevant assessment categories that capture a community's valuation of different development options. Communication between researchers and local stakeholders, however, can aid the selection process of relevant valuation categories. By using a flexible design and open feedback process the models can offer refined and integrated development scenarios as input for an informed decision-making process in which sustainable development options are identified, evaluated, and adjusted rather than offering the pretense of decision results. In this way, the interaction between experts and local experts allows for a process of valuation and re-evaluation of development options in which unsustainable practices can be detected and corrected early on. Figure 6 illustrates the integrated components of such a flexible assessment process.

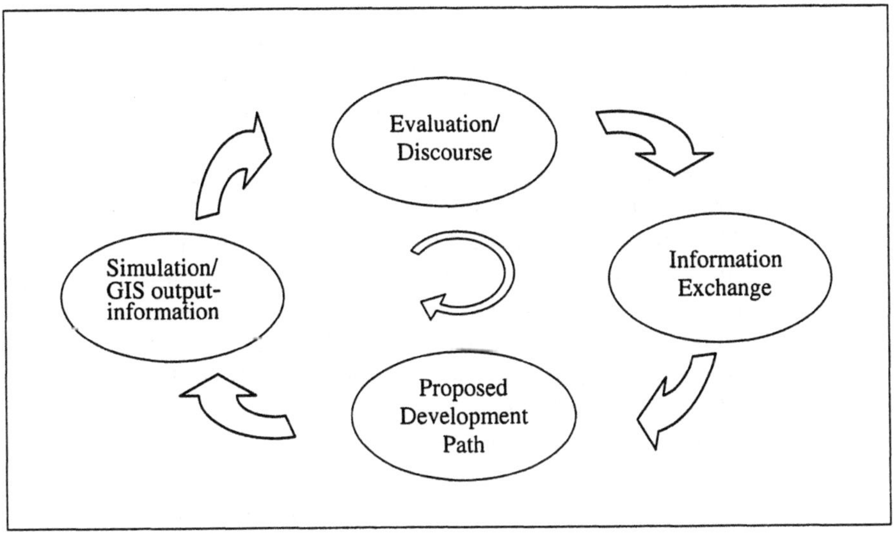

Figure 6. Integrated assessment process of sustainable development scenarios.

4.3 Stakeholders and the Lake George region

Putting a model to use in a stakeholder based or public decisions and valuation process rather than as a tool for improving scientific prediction moves a simulation model beyond a 'black box' that discourse participants must simply accept. Such model transparency is essential to leveling the playing field between different stakeholder groups as well as between 'experts' and 'local experts' (O'Hara 1996, Renn et al. 1995, Webler 1992, Mathews 1994). Otherwise a potential danger of using a rather technical communication tool like GIS, dynamic modeling or input-output analysis is that less technically versed discourse participants will feel voiceless and excluded from the debate. Caution about this potential biasing of a discourse process is especially in order since various discourse processes have pointed to the prevalence of 'expert' or 'hard discipline' biases even when only verbal or non-technical visual communication tools are used (O'Hara forthcoming b, Biesecker 1996).

In the case of the Lake George region tensions may arise particularly between more development oriented versus protection oriented, long term and short-term as well as year-round and seasonal residents, those dependent on the local economy as a source of income and those with income source outside the region. While these various interests may be overlapping and not easily identified with any one particular stakeholder group Table 1 attempts to categorise the region's main stakeholders and their primary interests.

Involving local participants in regional development decisions, however, is more than political expediency or an attempt to lower implementation and acceptance costs of potentially conflicting development agendas. The uncoerced communication process between mutually respectful individuals allows a discursive reason to become operative that goes beyond individual notions of reason and a discursive ethic that goes beyond preconceived ethical norms (Habermas 1984, 1996; Apel 1973, 1980; Wellmer 1986). The reason for this expanded discursive rationality is that discourse allows the life world, that is the larger social and environmental context of peoples' lives, to become visible. Individuals make judgements and assess options not in isolation but within a network of communicative relationships and interactions (Dryzek 1997, O'Hara 1996, Ulrich 1989).

Behavioral research has shown that such communicative interaction changes decision outcomes. For example, given the opportunity to discuss their decisions altered people's willingness to contribute to public goods (Caporael et al. 1989, Dawes et al. 1990). Discourse also invites participants to express their concerns and priorities in an integrated way rather than being asked to respond as consumers only, but not as citizens, or as producers, but not as family members and neighbors. In this way multiple valuation cri-

Table 1. Major stakeholders in the Lake George region.

Stakeholders	Type of Interests	Key Groups
Government Agencies US Environmental Protection Agency New York State Department of Environmental Conservation Department of Health Department of Public Works Adirondack Park Agency Lake George Park Commission Regional planning boards of area towns and villages	• Environmental conservation • Public health • Land use	• Lake George Park Commission • Municipal planning boards • Adirondack Park Agency
Elected Officials County executives Town supervisors Mayors Legislators	• Employment • Environmental conservation • Public health	• Municipalities
Private Sector Businesses Businesses and industry Utility companies Developers Realtors	• Economic development • New enterprises	• Realtors • Chamber of Commerce • Development corporations
Individuals Homeowners Boaters Campers Students	• Recreation • Quietness • Taxes • Cost of living	• Old homeowners • Campers
Regional Interest groups Lake George Association Neighborhood Associations (around 60) Lake George Basin Land Conservancy Adirondack Council Blue Line Council	• Water quality protection • Land use/ conservation • Economic development	• Lake George Association • Adirondack Council
Education and Research groups Darrin Freshwater Institute Rensselaer Polytechnic Institute SUNY at Albany	• Water quality analysis • Environmental modeling • Regional economic analysis	• Darrin Freshwater Institute

Source: adapted from Hubacek (1997).

teria are admitted to the discourse process, not simply those associated with any one system, group or context. Sagoff coined the term "citizen preferences" (Sagoff 1998: 219) to point to the social preferences operative in discourse processes. As a result, discourse processes can lead to decision outcomes in situations where more standard valuation methods fail. In addition, discourse based assessment offers the potential for uncovering hidden normative assumptions, behaviors and motivations that influence de-facto decision making and valuation processes. Viewed as descriptive tool (see Enderle's term descriptive ethics; Enderle 1989), the interaction between credentialed-expertise models and local-expertise valuation may form a much needed basis for improving information about operative decision norms and decision criteria in sustainable development.

5 Conclusions

Making sustainable development operational in a local community or region is a challenging task. Decision-makers are hard pressed to rely on expert knowledge for guidance as the debate about what exactly constitutes sustainable development continues. Yet the need for developing more sustainable development alternatives is strong particularly in ecologically sensitive regions which depend on maintaining their aesthetic beauty and high quality environment for their economic base. The Lake George region in upstate New York is such a region. Its natural beauty and pristine lake water are a main asset for its flourishing tourism sector. To develop viable development alternatives requires the ability to integrate information about the environmental impacts of human activities with information about natural systems processes, economic effects, and social impacts. One way to integrate and communicate such complex systems information in the case of Lake George is through graphical displays of different economic land-use scenarios and their respective water quality impacts. Starting with the most serious pollutants such a model can trace water pollution levels given a variety of 'natural' and 'human-induced' inputs. Such modeling results, however, cannot be considered a sufficient basis for making decisions about sustainable development alternatives. Selected economic, social and environmental criteria, which can serve as a basis for evaluating possible development scenarios must be identified as well, to move modeling results out of a 'black-box' state and into an informed decision making realm. A more careful reliance on indicators and valuation discussions in addition to visual displays systems models and GIS model results can also alleviate potential biases and even deceptions about the certainty versus uncertainty, scientific fact versus normativity of the information presented.

The informed debate about the relative and absolute importance assigned to selected valuation criteria offers, therefore, not only an important forum for integrating non-local and local expertise but also essential insights into the operative assumptions and normative presuppositions that inform any valuation process. The evaluative discourse of local decision makers and citizens thus offers the opportunity to observe motivations and rationales for supporting, opposing or prioritising particular development options and can make significant contributions to a better understanding of sustainability itself. Such improved insight, however, requires a heightened sensitivity to the links between 'what' valuation criteria are considered essential to sustainability and 'who' evaluates. To improve existing expert systems, as well as local expertise, those with context specific local knowledge, whose knowledge systems have been marginalised, must be consulted in the valuation process. Assessments of sustainability that ignore existing operative power structures, be they epistemological, economic, or political, simply perpetuate operative ignorance rather than advancing much needed theoretical and applied definitions of sustainability based on context specificity, detailed observation, and historical awareness,[6] as well as generalisable knowledge of expert systems. The unsustainability of our current development practices and the search for more sustainable alternatives confronts us with high uncertainty, high risk, and emergent properties. These characteristics push the limits of standard assessment methods. Integrating quantitative modeling techniques and qualitative discourse based valuation methods may offer a conceptual framework for considering communicable predictions and communication dependent unpredictability, fact and value, scientific knowledge and respect for our ignorance.

References

Apel, K.-O. (1980): Toward a Transformation of Philosophy. (Translated by G. Adey and D. Frisby) Routledge & Kegan Paul. London, Boston

Apel, K.-O. (1973): Das Apriori der Kommunikationsgemeinschaft und die Grundlagen der Ethik. In: Apel, K.-O. (Ed.): Transformation der Philosophie, Bd. 2, Frankfurt am Main, 358-435

Aulenbach, D.M. (1972a): Chemical Nutrients in Lake George. Rensselaer Polytechnic Institute Reports-72-19. Rensselaer Polytechnic Institute, Troy

Aulenbach, D., Clescri, N. (1972b): Sources and Sinks of Nitrogen and Phosphorous: Water Quality Management of Lake George. Rensselaer Polytechnic Institute-Freshwater Institute Reports 72-32. Rensselaer Polytechnic Institute, Troy

Aulenbach, D., Cleseri, N. (1973): Sources of Nitrogen and Phosphorous in the Lake George Drainage Basin: a Double Lake. Rensselaer Polytechnic Institute-Freshwater Institute Reports 73-1. Rensselaer Polytechnic Institute, Troy

---

[6] These characteristics are familiar to economists aware of the methodological approach associated with the Historical School of economics (Priddat 1995). Similar characteristics of scientific inquiry and method can also be found in philosophical Pragmatism and in feminist theory (Siegfried 1996).

Bell, J.A., Senge, P.M. (1980): Methods for Enhancing Refutability in System Dynamics Modelling, TIMS Studies in Management Sciences 14, 61-73

Biesecker, A. (1996): Power and Discourse. Some Theoretical Remarks and Empirical Observations. In: Biesecker, A., Elsner, W., Grenzdoerffer, K., Heide, H. (Eds.) Bremer Diskussionspapiere zur Sozialoekonomik. Nr. 14. Universität Bremen. Fachbereich Wirtschaftswissenschaften. Bremen, Germany

Boylen, C.W. (1985): Report on the Lake George Chemical Monitoring Program Rensselaer Polytechnic Institute-Freshwater Institute Reports 86-4. Rensselaer Polytechnic Institute, Troy

Boylen, C.W., Eichler, L., Clear, T.B. (1991a): Report on the Lake George Chemical Monitoring Program Rensselaer Polytechnic Institute-Freshwater Institute Reports 92-3. Rensselaer Polytechnic Institute, Troy

Boylen, C.W., Eichler, L., Clear, T.B. (1991b): Report on the Lake George Chemical Monitoring Program: 1980-1990 Rensselaer Polytechnic Institute-Freshwater Institute Reports. Rensselaer Polytechnic Institute, Troy

Brookshire, D.S., Thayer, M.A., Schulz, W., D'Arge, R. (1993): Valuing public goods: a comparison of survey and hedonic approaches. In: Markandya, A., Richardson, J. (Eds.): Environmental Economics: A Reader. St. Martin's Press, New York, 204-219

Caporael, L., Dawes, R.M., Orbel, J.M., van de Kragt, A. (1989): Selfishness Examined: Cooperation in the Absence of Egoistic Incentives. Behavioral and Brain Science 4, 683-698

Cater, E. (1995): Environmental contradictions in sustainable tourism. The Geographical Journal 161(1), 21-28

Cities International (1996):Vol VIII No III Third Quarter, http://www.icma.org/cities

Dawes, R.M., Alphons, J.C., van de Kragt, A., Orbel, J.M. (1990): Cooperation for the Benefit of Us: not me and not my conscience. In: Mansbridge, J.J. (Ed.): Beyond Self-Interest. The University of Chicago Press, Chicago and London

Dryzek, J. (1997): Discursive Democracy. Politics, Policy, and Political Science. Cambridge University Press, Cambridge/New York

Easterlin, R. (1995): Will Rising Income of All Increase the Happiness of All? Journal of Economics, Behaviour and Organization 27, 35-47

Easterlin, R. (1974): Does Economic Growth Improve the Human Lot? In: David, P., Reder, M. (Eds.): Nations and Households in Economics Growth: Essays in Honour of Moses Abramowitz. Academic Press Inc., New York

Eberle, D., Hayden, F.G. (1991): Critique of Contingent Valuation and Travel Cost Methods for Valuing Natural Resources and Ecosystems. Journal of Economic Issues XXV, 649-687

Eichler, M. (1996): Considering Sustainability from a Canadian Sociological Feminist Perspective. Paper prepared for UNESCO MOST Project on Sustainable Development as a Concept for True Social Sciences, Frankfurt, Germany

Enderle, G. (1989): Auf dem Weg zu einer ökologischen Wirtschaftsethik. In: Seifert, E., Pfriem, R. (Eds.): Wirtschaftsethik und ökologische Wirtschaftsforschung. Verlag Paul Haupt, Bern/Stuttgart, 237-249

Fedra, K. (1993): A Computer-Based Approach to Environmental Impact Assesment. RR-91-13, International Institute for Applied Systems Analysis, Laxenburg

Forrester, J.W. (1982): Principles of Systems. Second Edition, MIT Press, Cambridge, MA

Forrester, J.W., Senge, P.M. (1980): Tests for Building Confidence in System Dynamic Models, TIMS Studies in Management Studies 14, 209-228

Giddens, T.R. (1974): Nitrogen fixation in soil crusts of tall fescue sod. Soil Science 133(5), 295-297

Granger, H.J. (1989): Process Modeling and Geographic Information Systems (GIS) in River Basin Management. Water Science and Technology 19(9), 81-86

Habermas, J. (1984): The Theory of Communicative Action. Vol. 1, Reason and the Rationalization of Society. Beacon Press, Boston

Habermas, J. (1996): Justification and Application: Remarks on Discourse Ethics (translated by C. Cronin). MIT Press, Cambridge, Mass.

Hall, C., Cleveland, C., Kaufman, R. (1986): Energy and Resource Quality: the Ecology of the Economics Process. Wiley, New York

Hall, C., Jourdonnais, J., Stanford, J. (1989): Assesing the Impact of Stream Regulation in the Flathead River Basin, Montana U.S.A. I Simulation Modelling of System Water Balance Regulated Rivers: Research & Management, Vol 3, 61-77

Harris, C., Driver, B.L., McLaughlin, W. (1989): Improving the Contingent Valuation Method: A Psychological Perspective. Journal of Environmental Economics and Management 17, 213-229

Holling, C.S. (1978): Lessons for Ecological Policy Design: A Case Study of Ecosystem Management. Ecological Modelling 7(1), 1-53

Hubacek, K. (1997): The Interest Groups (Stakeholders) at Lake George. Course Paper. Advanced Ecological Economics. Rensselaer Polytechnic Institute, Troy, N.Y.

Hubacek, K., Shandas, V., Vazquez, J. (1997): Dynamic Simulation and Input-Output Modeling Course Paper. Quantitative Methods. Rensselaer Polytechnic Institute, Troy

Hunsaker, C.T., Jackson, M.J., James, W.J., Stevens, A. (1993): The Design of Environmental Geographic Systems. Phil. Trans. R. Soc. Lond. A. 324, 373-380

Jackson, J., Wyer, M.D., O'Neil, G., Crowther, J. (1988): Implementation of Low Cost AIS for Planning. Proceedings of 3rd International Conference of GIS/LIS, San Antonio, Vol. 2, 932-940

Keith, J., Fawson, C., Chang, T. (1996): Recreation as an Economic Development Strategy: Some Evidence from Utah. Journal of Leisure Research 28, 96-107

Kessell, S.R. (1990): An Australian Geographical Information and Modeling System for Natural Area Management. International Journal of Geographic Information Systems 4(3), 333-362

King, A.W. (1983): Assessing Land-Use Impacts on Natural Resources. Internal Paper of Environmental Science Division, Oak Ridge National Labs, Oak Ridge, Tennessee

Lam, D.C.L., Swayne, D.A. (1991): Integrating Database, Spreadsheet, Graphics, GIS, Statistics, Simulation Models and Expert Systems: Experiences with the Raison System on Microcomputers. NATO ASI Series, Bol, G26, Springer, Heidelberg, 429-459

Lotka, A.J. (1925): Elements of Physical Biology. Williams and Wilkins, Baltimore

Laurenroth, W.K., Burke, C., Parton, W.J. (1993): Regional and Temporal Variation in New Primary Production & Nitrogen Mineralization in Grasslands. Ecology 78, 1330-1340

Mathews, D. (1994): Politics for People: Finding a Responsible Public Voice. University of Illinois Press. Urbana Ill

Murdoch, J.C., Thayer, M.A. (1988): Hedonic Price Estimation of Variable Urban Air Quality. Journal of Environmental Economics and Management 15(2), 143-146

Norton, B., Toman, M. (1997): Sustainability: Ecological and Economic Perspectives. Land Economics 73(4), 553-68

O'Hara, S. (1983): Simulations of Nitrate Emissions from Agricultural Land Use, Simulated by Use of the CREAMS Model (in German). Gewässerschutz. Wasser. Abwasser 65, 569-576

O'Hara, S. (1996): Discursive Ethics in Ecosystems Valuation and Environmental Policy. Ecological Economics 16, 95-107

O'Hara, S. (1998): Internalizing Economics: Sustainability Between Matter and Meaning. Essays in Honor of Clement Allen Tisdell, Part IV. In: O'Brien, J.C. (Ed.): International Journal of Social Economics 25 (2/3/4), 175-195

O'Hara, S. (Forthcoming a): Economics, Ecology and Quality of Life: Who Evaluates? Feminist Economics

O'Hara, S. (Forthcoming b): The Challenges of Valuation: Ecological Economics between Matter and Meaning. In: Cleveland, C., Costanza, R., Stern, D. (Eds.): The Nature of Economics and the Economics of Nature. Edward Elgar, London

O'Hara, S., Mesner, S. (1998): The Limits of Economic Rationality: Social and Environmental Impacts of Recreational Land Use. Indian Journal of Applied Economics 7(2), 181-202

O'Neill, J. (1996): Cost-benefit analysis, rationality and the plurality of values. The Ecologist 26, 98-103

Park, R.A., Scavia, D., Clesceri, L.S. (1974): CLEANER, the Lake George Model. In: Russel, C.S. (Ed.): Ecological Modeling in a Management Context. Resources for the Future, Washington DC, 49-81

Park, C. (1979): Ecological and Environmental Management: A Geographical Perspective. Dawson & Westview Press, New York

Patten, B.C. (1971): Systems Analysis and Simulation in Ecology. Vol. I, Academic Press

Pearce, D.W., Turner, R.K. (1990): Economics of Natural Resources and the Environment. John Hopkins University Press, Great Britain

Pimentel, D. (1973): Food Production and the Energy Crisis. Science 182, 443-449

Priddat, B.P. (1995): Die andere Ökonomie. Eine neue Einschätzung von Gustav Schmollers Versuch einer ethisch-historischen Nationalökonomie im 19. Jahrhundert. Metropolis, Marburg

Rensselaer Darrin Freshwater Institute (1984): Report on the Lake George Chemical Monitoring Program. Rensselaer Polytechnic Institute-Freshwater Institute Reports 84-1. Rensselaer Polytechnic Institute, Troy

Renn, O., Webler, T., Rakel, H., Dienel, P., Johnsons, B. (1993): Public Participation in Decision Making. Policy Sciences 26, 189-214

Renn, O., Webler, T., Wiedeman, P. (1995): Fairness and Competence in Citizen Participation. Kluwer, Boston

Robinson, J., Tinker, J. (1995): Reconciling Ecological, Economic and Social Imperatives: Toward an Analytical Framework. SDRI Discussion Paper Series 95-1. Sustainable Development Research Institute, Vancouver

Rudzitis, G. (1989): Amenities, Migration, and Non-metropolitan Regional Development. A report to the National Science Foundation Dept. of Geography. University of Idaho, Moscow, ID

Sagoff, M. (1998): Aggregation and Deliberation in Valuing Environmental Public Goods: a look beyond contingent pricing. Ecological Economics 24(2,3), 213-230

Schmidt-Bleek, F. (1994): Wieviel Umwelt braucht der Mensch? MIPS - Das Maß für Ökologisches Wirtschaften. Birkhäuser Verlag, Berlin

Schwartz, P. (1991): The Art of the Long View. Doubleday, New York

Shyns, P. (1998): Crossnational Differences in Happiness: Economic and Cultural Factors Explored. Social Indicators Research 43, 3-26

Siegfried, C. (1996): Reweaving the Social Fabric: Pragmatism and Feminism. University of Chicago Press, Chicago

Sklar, F.H., Costanza, R. (1991): The Development of Dynamic Spatial Models for Landscape Ecology, Quantitiative Methods in Landscape Ecology. Springer, New York

Smith, V.K., Desvousges, W. (1993): The generalized travel cost model and water quality benefits: a reconsideration. In: Markandya, A., Richardson, J. (Eds.): Environmental Economics: A Reader. St. Martin's Press, New York, 184-193

Tietenberg, T. (1988): Environmental and Natural Resource Economics. (2nd ed.) Scott, Foresman and Company, Glenview, Boston, London

Tikunov, V.S. (1989): Modern Research Tools on the "Society-Natural Environment" systems in Soviet Geography. Journal of Environmental Systems 19(1), 59-69

Tisdell, C. (1991): Economics of Environmental Conservation. Elsevier, Amsterdam

Ulrich, P. (1989): Lassen sich Ökonomie und Ökologie wirtschaftsethisch versöhnen? In: Seifert, E.K., Pfriem, R. (Eds.): Wirtschaftsethik und ökologische Wirtschaftsforschung. Paul Haupt Verlag, Bern/Stuttgart, 165-172

United Nations Development Programme (1996): Human Development Report. Oxford Univerity Press, New York

Van Est, J.V., de Vroege, F. (1985): Spatially oriented information systems for planning and decision making in the Netherlands. Environment and Planning B: Planning and Design 12, 251-267

Vitousek, P., Ehrlich, P., Ehrlich, A., Matson, P. (1986): Human Appropriation of the Products of Photosynthesis. Bioscience 34(6), 368-373

Wackernagel, M., Rees, W. (1995): Our Ecological Footprint: Reducing Human Impact on the Earth. New Society Publishers. Gabriola Island, British Columbia and Philadelphia

Wallner, H.P., Narodoslawsky, M., Moser, F. (1996): Islands of Sustainability. Environment and Planning A. 25, 1763-1778

WCED (World Commission on Environment and Development) (1987): Our Common Future. Oxford University Press, Oxford

Webler, T. (1992): Modeling Public Participation as Discourse: An Application of Habermas's Theory of Communicative Action. Doctoral Dissertation. Clark University. Worchester, Massachusetts

Wellmer, A. (1986): Ethik und Dialog. Elemente des moralischen Urteils bei Kant und in der Diskursethik. Frankfurt

Wiggins, J.C., Hartley, R.P., Higgins, M.J., Whitaker, R.J. (1986): Computing Aspects of Large Geographic Information Systems for the European Community. Conference Proceedings of Auto Carto London, Vol. 2, 28-43

Witt, R.G. (1989): An Overview of GRID: a working global database. In: Zirm, K.L., Mayer, J. (Eds.): Envirotech Vienna 1989 - Computer Based Information Systems in Environmental Protections and Public Administration (Workshop). February 20-23 1989, International Society for Environmental Protection, Vienna/Hofburg, Austria

Part 2

Modelling as support for policy analysis

Model-based criteria for the effectiveness of conservation strategies – an evaluation of incentive programmes in Saxony, Germany

Karin Frank[1] and Irene Ring[2]

UFZ Centre for Environmental Research, Permoserstr. 15, D-04318 Leipzig, Germany
[1] Department of Ecological Modelling
[2] Department of Ecological Economics and Environmental Sociology

1 Introduction

Human activities have enormously accelerated habitat destruction and deterioration as well as landscape fragmentation. Industrial development has brought about land use forms which allow changes on a shorter temporal but a larger spatial scale, with serious consequences for all successional processes. As a result, many species have become endangered. Therefore, conservation strategies are needed which enable these effects to be effectively counteracted, reduced, or compensated for.

Conservation schemes need land. However, nature protection is in competition with other land use options that are generally more profitable, given the current legal framework. Under such conditions, one policy option is to levy charges or taxes on environmentally harmful activities. Another option is to award financial assistance to activities geared towards nature conservation, such as the protection, (re)establishment or maintenance of biotopes or valuable parts of the landscape. The latter approach can be implemented, for instance, by financial incentive programmes that provide positive economic incentives for certain target groups to enhance the conservational value of a landscape (Ring, Kneer and Frank 1998). Positive financial incentives address the problem of underinvestment in biodiversity (OECD 1994). There are several ways to counteract this effect: there are grants or direct payments (that can include environmental management agreements); the purchase of land can be financed to ease transformation into a protected area; and soft loans or tax concessions may be provided in agriculture, forestry and other activities that protect the environment. As the financial resources available for incentive programmes are limited, they should be invested with maximum ecological effect (Edwards and Abivardi 1998).

This paper analyses and evaluates positive economic incentives for nature conservation. A model-based approach is presented that allows the ecological effectiveness of incentive programmes for nature conservation to be evaluated from specific perspectives of biodiversity protection. As an example, this approach will be applied to selected incentive programmes in the German state of Saxony. These programmes will be evaluated in terms of their effectiveness, with the viability of a certain target species being taken as an indicator of biodiversity. Certain reserves in the programmes' effectiveness will be revealed and some ways of improving the situation will be suggested. To conclude, some principle consequences concerning the simultaneous analysis of both economic and ecological aspects of incentive programmes will be discussed.

2 A general approach for evaluating incentive programmes

We present an approach for evaluating nature conservation incentive programmes in terms of ecological effectiveness. An incentive programme is said to be ecologically effective if it allows the available financial resources to be optimally allocated, i.e. with maximum ecological effect.

2.1 Three levels for allocating financial resources

In the context of incentive programmes for nature conservation, there are three levels for which the question of the optimal allocation of financial resources is relevant. (1) Depending on the aspect of conservation which is of interest, different incentive programmes with certain relevance may apply. Here, the question is whether the allocation of total budgets to the individual incentive programmes is optimal in terms of ecological effectiveness. (2) Each incentive programme consists of different categories of management measures that can be supported. At this level, the allocation of partial budgets to the individual categories has to be analysed. (3) Within the realm of each category, different actors can apply for financial support for a multitude of specific management measures at different locations. Therefore, both measure- and location-specific differences in economic and landscape-ecological conditions become relevant. This may influence the ecological effect attainable. Hence, the way in which the resources are allocated to the individual applicants is a key factor of ecological effectiveness.

For each level, specific guidelines for optimal allocation are needed. The third level is of particular importance, for it is at this level that landscape intervention takes place. Here, the allocation of financial resources directly affects the attainable ecological effect. Therefore, we decided to start with the deduction of guidelines for the applicants' level.

2.2 Yardsticks for the ecological effect

The primary goal of nature conservation is to preserve or increase biodiversity. There are a number of quantifiers of biodiversity each concerning a specific aspect thereof, such as the survival chances of a target species or the number of species in a biotope. The actual value of such a quantifier closely depends on both the species' interaction and their specific perception of the given landscape. These processes, however, have the inherent property that nonlinearities, random or cumulative effects may occur. Consequently, the effect of a certain landscape manipulation on the quantifiers of biodiversity can only be predicted with difficulty. In this situation, mathematical models are useful. Models allow landscape manipulations to be simulated as special parameters changes (Verboom et al. 1993; Hanski 1994) and their effects on the quantifier of biodiversity to be calculated. However, it should be noted that a specific model is needed for each aspect of biodiversity.

The potential of models for tackling the problem of optimal allocation at the level of the applicants for incentive programmes is obvious. Alternative scenarios of allocating financial resources result in alternative landscape manipulations that can be simulated and compared in terms of the calculated effect on the quantifier of biodiversity. This enables the best scenario to be found and guidelines to be concluded for optimal allocation.

This information permits analysis of whether the key factors of ecological effectiveness are actually implemented in the incentive programme. This is necessary for correct decisions concerning the allocation of available resources and reveals possible improvements to the situation which can be discussed. The model must be optimally geared to the category of management measures under consideration, especially to its temporal characteristics ("non-recurring", such as the establishment of a certain biotope, or "recurring", such as the permanent maintenance of a biotope), as well as spatial characteristics ("patchy", if influencing a certain restricted area, or "exhaustive", if influencing the landscape on a larger scale).

2.3 An approach for evaluating incentive programmes in terms of ecological effectiveness

To distinguish between financial allocation at different levels and to deal with the peculiarities of effectiveness analysis in the field of nature conservation, we use a hierarchical approach:

1. Step: Determine the aspect of nature conservation in which you are interested.
2. Step: Determine what legal and administrative framework is relevant for useful management measures in the given context. This is necessary to reveal the administrative level where eventual changes can be implemented. Determine the range of incentive programmes implemented by the responsible authorities.
3. Step: Analyse each incentive programme in terms of (a) its relevance for the conservation purposes of interest, (b) its available total budget, and (c) the total supported area. For a more detailed analysis, we decided to start with the programme of highest conservation relevance.

4. Step: To evaluate a specific incentive programme, determine what categories of management measures are supported. Analyse each category in terms of (a) its available budget, (b) its temporal characteristics, and (c) its spatial characteristics (see above). To set priorities for a model-based analysis, we decided to start with the category with the highest budget.
5. Step: To analyse a specific category of management measures in terms of their ecological effectiveness, develop an appropriate model, simulate different scenarios of allocating financial resources, and compare them in terms of their effect on the relevant quantifier of biodiversity. Reveal (a) which scenario of allocation is optimal under the current conditions and (b) which factors are essential for ecological effectiveness. These results provide the basis for guidelines for decision making.
6. Step: Analyse the extent to which the relevant incentive programme takes the essential factors for ecological effectiveness into account. Finally, look for possibilities to subsequently implement the guidelines for optimally allocating the financial resources.

3 The incentive programmes of Saxony: a regional case study

In the following, the approach presented is applied to incentive programmes for nature conservation and landscape maintenance in Saxony (Germany). In this case study, we focus on nature conservation in open landscapes and its effect on the viability of a certain target species. Here, the mean lifetime T_m of the species represents an appropriate quantifier of its viability.

3.1 Incentive programmes for nature conservation in Saxony

To follow the presented approach, we have to determine (a) what legal and administrative framework is relevant for management measures aimed at nature conservation in open landscapes, (b) which authorities are found to be responsible in the given context, and (c) what relevant incentive programmes exist in the realm of each of these authorities (see Step 2).

3.1.1 Legal and administrative framework

Due to the federal structure of Germany, the federal state (*Land*) level is found to be an important political actor concerning the implementation of incentive programmes. In view of the future application of our results in the Leipzig area (Saxony, Germany), we analysed incentive programmes offering incentive measures for nature conservation at the level of the Free State of Saxony.

The political changes in 1989 led to the adaptation and implementation of both European and (West) German nature protection law in the five new federal states that had hitherto comprised the GDR (East Germany). Since 1 July 1990, the German Federal Conservation Act (BNatSchG) has applied in these states. In Saxony, the legal and administrative framework for nature protection was set up between 1991 and 1995 (Steffens 1997). The first law to implement the Federal Conservation Act was passed in 1991; one year later the Saxon Conservation and Landscape Maintenance Act (SächsNatSchG) came into force. Incentive programmes with relevance for nature conservation have been implemented in the realm of the environmental ministry (SMU: Saxon Ministry of the Environment and Development) and the agricultural ministry (SML: Saxon Ministry of Agriculture, Nutrition and Forestry)[1].

3.1.2 Incentive programmes by the environmental ministry

The first programme adopted by the SMU is a directive on incentive measures for nature protection and landscape maintenance (latest amendment: SMU 1997). In this programme, allocation possibilities embrace measures aimed at (a) species protection, (b) the establishment of biotopes or biotope networks, and (c) biotope or landscape maintenance. The directive also supports the purchase of land for conservation purposes in favour of third parties. A second programme is an administrative regulation on conservation contracting (SMU 1995), which is based on Section 39 of the SächsNatSchG. This regulation finances additional expenditure serving conservation purposes in the field of land use (e.g. the extensive use of meadows or fish ponds). Special regulations exist for agriculture and fishery. Both the directive and administrative regulation are restricted to protected areas in Saxony. Measures are only financed if the relevant areas lie within or adjacent to national parks, biosphere reserves, valuable biotopes or other protected areas. Whereas the directive is directly aimed at protection, the regulation is directed towards a type of land use that meets conservation goals.

3.1.3 Incentive programmes by the agricultural ministry

The agricultural ministry has introduced a cultural landscape programme (KULAP) that is part of the incentive programme on environmentally sound agriculture (SML 1995a). The latter programme serves the regional implementation of EU Regulation No. 2078/92. This means that the European Union participates in financing the Saxon programme on environmentally sound agriculture up to 75% of the maximum refundable amounts. Under KULAP, mainly extensification measures, but also a few biotope relevant measures such as the establishment of wetlands or the planting and maintenance of hedges, can be granted financial support. However, in contrast to the programmes introduced by the environmental ministry, the ma-

[1] Since 11 November 1998, these two ministries have been merged to form the Saxon Ministry of the Environment and Agriculture (SMUL).

jority of the management measures supported by the cultural landscape programme is not restricted to specific locations. KULAP is divided into two sub-programmes: KULAP Part I is aimed at extensive land use practices and predominantly supports area-related measures of grassland cultivation, while KULAP Part II supports investment schemes directed towards the protection, maintenance or (re)establishment of cultural landscapes.

3.2 Comparative analysis of the incentive programmes

Each of these incentive programmes is analysed in terms of (a) its relevance for conservation purposes, (b) its available total budget, and (c) the total supported area. This corresponds to Step 3 of the presented approach.

3.2.1 Relevance for conservation purposes

When comparing the incentive programmes in terms of their relevance for conservation purposes, a gradient is observed stretching from the pure protection of land over land use in protected areas to land use in cultural landscapes that meets conservation aims (Table 1).

Table 1. Incentive programmes for nature conservation and landscape maintenance in Saxony.

Incentive programme	**Directive on nature protection and landscape maintenance**	**Administrative regulations on conservation contracting**	**Cultural landscape programme**
Responsible ministry*	Environment (SMU)	Environment (SMU)	Agriculture (SML)
Predominant aim	Protection	Land use	Land use
Application area	In or adjacent to protected areas	In or adjacent to protected areas	Cultural landscape
Relevance for nature conservation			

* Since 11 November 1998, the Saxon Ministry of the Environment and Agriculture (SMUL) has been responsible for all programmes.

The directive on nature protection and landscape maintenance directly supports conservational measures, whereas the other programmes focus on the support of environmentally sustainable land use practices. Therefore, the directive represents the core programme for nature protection goals in Saxony.

3.2.2 Available total budget

The programmes considerably differ in the development of expenditure between 1992 and 1996 (Figure 1). In 1992, the expenditure of the environmental and agricultural ministries on their respective incentive programmes were almost equal. Since then, both conservation contracting (SMU) and KULAP Part II (investment measures, SML) have hardly changed. The directive on nature protection and landscape maintenance (SMU), the core programme for conservation purposes, shows a slight increase in expenditure from DM9.6 million in 1992 to DM12.4 million in 1996. The largest increase in expenditure concerns KULAP Part I, owing to the substantial expansion of the sub-programme in 1994. From that time on, allocations have for example been made for grassland cultivation with reduced means and a few other new measures. Thus, the area-related measures of the cultural landscape programme represent the category with by far the highest expenditure among the incentive programmes for nature conservation and landscape maintenance in Saxony.

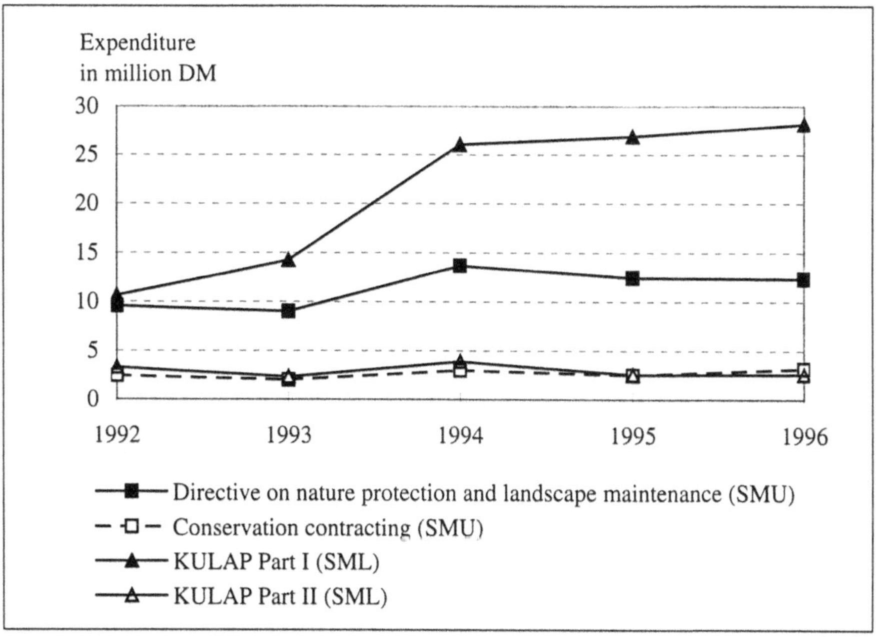

Sources: LfUG 1997; SML 1993, 1994, 1995b, 1996, 1997.

Figure 1. Expenditure on nature conservation and landscape maintenance in Saxony: environmental ministry (SMU) and agricultural ministry (SML).

3.2.3 Total supported area

Figure 2 depicts the total areas supported by the various incentive programmes as far as area is a relevant parameter. Both programmes launched by the environmental ministry have hardly changed as far as the total area supported is concerned since their implementation. Concerning the directive on nature protection and landscape maintenance, roughly 4,600 hectares of land received funds for biotope maintenance measures in 1996. Conservation contracting rated a little higher with almost 7,000 hectares, most support going to freshwater fishery. Thus, the environmental ministry supports little more than 10,000 hectares of land – only about 0.5% of the total area of Saxony, much less than the demand for nature conservation and landscape maintenance in Saxony stipulated by the Saxon Office for Environment and Geology. A budget of about DM60 million would be needed at the environmental ministry to support all necessary maintenance measures related to protected areas in Saxony (about 50,000 hectares) (Steffens 1997).

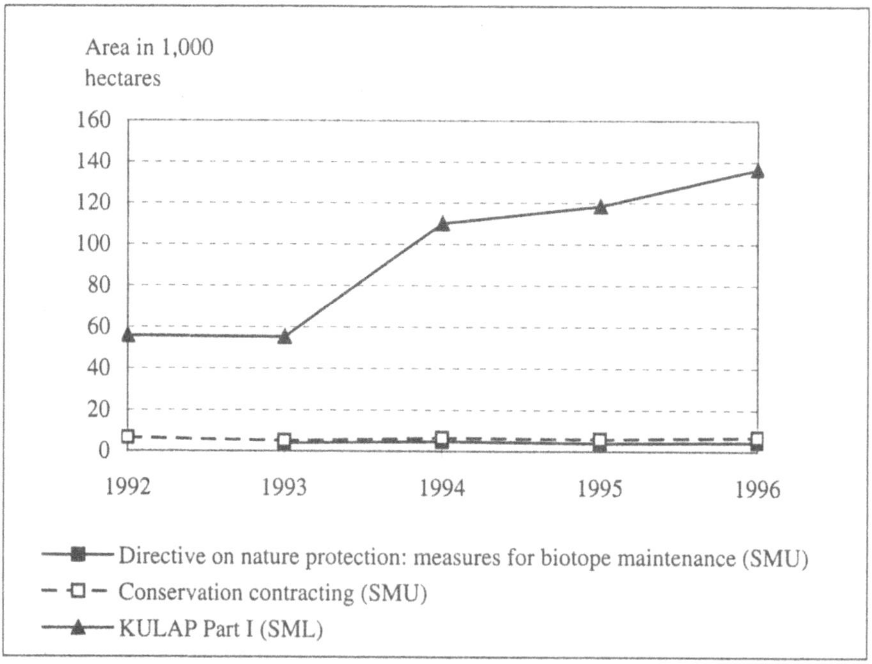

Sources: LfUG 1997; SML 1993, 1994, 1995b, 1996, 1997.

Figure 2. Areas supported by incentive programmes for nature conservation and landscape maintenance in Saxony.

Looking at the cultural landscape programme, Part I, we reach completely different figures. The original KULAP Part I was able to address about 56,000 hectares of the cultural landscape in Saxony (1992 to 1993). Following the implementation of the new KULAP Part I, in 1994, we notice a steady increase up to roughly 136,000 hectares of land supported by the programme. This area represents approx. 62% of the total grassland area and approx. 95% of the total pond area used for freshwater fishery in Saxony (SML 1997: 48). To summarise, the cultural landscape programme allows areas on a large spatial scale to be supported. This indicates the potential of land use practices that can be improved to the benefit of nature conservation.

3.3 The evaluation of the directive on nature protection and landscape maintenance

Further analysis concentrates on the directive on nature protection and landscape maintenance identified as the core programme for conservation purposes (Table 1). According to Step 4 of our approach, we have to determine which category of management measures shows the highest expenditure and what its temporal and spatial characteristics are.

3.3.1 Available budget for the categories of management measures

Figure 3 depicts the development of expenditure between 1992 and 1996 on different categories of management measures supported by the directive.

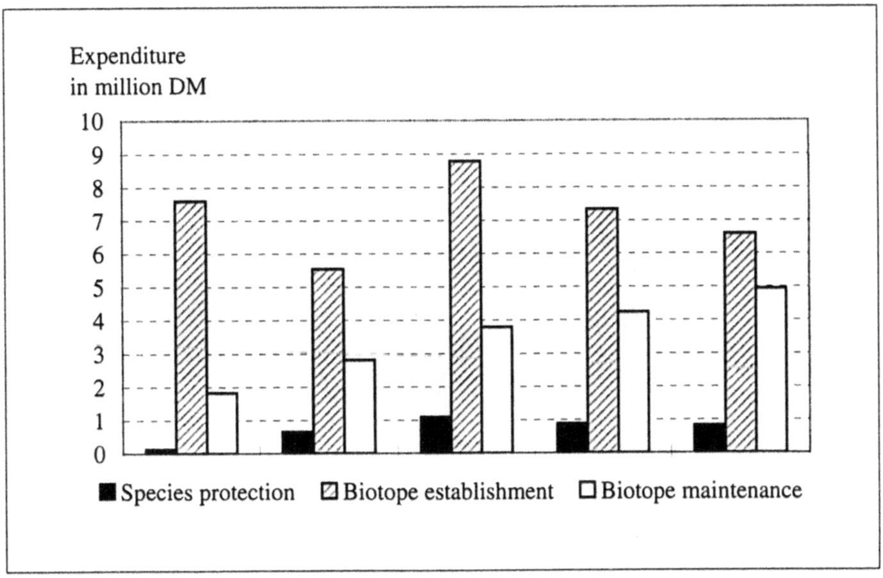

Source: LfUG 1997.

Figure 3. Directive on nature protection and landscape maintenance: development of expenditure on different measures.

Species protection clearly represents the category with the lowest expenditure, stabilising at just under DM1 million per year. Most expenditure went into biotope establishment, where an average of about DM7 million per year was invested. Expenditure on biotope maintenance has steadily increased since 1992, reaching almost DM5 million in 1996. This increase for maintenance measures has to be seen in the context of biotope establishment measures. (Re)established biotopes have to be maintained in the following years, especially when successional processes jeopardise the persistence of a biotope in its current state. Since biotope establishment is found to be the category with the highest available budget, we shall concentrate on this category as a starting point for further analysis.

3.3.2 The temporal and spatial characteristics of biotope establishment

The category of biotope establishment summarises a multitude of different management measures. They can be divided into measures inducing changes in the landscape settings and accompanying measures such as planning or public relations. Only the first type of measures is directly relevant for the ecological effect (see general approach above). From the temporal point of view, the relevant landscape changing measures can be characterised as individual "non-recurring" events. Their spatial characteristics ("patchy" or "exhaustive") primarily depend on the budget available.

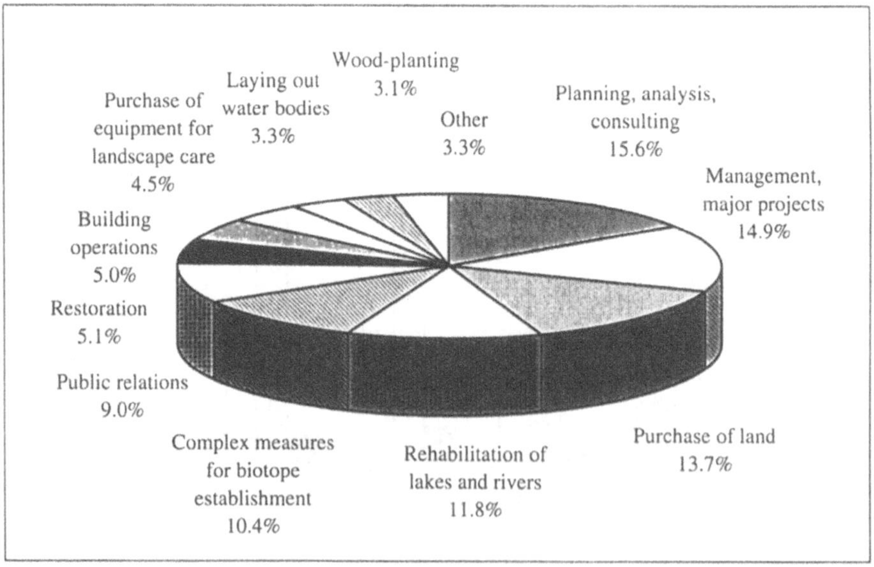

Source: LfUG 1997.

Figure 4. Relative expenditure on the category of biotope establishment within various management measures in 1996.

Figure 4 reveals a rather interesting picture. When studying the relative expenditure on different management measures in 1996, it can be seen that about 15% went into planning, analysis and consulting, and another 15% into management activities and major projects. An additional 19% was used for areas such as public relations, building operations or the purchase of equipment. Almost 14% was used to purchase land that was predominantly concentrated on ponds (LfUG 1997). This means that only about 33% of the relatively low total budget was available for landscape changing measures: 12% went into the rehabilitation of lakes and rivers, about 10% was used for complex measures of biotope establishment such as biotope connecting, and the other 11% was used for restoration, laying out water bodies and wood-planting.

This finding, together with the restriction that management measures can only be financed in or adjacent to protected areas (Table 1), gives rise to the conclusion that supported biotope establishment measures occur "patchily".

3.4 Guidelines for optimal biotope establishment

We now have a basis for a model-based analysis of the category of biotope establishment (Step 5 of the approach). An appropriate model will be developed that allows different scenarios of allocating financial resources to different applicants to be simulated and compared in terms of their effect on the mean lifetime T_m of the target species. Guidelines for optimal allocation will be deduced and the essential factors for ecological effectiveness determined.

3.4.1 The model

As we have seen, we are dealing with patchy biotopes which can be enlarged in size, improved in quality, or connected by corridors. The effect of all these measures on the mean lifetime T_m of the target species can best be analysed when a "metapopulation model" is used (this is especially useful when biotope networks are involved). The concept of metapopulation was introduced by Levins (1969): subpopulations of a species live in isolated habitat islands (patches) with some chance of local extinction. Single dispersing individuals, however, allow empty patches to be recolonised, thus compensating for local extinction. We use a model (Frank and Wissel 1998a) that allows the mean lifetime T_m of a metapopulation to be related to the patch-specific subpopulation features (e.g. the carrying capacities K_i), the patch configuration given by the distances d_{ij} between the patches, the pattern of connectedness (which patches are connected by corridors?), as well as some ecological characteristics of the target species (e.g. the individual dispersal ability or variability of the reproductive rates).

3.4.2 Simulating the allocation of financial resources

In the following, we address the management measure of enlarging biotope size for which a certain total budget B_{tot} is available. The crucial question the model has to answer is how the available budget should be allocated to the individual patches to maximise the mean lifetime T_m of the metapopulation. If p_i is the share of the total budget allocated to patch i, then a budget of $B_i = p_i \cdot B_{tot}$ is available to enlarge its area size A_i. This results in an increase of the carrying capacity $K_i = q\ A_i$ of its subpopulation with q denoting the species-specific population density that can be found in a biotope of the type considered. The essential factor, however, that determines the extent to which A_i and so K_i can be enlarged is the specific price per square metre c_i for land adjacent to patch i. With a budget B_i, an increase in K_i of $\Delta K_i = q \cdot \frac{B_i}{c_i}$ can be ensured, so that we obtain:

$$K_i^{new} = K_i + \Delta K_i = K_i + p_i \cdot \frac{q}{c_i} \cdot B_{tot} \tag{1}$$

By taking these settings for K_i^{new} as a basis, the metapopulation model allows the mean lifetime T_m to be analysed in terms of its dependence on the total available budget B_{tot}, the patch-specific land prices (c_i), and the shares (p_i) of allocation to the individual patches.

3.4.3 Guidelines for optimal allocation

In the following, different scenarios of allocating a given total budget B_{tot} ("All into the patch with the lowest land price" (Scenario 1), "Allocate according to the numbers of corridors adjacent to the patches" (Scenario 2), "Allocate uniformly" (Scenario 3)) are compared in terms of their effect on T_m. While the first and second scenario take the economic (landscape-ecological) differences between different locations into account, the third scenario ignores any differences. The results are shown for the exemplary metapopulation described by the pictogramme in Figure 5a and a species with high variability (Figure 5b) and low variability (Figure 5c) in reproductive rates (in this context, variability means the extent to which a species is sensitive to fluctuations in essential environmental factors such as the weather). Figures 5b-c reveal that (1) the mean lifetime T_m of the metapopulation always exhibits dependence on the available total budget B_{tot} that is much stronger than linear. (2) The different scenarios of allocation considerably differ in their effect on the mean lifetime T_m, even if the total budget B_{tot} is the same. But there is no general indication of which scenario is best. (3) There is a critical threshold value for the total budget B_{tot} below which the "All into the cheapest" scenario is found to be best. Above this threshold value, however, the other two scenarios are found to be more advantageous. The value of the critical total budget B_{tot} mainly depends on the land price per square metre c in the cheapest patch and the species-specific population density q. (4) A more detailed study (Frank and Wissel 1998b) has revealed that optimal allocation closely depends on both the pattern of connectedness and the species' variability of reproductive rates. It has been shown that, as long as the species are of a high variability (such as many small mammals or invertebrates), the resources ought to be allocated according to the numbers of corridors adjacent to the patches. This coincides with the finding in Figure 5b. If this variability is low (such as for larger mammals), the uniform allocation is optimal that conforms with the result in Figure 5c. But in this case, the corridor-oriented allocation scenario is also found to be quite effective. This allows the pattern of connectedness to be used as a general orientation to reveal the (sub-)optimal allocation strategy in the event of higher available budgets.

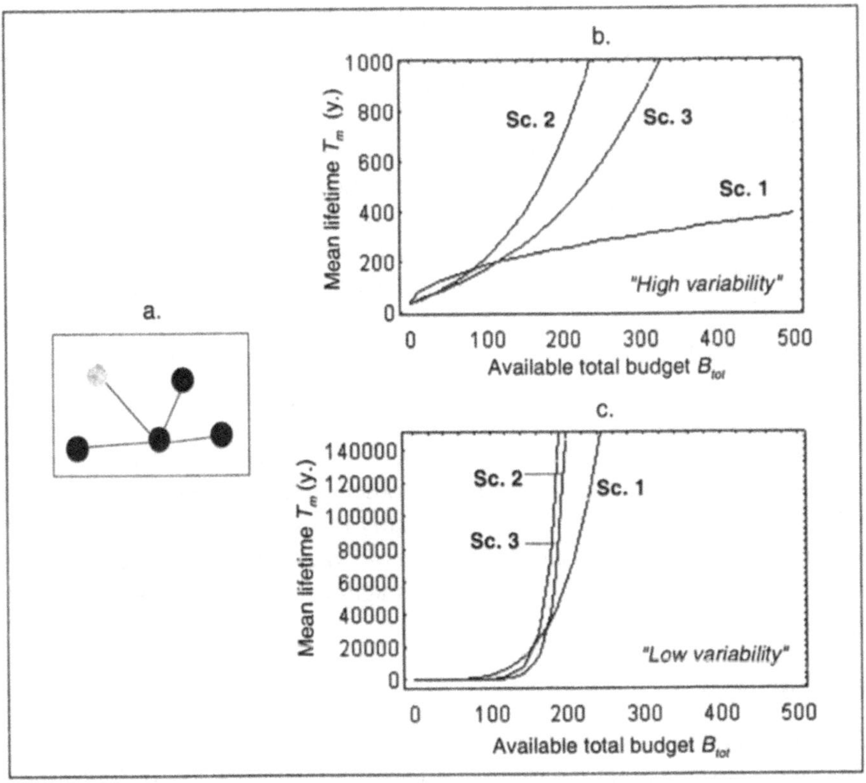

Figure 5. a) An exemplary metapopulation with 5 patches where the grey patch represents the patch of the lowest land price. b) and c) Mean lifetime T_m of the metapopulation versus available total budget B_{tot} for different scenarios of allocating the resources to the patches: "All into the patch with the lowest land price" (Sc. 1), "Allocate according to the number of corridors adjacent to the patches" (Sc. 2), "Allocate uniformly" (Sc. 3) for a species with high (b) and low (c) variability of the reproductive rates.

To conclude, the optimum revealed by the model gives some guidance for ranking different locations of biotope enlargement measures according to the attainable ecological effect. This can be realised by ranking the locations according to the land prices per square metre (in the case of low available total budgets) or according to the numbers of adjacent corridors (in the case of higher available budgets).

3.5 Consequences for the ecological effectiveness of the directive on nature protection

As the final step, some consequences for the ecological effectiveness of the directive on nature protection and landscape maintenance will be discussed.

Our model results give rise to the conclusion that the *location* of biotope establishment measures is a key factor of ecological effectiveness. So far, the directive has not allowed a spatial differentiation to be made. In this paper, guidelines have been deduced that enable a decision-maker to rank locations according to the attainable ecological effect for a certain target species. These guidelines can be implemented to increase the effectiveness of the directive.

For low budgets, the economic characteristics have been found to dominate. In these cases, it is best to concentrate the scarce resources to the patch (namely that with the lowest land price, thus enabling the largest area to be purchased) that guarantees the strongest increase in the carrying capacity K_i. This subsequently clarifies the usefulness of the directive's restriction to only support measures in or adjacent to protected areas. The higher the available total budget, the more limiting the landscape-ecological characteristics. Here, the pattern of connectedness provides guidance for the optimal allocation of financial resources.

Our model results also reveal that transferring a set of guidelines for optimal allocation from one situation to another is very problematical. As we have seen, the optimal strategy considerably changes when the total budget B_{tot} falls below or exceeds a critical threshold value. Note that B_{tot} is specific and may differ between different regions and/or different periods of implementation.

4 Conclusion

What is needed to evaluate the effectiveness of an incentive programme? Our analysis shows that the optimal allocation is never general, but instead closely depends on the total available budget of the programme and the aspect of nature conservation under consideration. Therefore a detailed economic evaluation of the incentive programmes is indispensable for ecological evaluation.

Our study also shows that models can be useful for evaluating incentive programmes for nature conservation in terms of their ecological effectiveness. The approach presented gives some kind of standard algorithm for evaluating the effectiveness of a given programme from a specific perspective of biodiversity protection. As a result, incentive programmes can be optimally geared to the legal, economic and ecological conditions of a given region. Furthermore, irrespective of whether the changes necessary really can be implemented, awareness of the key factors of ecological effectiveness fosters a better understanding of the system. All factors can be ranked according to their ecological importance for the aspect of biodiversity in mind. Presently, the model-based analysis as the core of this approach is still restricted to management measures that induce a certain change in the landscape settings; the ecological effect of an accompanying measure, e.g. public relation or environmental education, is hard to determine. To estimate the effects of at least some accompanying measures, it may be useful to take sociological expertise into account.

Each quantifier of biodiversity (here: the mean lifetime T_m of a certain target species) may be interpreted as an independent ecological 'currency'. Our results demonstrate that models allow pairs of ecological and economic currencies to be simultaneously analysed and their functional relationship to be revealed (see the T_m – B_{tot} – curves in Figures 5b-c). Since this can be done for each ecological currency, we have a basis for multi-criteria decision analysis (Ralls and Starfield 1995, Drechsler 1999, Grimm and Drechsler 1999). In this way, a multitude of different economic and ecological currencies can be simultaneously handled, increasing the chances of evaluating the effectiveness of incentive programmes from a more holistic perspective of biodiversity. However, such a procedure necessitates weighting all aspects of biodiversity considered in terms of their value for human society.

References

Drechsler, M. (1999): Entscheidungen im Naturschutz bei ökologischer Unsicherheit. Sonderheft 'Risikoanalyse im Naturschutz' der NNA (Nieders. Naturschutz-Akademie) Berichte (in press)

Edwards, P.J., Abivardi, C. (1998): The value of biodiversity: where ecology and economy blend. Biological Conservation 83, 239-246

Frank, K., Wissel, C. (1998a): Spatial aspects of metapopopulation survival: from model results to rules of thumb for landscape management. Landscape Ecology 13, 363-379

Frank, K., Wissel, C. (1998b): An approximation formula for the mean lifetime of metapopulations in heterogeneous landscapes. The American Naturalist (subm.)

Grimm, V., Drechsler, M. (1999): Risikoabschätzung und Entscheidungen in der Populationsgefährdungsanalyse (PVA). In: Breckling, B., Müller, F. (Eds.): Der ökologische Risikobegriff. Beiträge des Arbeitskreises "Theorie" in der Gesellschaft für Ökologie vom 4.-6. März 1998 im Landeskulturzentrum Salzau. Ecomed, Landsberg (in press)

Hanski, I. (1994): A practical model of metapopulation dynamics. J. Anim. Ecology 63, 151-163

Levins, R. (1969): Some demographic and genetic consequences of environmental heterogeneity for biological control. Bull. of Entomol. Society of America 15, 237-240

LfUG Sächsisches Landesamt für Umwelt und Geologie (Ed.) (1997): Abteilung Natur- und Landschaftsschutz, Dresden

OECD (1994): Economic Incentive Measures for the Conservation and Sustainable Use of Biological Diversity: Conceptual Framework and Guidelines for Case Studies. GD(94) 79, Paris

Ralls, K., Starfield, A.M. (1995): Choosing a management strategy: two structured decision-making methods for evaluating the predictions of stochastic simulation models. Conservation Biology 9, 175-181

Ring, I., Kneer, G., Frank, K. (1998): Incentives for nature conservation in urban landscapes. Environment and Planning C (subm.)

SML (Sächsisches Staatsministerium für Landwirtschaft, Ernährung und Forsten) (Ed.) (1993): Agrarbericht 1992. Dresden

SML (Sächsisches Staatsministerium für Landwirtschaft, Ernährung und Forsten) (Ed.) (1994): Agrarbericht 1993. Dresden

SML (Sächsisches Staatsministerium für Landwirtschaft, Ernährung und Forsten) (Ed.) (1995a): Umweltgerechte Landwirtschaft im Freistaat Sachsen. Hinweise zur Anwendung des Förderprogramms. Dresden

SML (Sächsisches Staatsministerium für Landwirtschaft, Ernährung und Forsten) (Ed.) (1995b): Agrarbericht 1994. Dresden

SML (Sächsisches Staatsministerium für Landwirtschaft, Ernährung und Forsten) (Ed.) (1996): Agrarbericht 1995. Dresden

SML (Sächsisches Staatsministerium für Landwirtschaft, Ernährung und Forsten) (Ed.) (1997): Agrarbericht 1996. Dresden

SMU (Sächsisches Staatsministerium für Umwelt und Landesentwicklung) (Ed.) (1997): Richtlinie des Sächsischen Staatsministerium für Umwelt und Landesentwicklung für die Förderung von Maßnahmen des Naturschutzes und der Landschaftspflege im Freistaat Sachsen vom 26. Juni 1997. Sächsisches Amtsblatt, Nr. 31, 31. Juli 1997, 811-813

SMU (Sächsisches Staatsministerium für Umwelt und Landesentwicklung) (Ed.) (1995): Verwaltungsvorschrift des Sächsischen Staatsministeriums für Umwelt und Landesentwicklung zum Vollzug des § 39 SächsNatSchG – Vertragsnaturschutz, Programm L vom 15. Mai 1995. Sächsisches Amtsblatt, 15. Juni 1995, 715-718

Steffens, R. (1997): Naturschutzarbeit in Sachsen – Ziele, Etappen, aktuelle Ergebnisse und Aufgaben. Naturschutzarbeit in Sachsen 39. Jg., 3-20

Verboom, J., Metz, J.A.J., Meelis, E. (1993): Metapopulation for impact assessment of fragmentation. In: Vos, C.C., Opdam, P. (Eds.): Landscape Ecology of a Stressed Environment. Chapman and Hall, 172-190

Joint abatement strategies: a dynamic analysis of acidification and tropospheric ozone

Erik C. Schmieman and Ekko C. van Ierland

Department of Economics and Management, Environmental Economics Group, Wageningen University, Hollandseweg 1, 6706 KN Wageningen, The Netherlands

1 Introduction

Acidification impacts water, soil and ecosystems. Tropospheric ozone (sometimes called ground level ozone, hereafter referred to as ozone or O_3) causes negative health effects and vegetation damage. Acidifying compounds such as sulphur dioxide (SO_2) and nitrogen oxides (NO_x) are often produced together, most typically by the burning of fossil fuels. Nitrogen oxides and volatile organic compounds (VOCs) are important factors in the formation of ozone. Currently, many ecosystems in the United States, Europe, and the emerging economies in Asia face acid depositions far in excess of their specified critical loads. Ozone exceeds critical levels in many cases. The excess acid depositions, the excessive ozone levels and the transboundary nature make it necessary to combat pollution on the continental level in the USA, Europe and Asia. The many interactions indicate that policies to reduce acidification influence ozone, and the other way around, ozone policies affect acidification. Figure 1 illustrates the main relations and interactions between economic activity, the sources of pollutants, the effects and receptors. This study pays special attention to the grey shaded boxes and their linkages.

The aim of this chapter is to investigate how dynamic aspects of acidification can be included in a model that calculates optimal time paths for the reduction of pollutants in a multiple pollutant multiple target setting. The study adds to the existing literature by focusing on three air pollutants (SO_2, NO_x, and VOCs) and two environmental problems (acidification of soils and tropospheric ozone). Using a numerical example, some aspects of the current policy plans based on the critical loads for acidity are evaluated. The impacts of acidification reduction strategies on the problem of tropospheric ozone are analysed in a cost-effectiveness study for a multiple pollutants multiple target setting.[1]

The chapter is organised as follows, in the next section we describe the interconnections between tropospheric ozone formation and acidification,

---

[1] Although, from economic viewpoint, it would be desirable to determine the best policies using cost-benefit analyses. However, valuing damages is a difficult (if not impossible) task. To overcome these difficulties this study performs cost-effectiveness analysis and provides insights in intertemporal cost-effective reduction strategies.

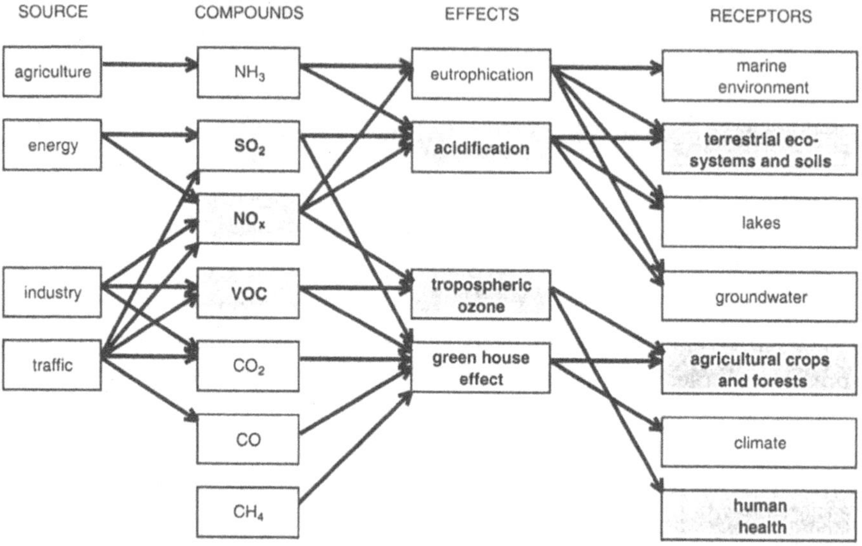

Figure 1. The regional air pollution problem. Relations between dominant sources, emitted compounds and their various receptors (based on Grennfelt et al. 1993 and Graedel and Crutzen 1993). This study pays special attention to the grey shaded boxes and their linkages.

including some of the relevant literature. We also discuss the mean features of ozone formation and dynamic aspects of soil acidification. In section 3 we formulate and discuss a model suitable for numerical analysis. We answer the question why it is important to include dynamic aspects of acidification and how the current reduction policies might be adjusted. Also the interrelationship between the problem of ozone and acidification is investigated. The last part concludes and gives suggestions for future research.

2 Tropospheric ozone formation and dynamic aspects of soil acidification

2.1 The formation of tropospheric ozone

The formation of ozone is mainly determined by the concentrations of NO_x and VOCs in the air along with the level of solar energy.[2] Extra complexity results from the non-linear relation between the concentration in the air of ozone and the concentrations in air of its precursors, NO_x and VOCs (see Figure 2).

[2] Ozone formation involves very complex chemical reactions. Kelly and Gunst (1990) and Heyes et al. (1995) give the most important features and relations between the major compounds.

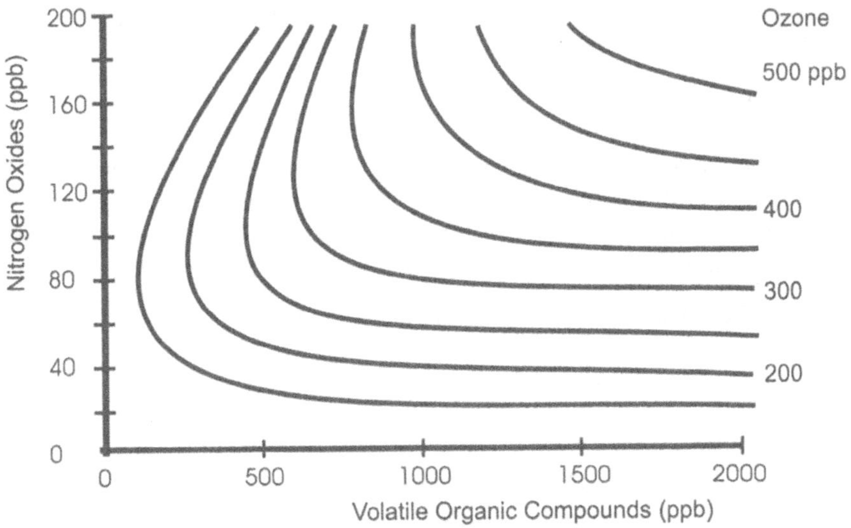

Figure 2. The relation between the concentration in the air (expressed in part per billion (ppb)) of VOCs, NO_x, and tropospheric ozone under certain conditions in an ozone isopleths diagram (based on Kelly and Gunst 1990).

In contrast to what one expects, a reduction in the NO_x emissions can lead to an increase in the ozone concentration in some countries. Reduction of NO_x emissions may increase ozone levels, especially in the UK, Germany, the Netherlands, Belgium, and Luxembourg (EMEP MSC W 1996). These countries, having relatively high NO_x densities, can be located in the upper left part of the diagram in Figure 2. VOCs abatement seems to be most effective for reducing ozone concentrations in these countries. Countries with relatively low NO_x concentrations such as Russia, the Ukraine, France, Italy and Spain (EMEP MSC W 1996), can be located in the lower right part of Figure 2. In these countries the reduction of NO_x seems to be most effective for reducing ozone concentrations.

To determine damage of ozone to health or vegetation it is important to take both the level and the duration of exposure into account. The accumulated ozone above threshold (AOT) index incorporates both aspects. For application in this study the most important features of AOT values, in this case AOT40, are shortly explained below.[3] The AOT40 exposure index accumulates the difference between the hourly measured ozone concentration (O_3 in ppb) values and 40 ppb for all hours in which 40 ppb are exceeded

[3] For details or definitions and possible applications and limitations of the AOT concept see EMEP MSC W (1996): in particular Chapter 6 and the references therein.

over the growing season, May, June and July (Tonneijck et al. 1998).[4] The AOT40 value is given in equation (1).

$$AOT40 = \int \max(O_3 - 40;0)dt \tag{1}$$

The Norwegian Meteorological Institute (1996) developed linear source-receptor matrices[5] for ozone formation. These matrices relate changes in emissions of VOCs and NO_x in an emitting country i to changes in ozone AOT values in a receiving country j (O_j, as an AOT40 value) related to a base value ($\overline{O}_j$) as is given in the following equation:

$$O_j = \overline{O}_j + W_{ij,no_x} \Delta NO_x + W_{ij,VOCs} \Delta VOCs \tag{2}$$

where $\overline{O}_j$ is the AOT40 value in the reference year, W_{ij,no_x}, $W_{ij,VOCs}$ are linear transport matrices and ΔNO_x and $\Delta VOCs$ represent changes in emissions in country i. Much criticism exists on the use of linear source receptor relations for ozone. For example, the ozone formation module in the RAINS model that is currently used at IIASA contains a non-linear relation including quadratic terms.[6]

Although the linearisation is under discussion we use linear source receptor relations to determine AOT40 values for ozone in a country in our model because of its straightforward application. For illustrative purposes we have chosen a set of coefficients reflecting a situation that is typical for the United Kingdom, the Benelux and Germany. This means that NO_x reduction (induced by acidification targets) might lead to higher ozone concentrations. Because of its short lifetime, no accumulation of ozone takes place.

---

[4] Also radiation energy plays a role, only hours in which the radiation energy exceeds 50 Watt per square meter are accumulated.

[5] A source receptor matrix or source receptor relation gives a relation between emission in a country and the influence on acid depositions or the influence on ozone formation in either the same or another country. According to EMEP MSC W (1996: 134) the use of source receptor matrices 'appear to offer the most promising approach to multi pollutant multi effect control strategy analysis', because of its straightforward application in integrated assessment modelling.

[6] For details see Heyes et al. (1997).

2.2 Dynamic aspects of soil acidification

2.2.1 Soil acidification in the literature

The introduction of the critical loads concept[7] in the late eighties created an indicator that could be used in policy plans which aim to reduce the problem of acidification. The relative simplicity of the concept lead to many applications in environmental economic literature. Many studies are performed that calculate cost-effective reduction of SO_2, NO_x and ammonia (NH_3) based on deposition calculations and critical loads.[8] Initially, the studies contained a limited number of critical loads. Increased knowledge of ecosystems and their response to acid depositions, and detailed mapping of critical loads make it possible to develop more detailed models that calculate cost-effective reduction strategies using many critical loads for various ecosystems. Currently the critical loads approach for acidification is widely spread in economic analysis.[9] More recently critical levels are formulated for ozone, see the next section for more details. Moreover, abatement policies for acidification and ozone presently in place in the European Commission and the United Nations Economic Commission of Europe (UN ECE) are based on a comparative static analysis of critical loads and critical levels. These studies mostly apply cost-effectiveness analysis.

Dynamic aspects on reduction strategies of acidification are dealt with in only a few environmental economic studies. Mäler (1994) states that static acid rain game models become quite different if it is assumed that damage is not determined by annual depositions but rather by the accumulated depositions. Not being able to incorporate accumulation of acid depositions Mäler focuses on dynamics induced by an acid rain game that is played repeatedly in the future. In 'the acid rain differential game' Mäler and De Zeeuw (1998) introduce a way to account for accumulation of acidification. They assume that when critical loads are exceeded the buffer stock for acidification decreases and when depositions are below critical loads the buffer increases again. A shortcoming of this description is that the behaviour of the buffer stock is not related to chemical processes in a soil and to the quality of a soil in a way that describes 'real' mechanisms related to acidification. The studies have in common that they focus on steady state outcomes in a game theoretical frame work. In contrast to Mäler and De Zeeuw (1998),

---

[7] A critical load is defined as a quantitative estimate of exposure to one or more pollutants below which harmful effects, which are judged to be significant on specified elements of the environment, do not occur according to present knowledge (Nilsson and Grennfelt 1988).

[8] See for example the RAINS model (Alcamo et al. 1990, Mäler 1989, Van Ierland 1991, Amann et al. 1992).

[9] See the references in footnote 8. Other applications are found in Altman et al. (1994), Amann and Klaassen (1995), Zylicz (1995), Amann et al. (1997), European Commission (1997) and Van Ierland and Schmieman (1999).

Kaitala et al. (1992) include an equation that describes dynamic soil acidification based on results from a dynamic soil acidification model. The equation they use calculates the temporal development of a chemical soil parameter, the base saturation which can be considered to be a soil quality indicator. They relate this indicator to reduced forest growth and hence to economic damages caused by acidification. Focusing on the application of game theory Kaitala et al. derive both cooperative and non cooperative solutions to an acid rain game between Finland and the USSR. Our study adds to the literature by integrating improved ecological modelling that incorporates dynamic aspects of acidification and economic modelling. It contrasts the results obtained from a dynamic model with those of more traditional comparative static models based on critical loads.

2.2.2 The mathematical specification

In this section we develop a reduced form[10] soil acidification model that describes the dynamics of soil acidification.

Dynamic aspects of soil acidification can be indicated by the temporal development of the base saturation of the soil. The base saturation is defined as the fraction of exchangeable base cations in the solid phase of a soil. The fraction base cation indicates the availability of nutrients in the soil. In turn this availability of nutrients influences growth of forests and other vegetation. Therefore, the base saturation is considered to be a soil quality indicator.

The base saturation at time t, $B(t)$, is defined as the stock quantity. The only relation that describes soil acidification dynamics in one simple equation we could find in the literature reads

$$\dot{B}(t) = \frac{dB(t)}{dt} = \alpha B(t) - \beta B(t)\ln B(t) - \gamma D(t)B(t) \tag{3}$$

The equation is taken from Kaitala et al. (1992) and is by those authors derived using a model developed by Holmberg (1990). To further simplify the equation we set α equal to zero by assuming that the term is captured by $\gamma D(t)$ as a kind of background deposition (Posch 1998). We express the base saturation as a fraction and not as a percentage. The dynamic behaviour of the base saturation in a soil can be given by the following state equation

$$\dot{B}(t) = \frac{dB(t)}{dt} = -\beta B(t)\ln B(t) - \gamma D(t)B(t) \tag{4}$$

with β and γ being coefficients which can be estimated using dynamic soil acidification models. $B(t)$ represents the base saturation expressed as a fraction and $D(t)$ is a deposition function depending on t. By a state transforma-

[10] Acidification models with many equations describing in detail soil and water chemistry are too complex to integrate with economic models, therefore we use a reduced form.

tion of $\phi(t) = \ln B(t)$ (and thus $B(t) = e^{\phi(t)}$) the state equation transforms into (omitting subscript t with respect to ϕ):

$$\dot{\phi} = -\beta\phi - \gamma D(t) \tag{5}$$

with $\beta > 0$ and $\gamma > 0$. Parameter β could be interpreted as a recovery rate while γ identifies how fast a soil responds to (changes in) depositions.

A lower base saturation will result in a more acidified and less fertile soil. Below a certain value for the base saturation, called the critical value, vegetation and ecosystems that depend on the soil face increased risks to damage. Below this critical value it is considered that increased risks exist for harmful effects in the long term.

The critical load for acid deposition is based on the critical base saturation (B_c) and is derived for a steady state condition that is for $\dot{\phi} = 0$. Using equation (5) and B_c which transforms to ϕ_c ($\phi_c = \ln B_c$), and assuming an infinite time horizon, we can derive the critical load (D_c) for acid deposition from the following expression:

$$D_c = \frac{-\beta\phi_c}{\gamma} \tag{6}$$

If we solve equation (6) for the critical base saturation ϕ_c it can be seen that ϕ_c is independent of the initial condition of the soil and independent of depositions before the time period under consideration (before t=0). Therefore, the analysis does not have to start before the process of acidification started (before industrialisation started).

With respect to the critical limit for the base saturation B_c and the critical load D_c four cases can be distinguished that depend on the initial situation B_0 and the long term constant deposition D_{con} (Posch 1998). For our model calculations we set the parameter values at β=0.015, γ=0.0001, and the critical value for the base saturation at B_c=0.10.[11] Using equation (6) we can compute the critical load, $D_c \approx 450$ acid equivalents per hectare per year (eq/ha/yr). From equation (6) we see that for a constant deposition below the critical load (100 acid eq/ha/yr) the base saturation will converge to $\beta \approx 0.51$. For a constant deposition of about twice the critical load (900 acid eq/ha/yr) B will converge to $B \approx 0.002$. See Figure 3 for the temporal development of the base saturation for different initial conditions of the soil.

[11] The values for β and γ are chosen arbitrarily but magnitudes are based on parameters estimated for a poor Finnish forest soil as applied in Kaitala et al. (1992). From soil scientific research we know that a reasonable critical limit for the base saturation is 0.05 or 0.10 (Posch 1998).

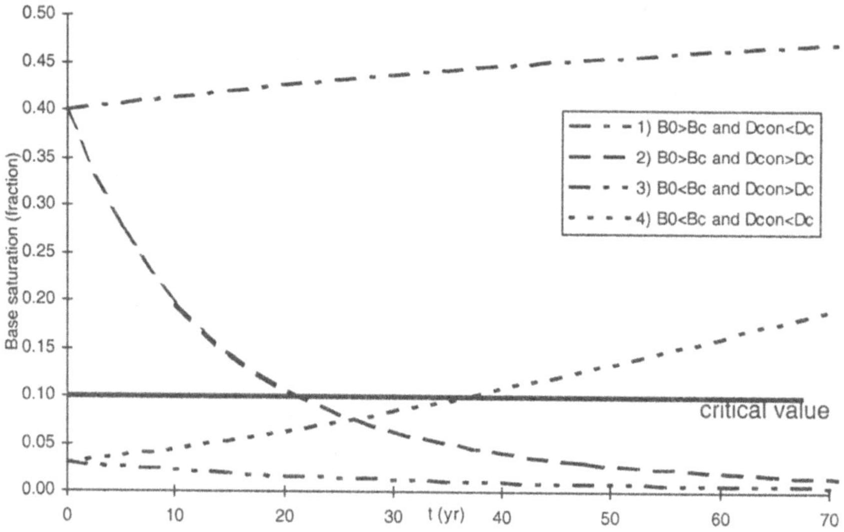

Figure 3. The temporal development of the base saturation (as a fraction) for a constant high (900 eq/ha/yr) and constant low (100 eq/ha/yr) acid deposition for four different cases, B_c=0.10 and the critical load ≈450 acid eq/ha/yr.

By formulating a model that incorporates soil dynamics one can determine when the critical base saturation (B_c) will be reached given initial conditions of the soil and assuming a known deposition function ($D(t)$). By using critical loads only, as is done in many studies, one cannot analyse the time paths and the temporal development of the condition of a soil itself.

In the next section we develop a model that accounts for the dynamic behaviour of soils and we use it to analyse optimal or cost-efficient time paths of emission reduction in a numerical example.

3 The model, simulations and analysis

To investigate cost-effective solutions we analyse the results of a numerical optimisation model that contains ozone formation (a flow pollutant), soil acidification (a stock pollutant), two emitting countries (i=1,2), two receptor countries (j=1,2), three emitted pollutants k (with k=1 for SO_2, k=2 for NO_x, and k=3 for VOCs) and two resulting environmental problems (in acidification of soils and tropospheric ozone). Abatement in country i at time t is given by $A_{i,k,t}$ (in kiloton with 1 kton equals 1,000,000 kg), the abatement costs functions ($C_k(A_{i,k,t})$) for technical end of pipe measures[12] are assumed to be constant in time (no technical progress). The functions are also

[12] The parameters $a_{i,k}$ and $b_{i,k}$ in equation (7) can be estimated using cost function data from the RAINS model.

assumed to be twice differentiable, convex and increasing in abatement (that is $C'_{i,k} > 0, C''_{i,k} > 0$) and abatement costs are given by

$$C_k(A_{i,k,t}) = a_{i,k} A^{b_{i,k}} \tag{7}$$

We assume unabated emissions constant[13] $\overline{E}_{i,k}$ (in kton). Because of technical limitations we assume that abatement cannot exceed 90% of initial emissions for every period ($A_{i,k,t} \leq 0.9 \cdot \overline{E}_{i,k}$). Emissions from country *i* are transported to country *j* by air, described in a transport matrix. Deposition of acid (acid equivalents per hectare per year, eq/ha/yr) in receptor country *j* is calculated by multiplying emissions of acidifying pollutants after abatement with the transport matrix[14] $M_{ij,k}$ (for k=1, 2 and with all elements in $M_{ij,k} \geq 0$, see equation (10)). The formation of ozone in receptor country *j* at time *t* ($O_{j,t}$) is determined by equation (11). In this equation $\overline{O}$ is a given AOT40 value in a base year, and the elements in the source receptor matrix $W_{ij,k}$ (k=2) can be positive, negative or zero.[15] For $W_{ij,k}$ (k=3) all elements are zero or positive. The two countries are assumed to have the same homogeneous soil (for reasons of simplicity). The impact of acid depositions on the base saturation are modelled using the relations developed in the prior section and are given by equation (10). To derive emission targets we restrict the (ln transformed) base saturation of the soil in a receptor country ($\phi_{j,t}$) not to decrease below the critical (ln transformed) base saturation (ϕ_c). We call the terminal time *T* the point in time that the soil will reach the lower bound of the base saturation (B_c). At this time the problem becomes a constraint problem. Total reduction costs (*TC*) are calculated as the sum of the discounted reduction costs in the two countries for the three pollutants. Total reduction costs consists of two parts, the first term in equation (8) (from t=0 to t=T) and the second term, the discounted reduction costs beyond time *T* necessary to maintain reduction levels to avoid a further decreasing base saturation:

$$TC = \sum_{j=1}^{2}\sum_{k=1}^{3}\int_{0}^{T} e^{-\rho t} C_{i,k,\tau}(A_{i,k,\tau})d\tau + \sum_{j=1}^{2}\sum_{k=1}^{3}\int_{T}^{\infty} e^{-\rho t} C_{i,k,t}(A_{i,k,t})dt \tag{8}$$

[13] This simplifies the problem and can be justified by assuming no economic growth and no growth in energy consumption.
[14] The transport matrices include a factor that translate depositons in kton to acid equivalents per hectar per year.
[15] As explained in section 2, reduction of NO_x can both increase or decrease AOT40 values.

We can rewrite[16] this expression, yielding a maximisation problem formulated as maximising the negative costs. The social planner now wants to find the abatement path $A_{i,k,t}$ that solves (omitting subscript t):

$$Max \quad V = \sum_{i=1}^{2} \sum_{k=1}^{3} - \int_{0}^{T} e^{-r\rho t} C_{i,k}(A_{i,k,t}) dt - \tfrac{1}{\rho} C_{i,k}(A_{i,k,T}) e^{-\rho T} \tag{9}$$

subject to

$$\dot{\phi}_j = -0.015\phi_j + 0.001 \sum_{k=1,2} M_{ij,k} (\overline{E}_{i,k} - A_{i,k}) \quad k = 1,2 \tag{10}$$

$$O_j - \overline{O}_j + \sum_{k=2,3} W_{ij,k} A_{i,k} = 0 \quad k = 2,3 \tag{11}$$

$$\overline{E}_{i,k} - A_{i,k,t} \geq 0 \tag{12}$$

$$\phi_j(t) - \phi_{c,j} \geq 0 \tag{13}$$

The initial condition for the soil is $\phi_j(0) = \phi_{0,j}$, with the initial value $\phi_{0,j}$ assumed to be known (the base saturation of a soil can be measured). To investigate cost-effective solutions for the dynamic acidification problem, we analyse the results of a numerical optimisation model that contains dynamics in soil acidification.[17] Table 1 shows the most important values we have used in our model. First we focus on dynamics in acidification in relation to dynamic cost-effectiveness. In a later section we analyse the interaction with the ozone problem.

Table 1. The most important data used in the numerical model runs.

	Country 1	Country 2
Emissions (for all t before abatement)		
SO_2 (kton/yr)	500	2,000
NO_x (kton/yr)	300	800
VOCs (kton/yr)	500	2,000
Initial values		
base saturation (fraction)	0.40	0.40
depositions (eq/ha/yr)	969	1,554
critical load exceedance (times critical load)	2.15	3.4
AOT40 for ozone (ppb h)	10,526	9,235
Critical base saturation (fraction)	0.10	0.10
Critical load (eq/ha/yr)	345	345
Discount rate (percentage)	5	5

[16] Using the concept of limits the second term can be rewritten as follows

$$\int_{T}^{\infty} e^{-r\tau} C(A_\tau) d\tau \equiv \lim_{b \to \infty} \int_{T}^{b} e^{-r\tau} C(A_\tau) d\tau = \left[\frac{-C(A_\tau) e^{-r\tau}}{r} \right]_T^b = \frac{C(A_T) e^{-rT}}{r}$$

[17] It is not the aim of this chapter to theoretically analyse this model. For a formal mathematical solution see Schmieman and Van Ierland (1998).

To investigate cost-effective solutions for the dynamic acidification problem, we analyse the results of a numerical optimisation model that contains dynamics in soil acidification. Two abatement scenarios are of particular importance and we compare them to show the main mechanisms. First, we examine the 'optimal abatement' scenario in which the model calculates cost-effective reduction of SO_2 and NO_x given a minimum standard for the quality of the soil (a lower bound on the base saturation). This scenario is called the Base Case. Second, we investigate 'the protocol implementation' scenario in which we assume that emission reductions are implemented analogous to the current European policies. These policies are based on the sulphur and nitrogen oxides protocols (United Nations 1985; United Nations 1988; United Nations 1991; United Nations 1994). Further we assume that emission reduction measures are linearly implemented between the year that the target becomes effective and the year the target is to be met. See Table 2 for details.

Table 2. The protocol implementation scenario, emission reduction targets for SO_2 and NO_x.

	Reduction (% of 1980 level)
SO_2 reduction path	
1980 - 1984	0
1985 - 1993	-30
1994 - 2000	-80
after 2000	-80
NO_x reduction path	
1980 - 1988	0
1989 - 1994	-20
1995 - 2005	-60
2006 - 2015	-80
after 2015	-80

3.1 Simulations and analyses

In the Base Case the discount rate (ρ) is set on 5% and the critical limit for the base saturation (B_c) is assumed to be 0.10, so $B(t) \geq 0.10$ for all periods. Cost-effective time paths of emissions, depositions, and the base saturation are presented in Figure 4. The soil in country 2 turns out to be the binding soil, which means that the soil in country 2 reaches the critical limit for the base saturation and determines the (boundary) solution of the problem. The critical limit for the base saturation is reached in about 31 years. Afterwards emissions and depositions remain constant ($D_1 \cong 200$ and $D_2 \cong 345$ eq/ha/yr) resulting in a steady state with the base saturation of the soil in country 1 equal to 0.26 (the base saturation in country 2 equals 0.10). An important notice is that according to both the depositions and the base saturation ecosystems are protected after the year 2010, because depositions are below critical loads and the base saturation stays on or above the critical value in both countries.

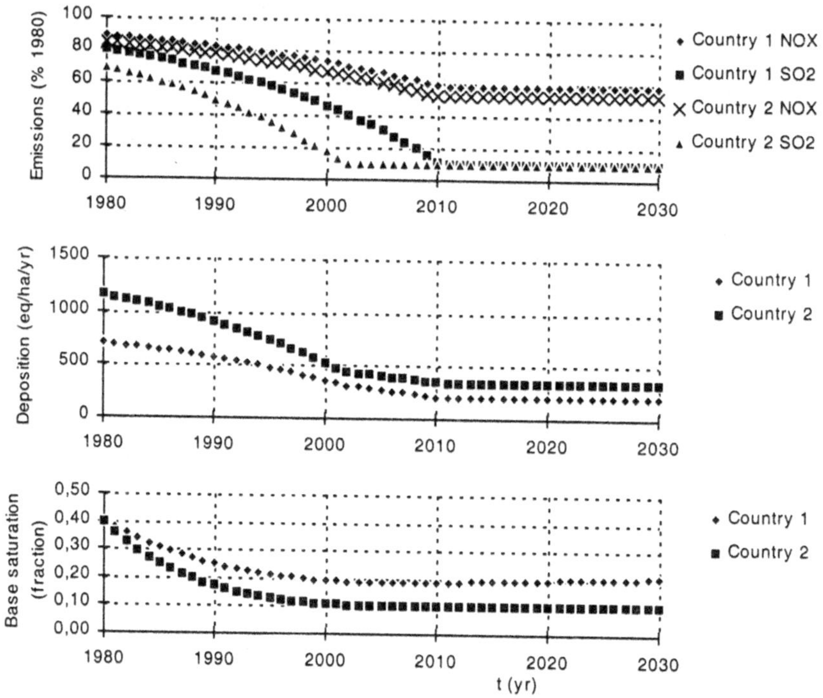

Figure 4. The Base Case, from top to bottom the temporal development of the percentage of initial emissions, the depositions (eq/ha/yr) and the base saturation (fraction) in country 1 and country 2.

We have performed some sensitivity analysis with respect to the discount rate and the critical value for the base saturation. Results for the discount rate are as expected. If we assume a low (high) social time preference by fixing the discount factor at 2% (10%), keep other things the same, reduction starts immediately at higher (lower) levels and abatement with relative high (low) marginal costs are cost-effective earlier (later) in time. The lower bound on the base saturation (B_c=0.10) becomes binding after about 40 (27) years. The soils will reach the same steady states at β_1=0.26 and B_2=0.10. With the critical value of the base saturation at B_c=0.10 (and ρ=0.05) the terminal time is nearly the same as in the base case (32 years). The base saturation in the soil in country 1 will converge to β_1=0.12 with a constant deposition of 327 acid equivalents per hectare per year.

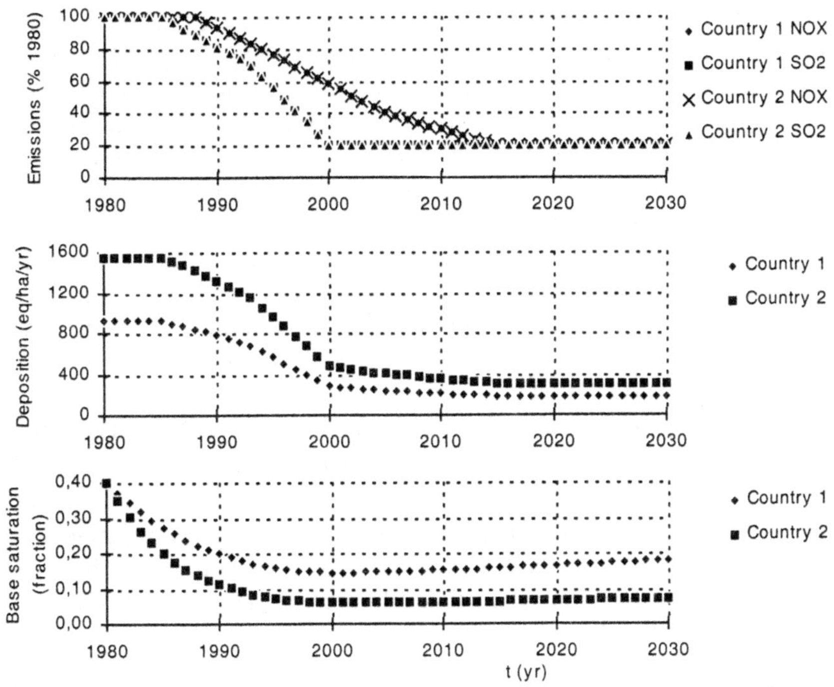

Figure 5. The protocol implementation scenario, from top to bottom the temporal development of emissions (% of initial emissions), depositions (eq/ha/yr) and the base saturation (fraction) in country 1 and country 2.

In the protocol implementation scenario emission (and deposition) time paths are fixed by means of policy plans and the model calculates the base saturation. See Figure 5 for emission and deposition patterns and the temporal development of the base saturation. According to the deposition levels in the middle graph of Figure 5 there are actual depositions below critical loads after 2000 in country 1 and after 2010 in country 2. Based on that one would conclude that ecosystems are protected from increased risk of damage due to acidification by 2000 and 2010 respectively. However, based on the base saturation one draws a different conclusion. In the protocol implementation scenario, the quality of the soil in country 2 indicated by the base saturation falls under the critical value in 1991 and stays under that value for more that 50 years after the full implementation of the protocols becomes effective in 2015 (provided that depositions remain constant afterwards). Accordingly, the soil in country 2 needs a long period to recover from the excess acid loads in the first three decades of the period under consideration. In this recovery period, also denoted as Damage Time Lag (Hettelingh and Posch 1994), the ecosystems depending on the soil face increased risk for acidification damage. This may result in reduced forest growth, a decrease in biodiversity or other negative effects.

This mechanism shows exactly what could happen if politicians agree on deposition targets based solely on critical loads being reached at some point in time. In the critical loads approach it is not taken into account to what extent soils are degraded and how long recovery may take. Insights in the temporal development of the quality of a soil can therefore be useful to redefine policy targets to avoid damage to ecosystems in the sometimes very long period the soil needs to recover from excess acid loads. It might even be the case that when the monetary value of damage is taken into account, early reduction or more stringent policy targets earlier in time may be cost-efficient. Moreover, a cost benefit analysis including dynamics in soil acidification and possible damage caused by low soil quality may result in shifting emission reduction closer to an earlier time.

Although not analysed, it should be noted that different soils (characterised by different values for the parameters β and γ) respond differently to excess acid loads. Therefore, for some soils a temporal exceedance of critical loads might not be a problem at all because they might respond so slow that they would never deteriorate to critical levels. On the other hand, a soil may respond so fast that critical levels are reached much faster and the quality of the soil will decrease even more.

3.2 Interaction between acidification and ozone policies

In this section we focus on the interaction between the problem of acidification and ozone. In the Base Case ozone formation is not restricted, therefore changes in ozone AOT40 values (see equation (2) and (11)) result only from changes in NO_x emissions that are induced by acidification policies. No abatement of VOCs takes place in both countries because no damage by ozone is included in the model and ozone formation is free (there are no restrictions on the maximum ozone level). Given the transport matrices for ozone it turns out that NO_x reduction increases ozone levels in country 1 and decreases ozone levels in country 2. Moreover, negative synergies exist between the problem of acidification and ozone in country 1 and positive synergies occur in country 2. Since the model assumes additive separable reduction cost functions, the synergies are fully determined (and explained) by the dependency in ozone formation. The temporal development of the ozone level as AOT40 value is given in Figure 6 (recall Figure 4 for the corresponding emission, deposition and base saturation patterns).

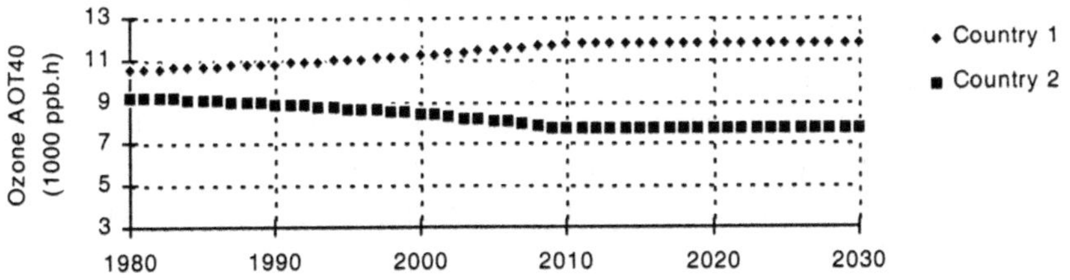

Figure 6. The base case: the development of the AOT40 in both countries (in 1,000 ppb h) when reduction policies are based on acidification targets and no additional VOCs reduction is imposed.

To further illustrate the cross effects between acidification policies and ozone formation AOT values for the protocol implementation scenario are shown in Figure 7 (recall Figure 5 for emissions and deposition patterns). The picture shows similar trends as in the cost-effective reduction scenario (the Base Case). The only difference is that time paths are non smooth because of the fixed emission reduction targets and the linear interpolation.

The most important conclusion is that the reduction of acidification by means of NO_x emissions reduction can lead to positive as well as negative cross effects on ground level ozone formation.

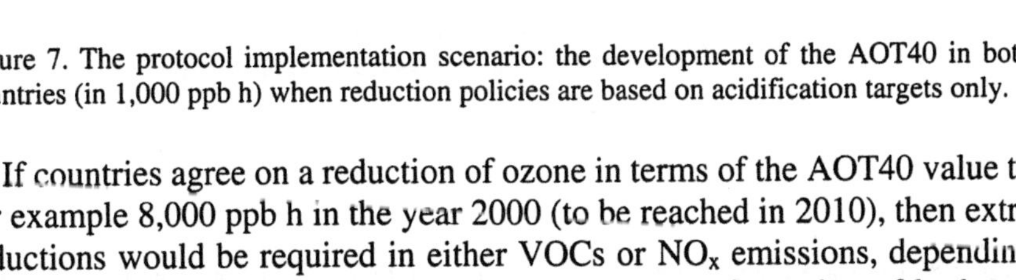

Figure 7. The protocol implementation scenario: the development of the AOT40 in both countries (in 1,000 ppb h) when reduction policies are based on acidification targets only.

If countries agree on a reduction of ozone in terms of the AOT40 value to for example 8,000 ppb h in the year 2000 (to be reached in 2010), then extra reductions would be required in either VOCs or NO_x emissions, depending on the cost-effectiveness and the influence on ozone formation of both options. As stated before, country A faces a high NO_x concentration in the air relative to the VOCs concentration and ozone formation behaves as in the upper left corner of Figure 2. In our calculation it turns out that it is cost-effective to relax NO_x abatement in country A after 2000 and to increase VOCs reduction (see Figure 8). This leads to a solution that goes together with a high NO_x concentration and a low VOCs concentration. The cost-effective solution does not lead to a desired result and extra restriction on NO_x emissions would be required to avoid such a solution.

If the qualitative behaviour of ozone formation can be described by the linear transport matrices used in this model, it could be concluded that pollution by ozone might increase due to acidification policies in some areas. For these areas it would be necessary to persuade extra policies with respect to VOCs reduction. Even if reduction of NO_x leads to ozone reduction in all cases it still might be possible to achieve more cost-effective solutions if the two environmental problems are jointly studied by taking into account the concerning marginal abatement costs. Therefore, these results show that a multiple pollutant multiple target approach can lead to better insights in reduction policies and to less costly abatement programmes.

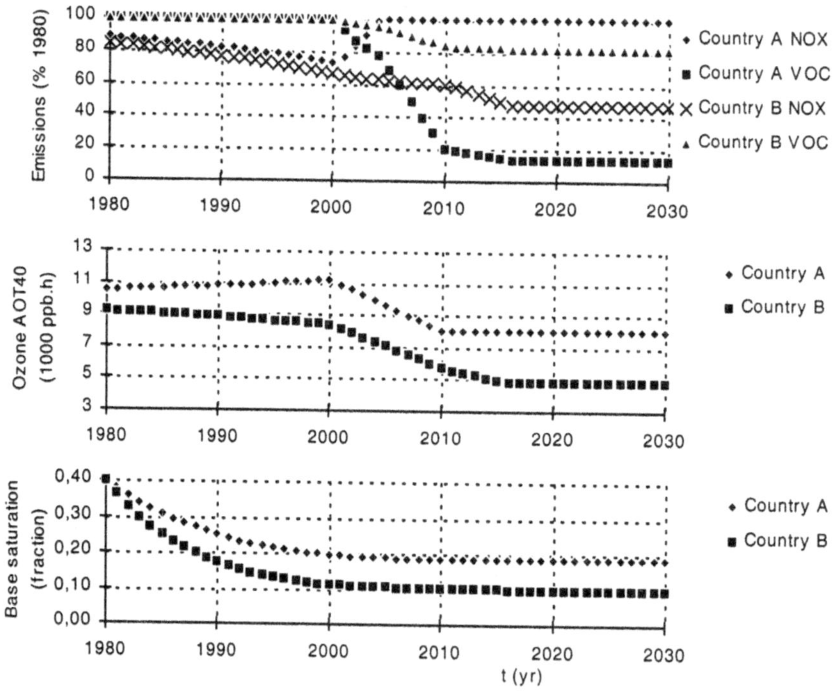

Figure 8. The Base Case with additional ozone policy targets for both countries. From top to bottom emissions (SO_2 not depicted), ozone AOT40 (1,000 ppb h) and the base saturation.

4 Conclusions and further research

A dynamic optimisation of cost-effective abatement strategies of a combined reduction of SO_2, NO_x and VOCs has been performed. SO_2 and NO_x are acidifying compounds, NO_x and VOCs are precursors of the toxic gas tropospheric ozone. The study provides a way to analyse optimal time paths of emission reduction for NO_x and SO_2 by showing how dynamic aspects of soil acidification could be incorporated in economic modelling. The study also relates acidification policies to tropospheric ozone. Because empirical application on a European scale would require huge amounts of data, the main mechanisms are shown by using a 2 country model with hypothetical data. Soil acidification dynamics are captured by one equation that can be estimated using a full and detailed dynamic soil acidification model. Ozone formation is described using a linearised approximation of non linear processes in ozone formation.

The results indicate qualitatively that an analysis of acidification in a dynamic setting gives useful additional insights to the currently used critical loads approach. Currently European acidification policies are strongly founded on the use of critical loads. In the resulting agreements deposition targets are formulated to be reached at some point in time. Nevertheless, in the period between when the agreement is accepted and the point in time when the targets will be met, depositions are exceeding critical loads. Soils will deteriorate but it is unknown to what extent. Insights in the temporal development of soil quality (for example by explicitly modelling the base saturation as is being done in this study) therefore can be useful to redefine policy targets to avoid damage to ecosystems in the period critical loads are exceeded. Different soil types respond differently to excess acid loads. Therefore, for some soils a temporal exceedance of critical loads might not be a problem at all, because they might respond so slow that they would never deteriorate to critical levels. On the contrary, a soil can respond so fast that critical levels are reached in a short period and the quality of the soil would decrease even more. By allowing intertemporal efficiency, reduction measures with low marginal costs are implemented early in time which leads to cost savings. The discount rate plays an important role in the optimal reduction path. A high discount rate tends to shift reduction to the future and the soil decays relatively fast, and total discounted reduction costs are valued lower and vice versa.

The influence of acid related policies on ozone precursors and ozone formation is also assessed. To further improve the model and for empirical application it would be desirable to include a model that better describes the non linear features in ozone formation. However, calculations with the linearised model illustrate how acidification policies interact with the problem of tropospheric ozone. The results show that additional policy measures with respect to VOCs might be required to reduce damage from ozone. It is also shown that both positive and negative cross-effects exists. Further investigation may show that a multiple pollutant multiple effect strategy can lead to additional cost savings.

References

Alcamo, J., Shaw, R.W., Hordijk, L. (1990): The RAINS Model of Acidification Science and Strategies in Europe. Kluwer Academic Publishers, Dordrecht

Altman, A., Amann, M., Klaassen, G., Ruszczynski, A., Schöpp, W. (1994): Cost-Effective Sulfur Emission Reduction Under Uncertainty. Report: 94-199, International Institute for Applied Systems Analysis, Laxenburg

Amann, M., Bertok, I., Cofala, J., Gyarfas, F., Heyes, C., Klimont, Z., Makowski, M., Shibayev, S., Schöpp, W. (1997): Cost-Effective Control of Acidification and Groundlevel Ozone. Report: Third Interim Report, International Institute for Applied Systems Analysis (IIASA), Laxenburg

Amann, M., Bertok, I., Cofala, J., Klaassen, G., Schöpp, W. (1992): Strategies for Reducing Sulfur Dioxide Emissions in Europe. SR-92-008, International Institute for Applied Systems Analysis, Laxenburg

Amann, M., Klaassen, G. (1995): Cost-Effective Strategies for Reducing Nitrogen Deposition in Europe. Journal of Environmental Management 43, 289-311

EMEP MSC W (1996): Estimating Dispersion of Acidifying Agents and Near Surface Ozone. Status Report 1/96 part one, The Norwegian Meteorological Institute, Norway

European Commission (1997): Elements of a Cost-Effective Emission Reduction Policy. Some Insights From the European Auto Oil 1 Programme Using the Leuven Model. II/022/97-EN, European Commission Directorate-General for Economic and Financial Affairs, Economic Services, Evaluation Transport, Environment and Energy Policies (II-B4), Brussels

Graedel, T.E., Crutzen, P.J. (1993): Atmospheric Change: An Earth System Perspective. W.H. Freeman and Company, New York

Grennfelt, P., Hov, O., Derwent, R.G. (1993): Second Generation Abatement Strategies for NO_x, NH_3, SO_2 and VOC. B1098, Swedish Environmental Research Institute, Sweden

Hettelingh, J.P., Posch, M. (1994): Critical Loads and Dynamic Assessment of Ecosystem Recovery. In: Grasman, J., Van Straten, G. (Eds.): Predictability and Nonlinear Modelling in Natural Sciences and Economics. Kluwer Academic Publisher, Dordrecht, 439-445

Heyes, C., Schöpp, W., Amann, M. (1995): A Simplified Model to Predict Long-Term Ozone Concentrations in Europe. Report: WP-95-034, International Institute for Applied Systems Analysis, Laxenburg

Heyes, C., Schöpp, W., Amann, M., Bertok, I., Cofala, J., Gyarfas, F., Klimont, Z., Makowski, M., Shibayev, S. (1997): A Model for Optimizing Strategies for Controlling Ground-Level Ozone in Europe. IR097-002/ January 1997, International Institute for Applied Systems Analysis, Laxenburg

Holmberg, M. (1990): Ion Exchange Dynamics and Soil Acidification: Model Development and Testing (Licentiate Thesis). Department of Mathematics and Systems Analysis, Helsinki University of Technology

Kaitala, V., Pohjola, M., Tahvonen, O. (1992): Transboundary Air Pollution and Soil Acidification: A Dynamic Analysis of an Acid Rain Game Between Finland and the USSR. Environmental and Resource Economics 2, 161-181

Kelly, N.A., Gunst, R. (1990): Response of Ozone to Changes in Hydrocarbon and Nitrogen Oxide Concentrations in Outdoor Smog Chambers Filled With Los Angeles Air. Atmospheric Environment 24a, 2991-3005

Mäler, K.G. (1989): The Acid Rain Game. In: Folmer, H., Van Ierland, E.C. (Eds.): Valuation Methods and Policy Making in Environmental Economics. Elsevier Science Publishers, Amsterdam, 231-252

Mäler, K.G. (1994): Acid Rain in Europe: A Dynamic Perspective on the Use of Economic Incentives. In: Van Ierland, E.C. (Ed.): International Environmental Economics: Theories, Models and Applications to Climate Change, International Trade and Acidification. Elsevier Science B.V, Amsterdam, 351-372

Mäler, K.G., De Zeeuw, A.J. (1998): The Acid Rain Differential Game. Environmental and Resource Economics 12, 167-184

Nilsson, J., Grennfelt, P. (1988): Critical Loads for Sulphur and Nitrogen. Report From a Workshop Held at Skokloster, Sweden 19-24 March, 1988. Report: 1988:15, Kobenhavn

Posch, M. (1998): Personal Communication. April 1998, Bilthoven, The Netherlands

Schmieman, E.C., Van Ierland, E.C. (1998): Joint Abatement Strategies: A Dynamic Analysis of Acidification and Tropospheric Ozone. Working Paper 1998-3, Wageningen Agricultural University, Wageningen

Tonneijck, A.E.G., Van der Eerden, L.J., Wijnands, J.H.M., Bunte, H.H.J., Bremmer, J., Hoogeveen, M.W. (1998): Economische Aspecten van het effect van Luchtverontreiniging op de Gewasteelt in Nederland. Report 90, LEI-DLO, Den Haag

United Nations (1985): Protocol to the 1979 Convention on Long-Range Transboundary Air Pollution on the Reduction of Sulphur or Their Transboundary Fluxes by at Least 30 Per Cent. ECE/EB.AIR/12, United Nations, Geneva

United Nations (1988): 1988 Protocol to the 1979 Convention on Long-Range Transboundary Air Pollution Concerning the Control of Emissions of Nitrogen Oxides and their Transboundary Fluxes. ECE/EB.AIR/21, United Nations, Geneva

United Nations (1991): Protocol to the 1979 Convention on Long-Range Transboundary Air Pollution Concerning the Control of Emissions of Volatile Organic Compounds or their Transboundary Fluxes. ECE/EB.AIR/30, United Nations, Geneva

United Nations (1994): Protocol to the 1979 Convention on Long-Range Transboundary Air Pollution on Further Reduction of Sulphur Emissions and Decision on the Structure and Function of Implementation Committee, as well as Procedures for Its Review of Compliance. ECE/EB.AIR/40, United Nations, Geneva

Van Ierland, E.C. (1991): The Economics of Transboundary Air Pollution in Europe. Environmental Monitoring and Assessment 17, 101-122

Van Ierland, E.C., Schmieman, E.C. (1999): Sustainability and Joint Abatement Strategies Under Multiple Pollutants and Multiple Targets: the Case of Tropospheric Ozone and Acidification in Europe. In: Gowdy, J., Köhn, J., van der Straaten, J. (Eds.): Sustainability in Action: Regional and Sectoral Case Studies. Edward Elgar, Cheltenham

Zylicz, T. (1995): Cost-Effectiveness of Air Pollution Abatement in Poland. Environmental and Resource Economics 5, 131-149

Incorporating resistance in pesticide management: a dynamic regional approach

Matthew J. Kotchen[1]

School of Natural Resources & Environment, University of Michigan,
Ann Arbor, MI 48109-1115, USA

1 Introduction

Pesticide resistance in agricultural systems has been recognised as one of the world's top environmental problems for nearly two decades (UNEP 1979). Occurring in over 500 species of insects (Georghiou 1990), resistance is a genetic phenomenon whereby resistance-conferring genes accumulate in pest populations. Agricultural producers contending with pests that reduce the quality and/or quantity of outputs apply pesticides to increase profits or to decrease income variability. As resistance begins to accumulate, however, these treatments become less effective. Attempting to maintain expected crop yield, producers typically apply additional pesticide applications, yet over time, this practice compounds the problem by increasing environmental selection for resistant traits (Croft and Dunley 1993).

The accumulation of resistance in pest populations imposes substantial economic costs to agricultural production. Resistant pests continue to destroy crops, and the coincidental removal of natural enemies through pesticide treatments exacerbates the problem. A study of California cotton production, for example, reveals resistance costs of approximately \$45 to \$120 per hectare, totalling \$348 million per year (Pimentel et al. 1992). Extrapolating these results to other pesticide-intensive crops, nation-wide costs of resistance in the United States are estimated at \$1.4 billion per year (Pimentel et al. 1992). Despite attempts to deal with this problem, pesticide resistance continues to develop as a biological problem with economic consequences. Devising successful management strategies encompassing property rights and the complexity of biological and economic systems has proven difficult.

This paper proposes a regional model of how pesticide management strategies can incorporate resistance costs. The analysis relies on the assumption that management decisions affect the rate of resistance development, and trade-offs exist between current benefits and future costs of pesticide use. Treating pest susceptibility, or absence of resistance, as a resource,

[1] The author is grateful to Andrew Plantinga and Bernd Klauer for providing helpful comments on earlier versions of this paper.

a method is derived to determine optimal pesticide use rates.[2] The temporal dimension of regional resistance accumulation is captured with a multi-period, dynamic optimisation model.

2 The need for regional management

Several factors influence the rate of spread, persistence, and general dynamics of resistance accumulation. These include an organism's: genetic features, such as number, dominance, and fitness of resistant genes; mode and rate of reproduction; and population dynamics and migration characteristics (Georghiou and Taylor 1986). Chemical factors such as pesticide type, frequency of applications, and dosage potency also influence resistance patterns (Green et al. 1990). Together, these natural and anthropogenic variables affect the ability of individual farmers to manage pesticide resistance.

Pest mobility and biological interactions often lead to pesticide resistance spillovers, in which pest resistance in one area is transported to another. This creates situations where individual farmer's actions are rarely isolated from those of others. The more pests are shared across farms, the more resistance-influencing actions will result in externalities affecting the usefulness of pesticides on farms within a common region (Carlson and Wetzstein 1993). The extent of these interactions will increase with higher levels of pest mobility, spatial uniformity, and resistance severity. These characteristics have led researchers to consider maintaining pest susceptibility as an open-access resource, whereby problems typically associated with managing common property resources apply (Clark and Carlson 1990). That is, individual farmer incentives to control pests may lead to levels of pesticide use that increase resistance within a region, and the added costs of resistance to others within the region will not fully factor into the farmer's decision. The unfortunate result of this condition is inefficient levels of resistance accumulation at a cost to all those within the region.

As with most common property resources, regional management is one way to internalise adverse externalities. Whereas individual farmers will tend to overapply pesticides, regional decisions are more likely to equate true marginal benefits and marginal costs (Miranowski and Carlson 1986). Thus, regional pesticide management is likely to result in more efficient control of the economic costs of resistance. Recognising advantages of regional management, various voluntary and compulsory organisational structures have emerged to control pesticide use. These range from community groups, co-operatives, and state and local authorities. The success of

---

[2] The method does not, however, address environmental externalities beyond resistance accumulation. While internalising costs associated with effects such as water contamination and harmful effects to fish and wildlife is possible, their consideration is beyond the scope of this paper.

regional initiatives to manage pesticide resistance depends on the effectiveness of these organisations. Studies have shown how regional pesticide management can result in higher individual, producer profits (e.g., Ahouissoussi et al. 1995; Carlson and Suguiyama 1985). Thus, regional management may not only be important for controlling pesticide resistance; such organisations may be more profitable.

Accordingly, the model developed in this paper is intended for implementation at the regional level. For reasons described above, a regional agency is thought to provide the only mechanism for successfully managing pesticide resistance. The technique could be applied to individual producers, but the negative consequences of resistance spillovers would remain. Therefore, regional management is necessary to internalise the negative externality of resistance spillovers, and regions should be determined based on degrees of pest mobility and spatial uniformity. While the specific organisational structure of the regional agency is not specified, the overall goal of maximising profits for all producers within the region is assumed.

3 The limitation of threshold models

Considering genetic and life history information on agricultural pests has become increasingly important to integrated pest management (IPM) strategies, which seek to farm more ecologically. An integral part of the IPM paradigm is the use of threshold decision models, which link pesticide use with actual pest numbers (Peck and Ellner 1997). In effect, crops are not treated with pesticides until insect populations reach damaging levels. The threshold decision framework is a widely used tool by agricultural producers for reducing pesticide loading in agroecosystems, yet incorporating resistance costs is limited by the static approach inherent to these models.

Threshold models are useful when producers must make decisions about whether or not to apply pesticide treatments. Assuming producers attempt to maximise profits when managing pests, threshold models are a single period application of the marginal principle. The decision relies on whether the marginal value of crop saved equals the marginal cost of treatment, and this condition occurs at some critical pest density, above which treatment is advisable. Thus, the problem is to determine the critical pest density. When managing pesticide use at the regional level, the problem is expanded to determining the critical pest density within the entire region.

Modifying an analysis presented by Carlson and Wetzstein (1993), a basic regional threshold model without treatment can be written as:

$$\pi = p(y - mN) - c \tag{1}$$

where π is regional profits, p is crop price, which is assumed to be constant for all producers in the region, y is expected yield in the region with no pest damage, m is damage in physical units of lost yield per pest unit,

N is the spatial density of pests within the region, and c is regional production costs.

This model follows the general rationale that profits are equal to total revenues (py) minus the costs of production (c) and the costs of pest damage (pmN). An expansion of (1) to include pesticide treatment can then be written as:

$$\pi = p[y - m(1-b)N] - c - \tilde{c} \qquad (2)$$

where b is the percent reduction in pest numbers, and $\tilde{c}$ is the regional cost of pesticide treatment. Now, subtracting (1) from (2) yields a condition where only the marginal benefits and costs of the pesticide treatment are considered. Since the decision is only whether to apply a single treatment, the marginal cost is $\tilde{c}$, and the marginal benefit is equal to the marginal value of crop saved, or $pmbN$. The critical pest density (N^*) can then be determined by equating marginal benefits and marginal costs and solving for N^*, which yields:

$$N^* = \frac{\tilde{c}}{pmb} . \qquad (3)$$

Thus, marginal benefits exceed marginal costs at pest densities greater than N^*, at which point pesticide treatment begins to be profitable. At pest densities below N^*, treatment would not be advisable.

Threshold models of this type are useful for determining the appropriateness of pesticide treatments, but more detail is frequently necessary to capture actual biological and economic dynamics (Smith et al. 1987). Resistance build-up, for example, is one factor regional managers will not adequately consider if only threshold principles are used to determine pesticide use. A recent study by Peck and Ellner (1997) found that using regional economic thresholds can influence the rate of resistance build-up, but their paper did not mention how consideration of resistance within a threshold decision framework is limited. The static character of threshold models only enables existing levels of resistance to be incorporated. This would translate into adjusting the parameter b in (2). While such an approach does consider reduced susceptibility a cost of production, there is failure to recognise how resistance build-up is a dynamic function of previous pesticide applications, and current decisions influence future conditions. Therefore, fully incorporating resistance costs requires use of a dynamic optimisation model.

4 Dynamic optimisation with resistance costs

Dynamic optimisation models, unlike threshold models, enable consideration of an objective over several sequential periods. Attention is given to the fact that foregone benefits in current periods may result in greater benefits over several periods. In particular, recognition is possible of the way pesticide management decisions affect the rate of resistance development, and trade-offs exist between current benefits and future costs, where current benefits are a reduction in pests and future costs are increased pest resistance.

The threshold model in (2) provides a foundation for developing a dynamic optimisation model that incorporates resistance costs over time. To focus on the relationship between resistance and pesticides, all factors of production, except the frequency of pesticide applications, are assumed to be constant. Crop price is also assumed to remain constant between periods. Three periods are used as the time horizon to demonstrate the model's features while maintaining simplicity of presentation. The model can be written as:

$$\begin{aligned} &\textit{Period 0:} \quad \pi_0 = p[y(A_0) - mNR] - c - \tilde{c}(A_0) \\ &\textit{Period 1:} \quad \pi_1 = p[y(A_1) - mNR(A_0)] - c - \tilde{c}(A_1) \\ &\textit{Period 2:} \quad \pi_2 = p[y(A_2) - mNR(A_0, A_1)] - c - \tilde{c}(A_2) \end{aligned} \tag{4}$$

where π_t is regional profits in period t; A_t is regional frequency of pesticide applications in period t; p is crop price; $y(A_t)$ is regional yield as a function of A_t; m is damage in physical units of lost yield per pest unit; N is spatial density of pests within the region; R is the proportion of resistant pests, which may be given in period 0 and is a function of (A_0) and (A_0, A_1) in periods 1 and 2, respectively; c is regional production costs without treatment; and $\tilde{c}(A_t)$ is regional cost of pesticide treatment as a function of A_t.

Unlike threshold model (2), this model considers expected yield (y) and costs of pesticide treatment $(\tilde{c})$ as functions of pesticide use rate. The proportion of resistant pests (R) replaces $(1-b)$ in (2) and becomes a function of pesticide use rates in previous periods. As demonstrated in (4), the operational assumption is that reducing pesticide use rates is the only way to reduce pesticide resistance.

Given the generalised model in (4), biological and economic theory provide insights as to the functional relationships between pesticide use rate and y, $\tilde{c}$, and R. Signs of the first and second derivatives may be inferred in the following way. As pesticide use rate increases, the crop yield will increase at a decreasing rate (Comins 1986); $y'(A_t) > 0$ and $y''(A_t) < 0$. Assuming previous capital investments for pesticide applications, the cost of treatments per period will increase with the number of treatments at a constant rate, since there will only be material and application costs; $\tilde{c}'(A_t) > 0$ and $\tilde{c}''(A_t) = 0$. Increases in prior cumulative pesticide use (A_Z) will lead to increases in resistance at an increasing rate (Comins 1977); $R'(A_Z) > 0$ and $R''(A_Z) > 0$. Thus, some common functional forms are assumed for the purposes of further analysis:

$$\begin{aligned} &\textit{Period 0: } \pi_0 = p[\ln A_0 - mN\gamma] - c - \alpha A_0 \\ &\textit{Period 1: } \pi_1 = p[\ln A_1 - mN\gamma e^{A_0}] - c - \alpha A_1 \\ &\textit{Period 2: } \pi_2 = p[\ln A_2 - mN\gamma e^{A_0 + A_1}] - c - \alpha A_2 . \end{aligned} \tag{5}$$

Specifically, $y_t = \ln A_t$; $c_t = \alpha A_t$, where α is some constant greater than 0; and $R_t = \gamma e^{A_Z}$, where $\gamma \in (0,1)$ is a constant representing the initial proportion of resistant pests.

Given the specified functional forms in (5), the regional management objective is to maximise profits over time by selecting the appropriate number of pesticide applications per period (A_t). Profit is the present value sum of net revenues in current and future periods; therefore, returns in periods 1 and 2 must be converted to present values. The formal objective function can be written as:

$$Max\ \pi = \pi_0 + \lambda_1 \pi_1 + \lambda_2 \pi_2 \tag{6}$$

where $\lambda_i = 1/(1+r)^t$, and r is the discount rate. Solving this maximisation problem with a recursive solution procedure ensures the optimal choice of A_t in current periods is consistent with optimal choices in previous and future periods (Bellman 1957). That is, determining optimal pesticide use rates in reverse chronological order captures interaction between periods.

The first step is to maximise period 2 with respect to pesticide use in period 2. This gives the optimal level of pesticide use in period 2, the final period. Next, the objective is to maximise period 1 with respect to pesticide use in period 1. This, however, includes the solution to the first step and yields optimal levels of pesticide use in period 1 for period 1 and period 2. Finally, period 0 is maximised with respect to optimal pesticide use in period 0, but this time, the maximisation includes periods 1 and 2 as well. Thus, the overall solution is the choice of optimal pesticide use over all periods.

The optimal conditions derived from the recursive solution procedure can be written as:

$$\begin{aligned} &\textit{Period 0: } \frac{p}{A_0} = \alpha + pmN\gamma(\lambda_1 e^{A_0} + \lambda_2 e^{A_0 + A_1}) \\ &\textit{Period 1: } \frac{p}{A_1} = \alpha + \lambda_2 pmN\gamma e^{A_0 + A_1} \\ &\textit{Period 2: } \frac{p}{A_2} = \alpha \end{aligned} \tag{7}$$

where α is the cost per pesticide treatment. These conditions for each period identify the point where marginal benefits of pesticide use (p/A_t) equal marginal costs, including the costs of future resistance. The marginal cost in period 2 is simply the marginal cost of the pesticide application (α), since no future periods are within the model's scope. Periods 0 and 1, however, include the additional discounted marginal costs of future resistance, which is $pmN\gamma(\lambda_1 e^{A_0} + \lambda_2 e^{A_0+A_1})$ and $\lambda_2 pmNe^{A_0+A_1}$, respectively. Whereas period 1 only includes resistance costs for period 2, period 0 includes resistance costs for periods 1 and 2. Thus, the optimal levels of pesticide use for each period (A_t^*) can be expressed as an implicit function of parameters: $A_0^*(p,\alpha,r,m,N,\gamma,A_1)$, $A_1^*(p,\alpha,r,m,N,\gamma,A_0)$ and $A_2^*(p,\alpha)$.

5 Advantages and limitations of the model

The marginal conditions derived from the model demonstrate how regional resistance costs can be incorporated in pesticide use decisions. The standard economic solution of setting marginal benefits equal to marginal costs is maintained. The model's dynamic character, however, enables the marginal costs of each period to include the discounted marginal cost of resistance in subsequent periods. Thus, the cost of future resistance affects the marginal conditions from which pesticide use is derived. This approach moves beyond the static limitations of threshold decision models. While only three periods are used for demonstrative purposes, the time horizon could readily be extended.

Advantages are associated with the model's ability to incorporate actual biological conditions. Management regions could be determined based on the degree of spatial pest interactions or relative isolation. This approach would be best equipped to internalise externalities associated with individual management. The dynamic optimisation could also incorporate genetic information that may be known prior to pesticide applications. The nature of resistant genotypes and initial gene frequencies affect the rate of resistance development. Improvements in genetic technology and the high probability of specific pesticides having been used elsewhere make such preliminary information increasingly available. While the model is capable of incorporating this information, there is no such requirement. Information about initial levels of resistance could be captured in R of (4), or alternatively, $(1-b)$ from (2) could be used as an approximation. A two-period Lagrangian model presented by Regev et al. (1983) to consider resistance build-up does not provide this option. They assumed all prior information would remain unknown.

The specified relationship between resistance build-up and pesticide use provides another advantage. No general functional relationship exists for all management situations, yet a reasonable starting point is that resistant genes exist at low equilibrium frequencies determined by the natural processes of pre-treatment mutation and adverse selection. Preferential selection for these genes begins once treatment regimes are initiated. Pesticide efficacy will continue until resistant genes begin spreading more and more rapidly through the population, at which point control measures fail (Comins 1986). Attempting to match these observed genetic dynamics, an exponential relationship between pesticide use and resistance build-up is specified. This contrasts other studies that may have oversimplified the genetic dynamics by specifying a linear functional relationship (Regev et al. 1983).

Specifying the exponential function is an improvement for generalised scenarios, but there is even more potential to develop the relationship between pesticides and resistance for particular pest situations. May and Dobson (1986), for example, have developed more detailed models for the timing of resistance development. Moreover, Comins (1977) predicted specific resistance dynamics for the sugarcane froghopper using a deterministic density dependent Mendelian model. Similar analyses conducted for other pest situations would be useful to include in pesticide management models. This information, however, may be difficult to obtain, and functions such as the exponential increase the model's generality, which is not trivial since the simplicity of models is important to pesticide managers when considering the relative usefulness of decision tools (Musser et al. 1986).

Failure to consider alternative IPM strategies or technological advancements is a limitation of the regional model presented here. The assumption is that only one technique is used to manage pests, and decreasing the frequency of pesticide applications is the only way to reduce resistance. While this assumption characterises the majority of large-scale agricultural producers, alternative IPM strategies frequently involve a diversity of techniques to control pests, which are not captured by this analysis. Alternating years of treatments and rotating through different pesticides are examples. The problem is that such techniques are under-utilised. Changes in weather patterns, new developments in pesticides, or biotechnologies may also threaten the efficiency of following the program outlined by the model. Current foregone profits to compensate future resistant costs may be lost if resistance levels are altered by climatic conditions or new developments emerge. Selecting appropriate time horizons for application of the model, however, could begin to incorporate factors such as assessments about the probability of new developments.

There must also be recognition that the optimal conditions derived in this model do not incorporate all social costs of pesticide use. The total costs resulting from environmental externalities associated with pesticides have been estimated in the United States at $8 billion annually (Pimentel et al. 1992). These include human health effects, contaminated products, fish and wildlife poisonings, and destruction of beneficial predators and parasites. Incorporating resistance is one step in the process of internalising adverse externalities of pesticide use, but research and policies designed to include these other social costs should be a priority as well.

In sum, pesticide resistance is an important factor in determining appropriate pest control strategies. Pest susceptibility is a valuable biological resource that imposes substantial economic costs when diminished. Regional management is an important means to controlling resistance build-up. The use of threshold decision models in IPM strategies is an effective way to reduce pesticide loading in agroecosystems; however, the decision framework is limited in its ability to incorporate resistance. Fully considering resistance in regional management strategies requires the use of a dynamic optimisation model. Building on the threshold approach, the model presented in this paper provides a conceptual approach as to how resistance can be incorporated in regional pesticide management. The analysis expands upon other techniques by attempting to integrate the complicated dimensions of property rights and biological and economic dynamics.

References

Ahouissoussi, N., Wetzstein, M., Duffy, P. (1995): Economic Returns to the Boll Weevil Eradication Program. Journal of Agricultural and Applied Economics 25, 46-55

Bellman, R. (1957): Dynamic Programming. Princeton University Press, Princeton New Jersey

Carlson, G.A., Suguiyama, L. (1985): An Economic Evaluation of Area-Wide Cotton Insect Management: Boll Weevils in the South-eastern United States. North Carolina Agricultural Research Service Bulletin Number 473, Raleigh, North Carolina

Carlson, G.A., Wetzstein, M.E. (1993): Pesticides and Pest Management. In: Carlson, G., Zilberman, D., Miranowski, J. (Eds.): Agricultural and Environmental Resource Economics. Oxford University Press, New York, 268-318

Clark, J.S., Carlson, G.A. (1990): Econometrically Distinguishing Between Private and Common Property: The Case of Pesticide Resistance. Journal of Environmental Economics and Management 19, 45-60

Croft, B.A., Dunley, J. (1993): Habitat Patterns and Pesticide Resistance. In: Kim, K.C., McPherson, B.A. (Eds.): Evolution of Insect Pests. John Wiley & Sons, New York, 145-162

Comins, H.N. (1986): Tactics for Resistance Management Using Multiple Pesticides. Agriculture, Ecosystems and Environment 16, 129-148

Comins, H.N. (1977): The Management of Pesticide Resistance. Journal of Theoretical Biology 65, 399-420

Georghiou, G.P. (1990): Overview of Insecticide Resistance. In: Green, M.B., LeBaron, H.M., Moberg, W.K. (Eds.): Managing Resistance to Agrochemicals: From Fundamental Research to Practical Strategies. American Chemical Society, Washington DC, 18-41

Georghiou, G.P., Taylor, C.E. (1986): Factors Influencing the Evolution of Resistance. In: National Research Council (Ed.): Pesticide Resistance: Strategies and Tactics for Management. National Academy Press, Washington DC, 157-169

Green, M.B., LeBaron, H.M., Moberg, W.K. (Eds.) (1990): Managing Resistance to Agrochemicals: From Fundamental Research to Practical Strategies. American Chemical Society, Washington DC

May, R.M., Dobson, A.P. (1986): Population Dynamics and the Rate of Evolution of Pesticide Resistance. In: National Research Council (Ed.): Pesticides Resistence: Strategies and Tactics for Management. National Academy Press, Washington DC, 170-193

Miranowski, J.A., Carlson, G.A. (1986): Economic Issues in Public and Private Approaches to Preserving Pest Susceptibility. Pesticide Resistance: Strategies and Tactics for Management. National Academy Press, Washington DC

Musser, W., Wetzstein, M., Reece, S., Varca, P., Edwards, D., Douce, G. (1986): Beliefs of Farmers and Adoption of Integrated Pest Management. Agricultural Economics Research 38, 34-44

Peck, S.L., Ellner, S.P. (1997): The Effect of Economic Thresholds and Life-History Parameters on the Evolution of Pesticide Resistance in a Regional Setting. The American Naturalist 149(1), 43-63

Pimentel, D., Acquay, H., Biltonen, M., Rice, P., Silva, M., Nelson, J., Lipner, V., Giordano, S., Horowitz, A., D'Amore, M. (1992): Environmental and Economic Costs of Pesticide Use. BioScience 42(10), 750-760

Regev, U., Shalit, H., Gutierrez, A. (1983): On the Optimal Allocation of Pesticides With Increasing Resistance: The Case of Alfalfa Weevil Control. Journal of Environmental Economics and Management 10, 86-100

Smith, G.S., Wetzstein, M.E., Douce, G.K. (1987): Evaluation of Various Pest Management Characteristics. Southern Journal of Agricultural Economics 19, 93-101

United Nations Environmental Program (UNEP) (1979): The State of the Environment: Selected Topics – 1979. UNEP Governing Council Seventh Session. Nairobi, Kenya

Some evidence of the relative efficiency of multiple-instrument policies for controlling agricultural nonpoint pollution: an application to nitrate pollution

Athanasios Kampas and Ben White

Department of Agricultural Economics and Food Marketing,
University of Newcastle, Newcastle upon Tyne, NE1 7UR, UK

1 Introduction

Controlling water pollution from agriculture is intrinsically difficult. In most cases, pollution occurs over a wide area and its sources are diffuse and difficult to identify. In addition, water pollution levels can vary substantially over space and time, and depend not only on rainfall pattern and land type, but also on farmers' decisions. These decisions include land use choices, crop choices, production techniques and the intensity of inputs used. Under the conventional assumption of farmers' rationality,[1] such decisions are determined by relative prices as well as by government support policies.

Nonpoint pollutants from fertilisers, pesticides and sedimentation have been described as the 'second generation' pollutants by Braden and Segerson (1993): considerable progress has been made in regulating point pollutants, but relatively little progress has been made towards regulating nonpoint pollution efficiently. The fundamental obstacles in controlling nonpoint pollution are the high costs of observing the production activities of producers across their land area and modelling the complex environmental fates of nitrogen inputs to assess the costs of emissions. These information problems render the preferred instruments, namely taxing or regulating emissions, infeasible. Instead regulators must resort to second-best policies which target observable variables such as land use and livestock numbers.

The control and management of agricultural pollution, primarily nitrate, is an issue of major concern within the European Union. Concerns have been raised on the direct health impact of nitrate pollutants in the drinking water and relevant standards have been laid down in the Nitrate Directive (91/676). The Nitrate Directive can be seen as belonging to the long tradition of EC water policy. The first EC water Directive was the Surface Water for Drinking Directive (75/440), which coincided with the First Action Programme on the Environment. Other examples include the Surface Water

[1] Here, rationality refers to the allocative principle of profit maximisation, which is an operational assumption of producers' behaviour rather than an iron law. A comprehensive analysis of its limitations and the associated problems can be found in Sen (1977) and Field (1984).

Directive (75/464), the Drinking Water Directive (80/778) and the Groundwater Directive (80/68). The monitoring required under these Directives has gradually shifted attention from the regulation of point sources to less visible and chronic forms of diffuse pollution, particularly those associated with agriculture (Ward 1998). In addition, a Water Framework Directive (COM(97) 49) has been recently proposed to revise, unify and update the existing fragmented structure of water policy in the EU (EC 1997). Alternatively, the Nitrate Directive can be viewed as a component of the greening process of the CAP after the MacSharry reform, since although the Directive was agreed in 1991, there has been a further extension of Nitrate Sensitive Areas under the Agri-Environmental Regulation.

The aim of this paper is to assess a range of feasible nitrate reduction policies for the Kennet, a tributary of the Thames in South-East England. The approach is to develop a model which combines an economic model with a simple model of the hydrology. From this combined model it is possible to assess the first-best solution for a given reduction in the level of nitrogen emissions and then use this as a benchmark against which we can compare feasible second-best instruments. The remainder of this paper is organised as follows. The next section critically reviews theoretical models of the optimal regulation of nonpoint pollution and develops a theoretical framework for analysis. Section 3 describes the form of the empirical model. Section 4 outlines the data available. Section 5 presents some results on the relative efficiency of alternative policies for nitrate regulation. Section 6 concludes.

2 Theoretical models and economic efficiency

2.1 The 'standard' solution to nonpoint pollution problems

The last fifteen years have seen a number of contributions to the theoretical debate on suitable effective instruments for nonpoint pollution, commencing with Griffin and Bromley (1982), through Segerson (1988), and Xepapedeas (1991, 1994, 1995). The theme running through this literature is that of modifying the emission tax approach to point pollution to reflect the realities of nonpoint pollution: namely that the emissions of individual producers are unobservable, or only observable at a high cost.

The simplest form of the problem is conceived as follows. The regulator aims to maximise the benefits over the damage of emissions

$$\max_{e} = \sum_{i} B_i(e_i) - D(e); \quad subject\ \ to\ \sum_{i} e_i = e \tag{1}$$

where e_i is the level of emissions of producer *i*, the benefit of emission function $B_i(.)$ is defined as the maximum profit for every level of emissions and $D(.)$ is a function of the damage of emissions

$$B_i(e_i) = \max_{q_i} \pi(q_i, e_i) = \max_{q_i} \{pq_i - c_i(q_i, e)\} \quad (2)$$

where *p(.)* is the profit function, *p* is product price, q_i quantity of product and $c_i(.)$ is a cost function. It is well known that in the case of perfect information, certainty and a perfectly competitive market structure, the optimal tax is defined by:

$$B_i'(e_i) = D'(e) = t \quad (3)$$

However, if the emissions of individual producers are not observable, but the ambient concentration is observable, then Segerson (1988) proposes an ambient tax/subsidy mechanism of the form:

$$T_i(e) = \begin{cases} t_i(e - \tilde{e}) + k_i & \text{if} \quad e > \tilde{e} \\ t_i(e - \tilde{e}) & \text{if} \quad e \leq \tilde{e} \end{cases} \quad (4)$$

$T_i(.)$ is the ambient charge scheme, t_i is the tax/subsidy component and k_i is a fixed penalty imposed when ambient levels of emissions exceed the cut-off level, $\tilde{e}$. Thus, the problem for the individual producer is to maximise benefits over the ambient charge scheme:

$$\max_{e_i} = B_i(e_i) - T_i(e_i) \quad (5)$$

Then by the individual ambient tax it is possible to ensure that producers restrict themselves to the optimal level of emissions.

The major advantage of an ambient charge scheme is that it does not require continual monitoring of emissions, and as a consequence it is often considered the preferred instrument to control a nonpoint pollution problem. However, a number of problems are associated with its potential implementation. Firstly, there is little scope under current legislative structures to impose individual taxes. Secondly, individual taxes would require a wealth of information to set the correct level of the ambient charge scheme (Cabe and Herriges 1992). Thirdly, these taxes are based upon a measure of ambient pollution which is difficult and expensive to establish due to stochastic climate effects and might therefore be the subject of litigation by farmers who wish to avoid paying tax. Finally, as Xepapadeas (1995) has shown, its attractiveness is based on the assumption of a non-stochastic ambient pollutant concentration. If this assumption is relaxed then ambient taxes could impose high compliance costs on farmers, especially when the variance of ambient pollutant is large.

2.2 An alternative approach

The aforementioned literature focuses on policy instruments based on emissions whilst ignoring other restrictions on the range of policies which can be considered. Here it is argued first that it is unlikely that ambient charges would ever be considered by a regulator due to the legal problems of discriminatory taxation. The issue of information and transaction costs is critical in terms of negotiating and monitoring compliance with any contract. If this broader set of administrative costs is taken into account, then the optimal policy might involve a quite different set of target variables in contrast to the standard model. In particular, the benefits of emissions function $B_i(e_i)$ can no longer be defined since it may be optimal for the regulator to target particular inputs because they are cheaper to monitor. For instance, land use is relatively cheap to monitor while livestock numbers are more expensive and nitrogen inputs more expensive still. Thus, the profits associated with a level of emissions will depend not only on the emissions generated but on the range of input restrictions selected.

On this basis the regulator's objective function is to maximise the sum of restricted profits while satisfying an overall standard on emission levels:

$$\max_{x^s} \sum_i \{\pi_i^s(p, w, x^s) - m_i\} \quad subject \ to \quad e_i = \phi(x); \sum_i e_i \leq \tilde{e} \tag{6}$$

where p and w are product and input prices respectively, $\pi_i^s(.)$ is the restricted profit function for producer i, x is the vector of inputs used, x^s is the vector of input restrictions, m_i is the monitoring costs of producer i, e is the level of emissions as a function $f(.)$ of all inputs, both restricted and unrestricted, and the policy target is to limit emissions to less than $\tilde{e}$. The reported monitoring costs of NSA's were chosen as a proxy for m_i (Agriculture Committee 1997).

Input taxes have long been deemed as alternatives to direct taxes on emissions (Holtermann 1976; Common 1977; Griffin and Bromley 1982). The major assumption is that emissions come into being only when inputs are used, and therefore there is an option to tax inputs instead of emissions. A tax on inputs has the advantage of lower monitoring costs in comparison with the emission tax option. Stevens (1988) has shown that input tax and emissions tax can be equally efficient given that the production of emissions is characterised by constant returns to scale. If there are increasing returns to scale, emissions tax is more efficient and vice versa. The difficulty arises when some emission functions are characterised by decreasing returns to scale and some others by increasing returns to scale, at which point it becomes impossible to predict the ex-ante efficiency rank between input and emissions taxes. The obvious disadvantage of taxing inputs is associated with the heterogeneity of polluting sources which requires tax rates to vary across inputs in different regions, which is nearly impossible to apply.

For input taxes, it is typically expected that large marginal taxes may be required to elicit more than marginal reductions in input use (Anderson et al. 1990). This is due to the fact that quite low price elasticity for nitrogen fertiliser is expected because such elasticity varies directly with the share of total production costs associated with a given factor and the elasticity of substitution between a given factor and other inputs (Johnson et al. 1991). Estimates of price elasticities of nitrogen fertilisers for the UK can be found in Burrell (1989) and in Rayner and Cooper (1994).

Thus, it is not surprising that Botterweg et al. (1994) have found that unrealistically high taxes on N-fertiliser are needed to reduce leaching. However, other studies such as Giraldez and Fox (1995) concluded that a tax rate of 55% was necessary to reduce nitrogen application to such levels that a given standard of ambient pollution can be achieved. It is apparent that the majority of studies are site-specific and no general conclusions can be drawn which are universally valid. The relevant point is the qualitative nature of such comparisons rather than the cardinal ranking of policy measures. Efficiency comparisons of input tax versus other alternatives can be found in Huang and Lantin (1993), Pan and Hodge (1994) and Swinton and Clark (1994), and Wu et al. (1995) among others.

The standpoint adopted in our case study is that the regulation of non-point source pollution could be more efficient if it were based on a set of feasible second-best policy instruments, such as input restrictions, rather than on unobservable emissions as a first-best solution requires. Restrictions on fertiliser use can be achieved by a fertiliser tax or a nitrogen quota, while set-aside is a typical example of land restriction.

3 Data sources and modelling approach

3.1 Land cover

It has been established in other studies, e.g. Moxey and White (1994), that as spatially resolved agricultural land cover data is not available for the UK, it is necessary to predict how the land cover is distributed at the regional level by areal interpolation. The ITE satellite data Land Cover Map for Great Britain is used to give the distribution of the broad categories of land in the Kennet catchment. These broad categories, for instance 'arable' and 'agricultural grassland', are then subdivided using GIS with soil data to locate the land cover types recorded within the Agricultural Census at the level of Parish Groups. This allows us to give an approximate distribution of cropping by soil type for the Kennet catchment. The method followed is taken from Miles et al. (1996). However, as parish groups are relatively large compared to the catchment, it was decided to use the data reported at the parish level in 1988 to give a more accurate estimate of land cover.

3.2 Crop yields

Crop yields are based upon estimated production functions for nitrogen response from experimental data for winter wheat, oilseed rape, winter barley and spring barley (England 1986).

3.3 Nitrogen emissions

Experimental data on nitrogen losses is available for a small number of specific sites; however, it is not generally available for the combinations of soil and crops encountered in the Kennet catchment. Therefore it was decided to use a set of nitrogen models to first estimate nitrate losses and then estimate the rate of nitrate leaching.

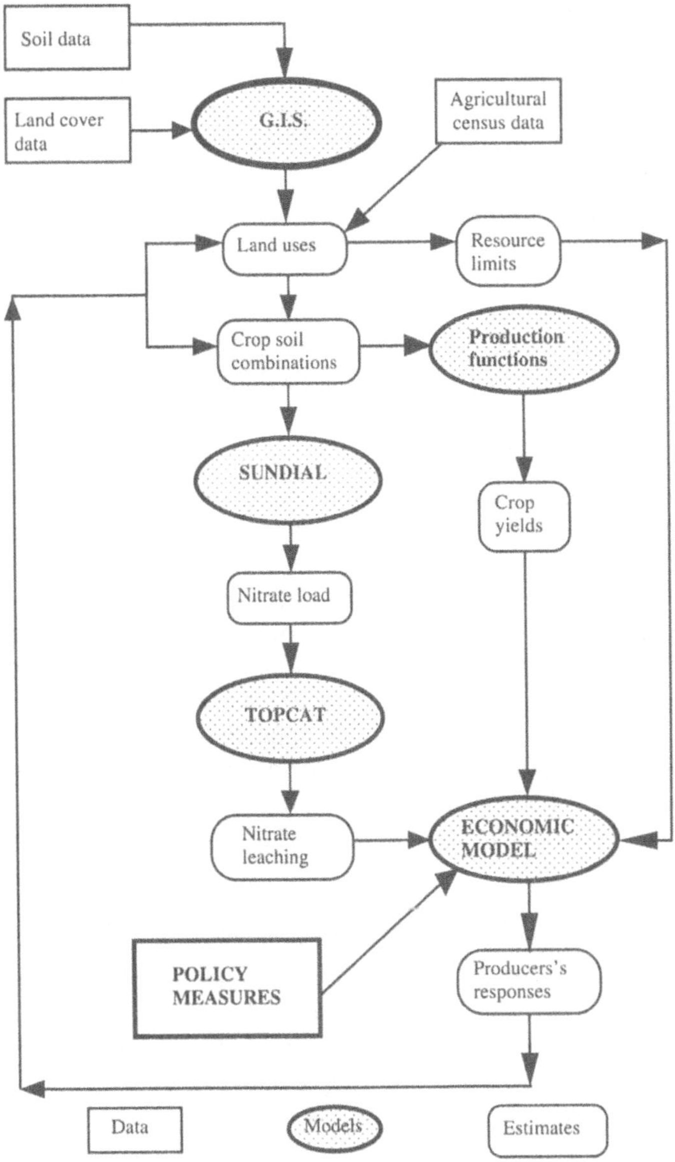

Figure 1. Outline of the modelling framework.

A biophysical model was used, the "SUNDIAL" developed by Rothamsted Experimental Station (Jenkinson et al. 1994; Smith et al. 1996), which measures nitrogen losses under arable crops using soil, crop, fertiliser and weather combinations as inputs. Furthermore, a hydrological model, TOPCAT (Quinn et al. 1996), converts estimates of soil nitrate losses into the ambient concentration of nitrates in the drain flow.

The results from the various models are represented as functions to allow them to be included in the mathematical programming model described in the next section. Nitrate loss functions were estimated econometrically from the results of the biophysical models using MICROFIT 3.0 (Pesaran and Pesaran 1991). Different functional forms were tested and the final choice was based on conventional statistical criteria and the PE test for non-nested models (MacKinnon and Davidson 1983).

Losses from the root zone may be stored in the sub-soil and then gradually leached into ground and surface water. The TOPCAT model estimates the pattern of daily leaching given rainfall variability. Output from this model allows us to estimate the variability of nitrate emissions to groundwater either in terms of the nitrate concentration of water or the total nitrate losses. Figure 1 gives the outline of the modelling approach and data used.

4 Economic model

The economic model assumes that producers in the catchment maximise returns over nitrogen fertiliser cost subject to rotational constraints. A similar partial optimisation framework has been used by Larson et al. (1996) in order to assess the efficiency of a number of second-best alternative policies. The Kennet catchment is divided into land classes on the basis of the soil map. This gives three land classes characterised as clay good, loam good and loam poor, according to their soil texture and drainage properties. The areas of crops are restricted by rotational constraints which reflect cropping patterns. Nitrogen losses are modelled as a two-stage process. Estimates of nitrate losses are derived from SUNDIAL and then estimates of average nitrate concentrations in the drainage flows are calculated from the TOPCAT model.

4.1 The deterministic version of the model

It is assumed that the regulator wishes to minimise the sum of abatement costs for all the producers in the catchment in achieving an arbitrary specified cut-off level of emissions. An allocation of average abatement levels is cost-effective if it solves the following problem:

$$\min \sum_i C(e_i) \;\; subject \;\; to \;\; \sum_i e_i \leq \tilde{e} \tag{7}$$

where $\sum_i C(e_i) = \sum_i \{\pi_i(p,w) - \pi_i^s(p,w,x^s) - m_i\}$ (8)

The objective function indicates that the regulator wishes to minimise the income forgone due to the presence of environmental regulations. The function *C(.)* represents the abatement costs, which are equal to the difference between unrestricted and restricted profit. Since all prices are exogenously determined, the minimisation of abatement costs is equivalent to maximising the restricted profit (Cornes 1992). The regulator may have to compensate producers for their loss of income, but these transfers do not affect the objective function.

4.2 The stochastic version of the model

Variability in the level of rainfall means that the daily emissions of nitrate in water percolating through the soil are highly variable. Due to this variability, a policy which targets mean emissions is liable to give nitrate concentrations in excess of the concentration standard on a number of days. It is known (Kall 1976; Prekopa 1995) that replacing the stochastic variables by their expected values leads to a well-defined problem but may produce unreliable solutions.

Therefore, it is more realistic to specify the policy as a reduction in nitrate emissions to a point where the probability of the standard being exceeded is equal to some acceptable level. This is then a problem in chance-constrained programming where the probability of a constraint being satisfied determines the chance constraint. In the case of nitrate emissions, the chance constraint in its most general form is given by:

$$\Pr(\sum_i e_i \geq \tilde{e}) \leq \alpha \qquad (9)$$

i.e. the probability that emissions are greater than $\tilde{e}$ must be less than the acceptable reliability level α.

In general, there are two different approaches to approximate the probabilistic constraints. The first is to estimate the unknown probability from empirical data, and the second is to assume a certain parametric distribution of the random variables (Growe 1997). The second approach was chosen due to the first being characterised by a number of unresolved issues. In the second approach there are two ways of incorporating the constraint (9) into the nonlinear programming problem: a) the parametric approach, where emissions are assumed to follow either a normal or lognormal distribution, and b) the non-parametric approach, which employs Chebyshev's inequality as an approximation of the probability bound. Typically the underlying distribution of the emission variable is unknown and therefore there is no clear-cut choice of method. Among the parametric approaches, that based on normality assumption is the most often applied (McSweeny and Shortle 1990; Halstead et al. 1991), although there is scientific evidence that pollutant concentrations follow lognormal distribution (Ott 1990). Notwithstanding, both parametric approaches may not provide a very good match to any real data (Warric et al. 1990; Blackwood 1995). The approach we take here is to compare the results of all three.

If we assume that emissions are independent and normally distributed then the chance constraint is given by:[2]

$$\tilde{e} - \sum_k \sum_j e_{kj}\, a_{kj} \geq k_a \sqrt{\sum_k \sum_j \sigma_{kj}^2\, a_{kj}^2} \qquad (10)$$

where K_a is the z-value for reliability level α, s_{kj} is the emissions variance of crop k grown in j land, e_{kj} the average emissions from crop k grown in j land and a_{kj} is the j land devoted crop k. For discussion and derivation of the above approximation see Vajda (1972) and Beavis and Walker (1983).

By contrast, if we assume that emissions are lognormally distributed then the chance constraint is given by:

$$\log \tilde{e} - m_1 \geq K_a \sqrt{\sigma_1^2} \qquad (11)$$

where $m_1 = \ln(\sum_k \sum_j e_{kj} a_{kj}) - 0.5\sigma_1^2$ and $\sigma_1^2 = \ln\{\frac{\sum_k \sum_j \sigma_{kj}^2 a_{kj}^2}{(\sum_k \sum_j e_{kj} a_{kj})^2} + 1\}$

For discussion and derivation of the above approximation see Fenton (1960) and Zhu et al. (1994). Finally, the non-parametric chance constraint is based on Chebyshev's inequality:

$$\tilde{e} - \sum_k \sum_j e_{kj}\, a_{kj} \geq a^{-0.5} \sqrt{\sum_k \sum_j \sigma_{kj}^2\, a_{kj}^2} \qquad (12)$$

For derivation of the above approximation see Wets (1983) and Kim et al. (1990).

5 Results

These results present an assessment of the relative efficiency of second-best policies when compared to the hypothetical first-best solution of direct emission control.[3] We only consider the more realistic stochastic version of the model.

The first-best solution provides a benchmark against which other alternative policies can be compared. For the first-best solution we compare the

---

[2] Note that $\sum_i e_i = \sum_k \sum_j e_{kj}$ the sum of nitrate emissions from all the producers, is equal to the sum of emissions from all crops in all land types.

[3] The first-best solution corresponds to the least cost principle of Baumol and Oates (1988) and is defined as "efficiency without optimality". We obtain such a solution by solving problem (7), imposing direct nitrate emissions standards stipulated by the Nitrate Directive.

non-parametric chance constraint with the parametric chance constraint based on normal and lognormal distribution. The standard is set by total nitrate leaching not exceeding the equivalent of 22,025 kg/ha based on the EU standard.[4] The results shown in Figure 2 indicate how critical the assumption made about the distribution of emissions is in determining the efficient policy.

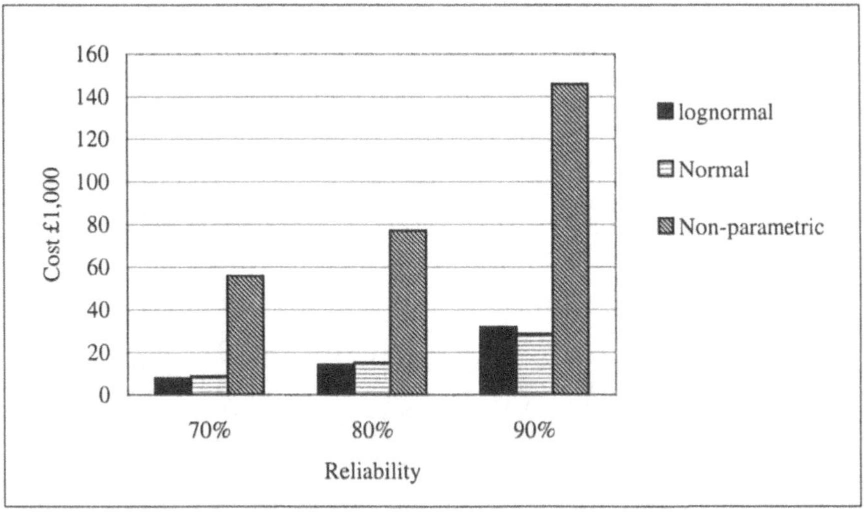

Figure 2. Abatement cost of the first-best solution.

A couple of points have to be emphasised. Firstly, the non-parametric approach leads to a very conservative solution, a point already made by Wets (1983). Figure 2 illustrates such a result. Secondly, the effects of selecting either a lognormal or normal distribution have little effect on abatement costs. The literature is inconclusive on this point. For example, Zhu et al. (1994) found that the normality assumption consistently provides lower abatement costs, while Xu et al. (1996) argued the opposite. In our case it is apparent from Figure 2 that normality gives higher abatement costs for reliability levels of 70% and 80%, but lower ones for a 90% reliability level.

Finally, the information costs of monitoring emissions make the first-best solution impossible to attain. The only reason for presenting the abatement costs of the first-best solution is to emphasise the importance of the choice between parametric and non-parametric approximations of the chance constraint. Therefore, the policy-maker must choose between a number of feasible second-best policies, some of which may include combinations of different instruments. The relative cost-effectiveness of a number of second-best policy alternatives is based on parametric approximations since the

[4] This is inferred from the EU limit of 11.3 mg/l using the hydrological model TOPCAT.

evidence found in the literature indicates that the distribution of pollutants may be either normal or lognormal (Ott 1990; Warrick et al. 1996). The policies examined include: a) a uniform nitrogen tax; b) land use constraints; c) targeted input quotas; d) a combination of input tax (20%) plus land use constraints; and e) a combination of output tax (20%) plus land use constraints[5]. Figure 3 summarises the impact of second-best policies on the abatement costs.

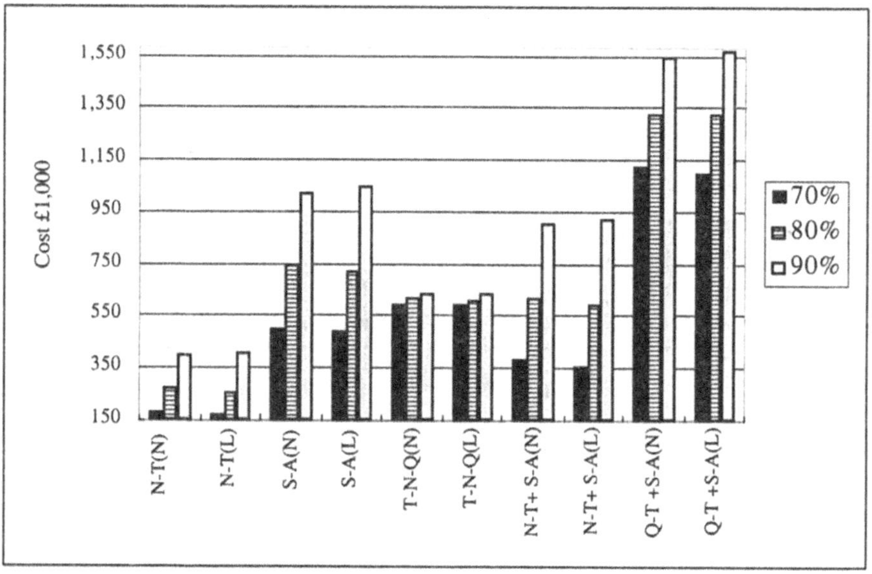

Figure 3. Abatement cost of second-best policy scenarios.

Definitions : (N): Normal distribution
(L): Lognormal distribution
N-T: Nitrogen tax
S-A: Set-aside
T-N-Q: Targeted input quotas
N-T+S-A : Combination of nitrogen tax and set-aside
Q-T+S-A: Combination of output tax and set-aside

There is an obvious inefficiency of land restrictions compared to the N-tax solution. An intuitive explanation of this result is that it is more efficient to marginally reduce the nitrogen level across the area through taxation than

[5] The fact that the price elasticity of nitrogen fertiliser with respect to the output price has been found to be greater in absolute terms than its own price elasticity has raised the possibility of introducing fertiliser limitations through output price reductions (Karagiannis 1998).

to reduce the land area available for production. The difference between these costs represents the maximum the regulator would be willing to pay to administer a more costly system of land restrictions, which is the current policy used in Nitrate Sensitive Areas.

Current abatement costs through targeted N quotas display very small variation for different reliability levels, and they also constitute a less expensive policy than set-aside the higher the reliability required. This result comes out in favour of quotas, although additional considerations are required for implementing and enforcing such a quota system.

Braden and Segerson (1993) and Schmutzler and Goulder (1997) propose that policies which combine instruments may be more efficient than single-instrument policies, given that the combined policies exhibit a certain degree of complementarity. However, the possible complementarity of policy instruments is not known a priori and it is rather an empirical issue. Set-aside which induces a change in area might be more efficient when combined with a policy which reduces nitrogen inputs, such as an input tax or even a price reduction policy. The combination of set-aside and N-tax reduces costs over the land restrictions alone, but is more expensive than nitrogen taxes. Finally, the combination of output tax and set-aside is by far the more expensive policy choice to regulate nonpoint pollution.

6 Conclusions

This paper presents an analysis of the nitrate management of a small catchment in South-East England. The first-best solution which allows direct emission controls is compared with alternative policy instruments. It is concluded that the two feasible policies nitrogen taxes and land restrictions are significantly more costly to producers or the regulator than the first-best solution. Land class specific nitrogen input quotas is a strong candidate in case of uncertainty and relative appealing policy. However, account would have to be taken of additional administrative and monitoring costs.

The current Nitrate Sensitive Area Scheme uses a voluntary land use restriction. The evidence here is that this is relatively expensive compared to the first-best solution, but relatively cheap to monitor because land cover is readily observed. Finally, the combination of set-aside with N tax seems to be quite a promising and effective policy choice.

Our results address only one criterion for ranking alternative policy scenarios, that of cost-effectiveness. However, a number of other criteria exist, including the ease of monitoring/enforcement and political considerations (see for example Bohm and Russell 1985; Hodge 1991). Although there is substantial agreement among economists in favour of economic incentives for environmental protection, corrective taxes[6] are not used in practice

[6] Corrective taxes are sometimes referred as environmental or green taxes.

(Hanley et al. 1990; Arnold 1995), indicating that there is great divergence between the recommendations of normative economic theory and positive political reality. In contrast to the normative analyses, positive studies try to explain why one instrument was chosen over another in a particular context. Hahn (1990) presents a theory of political conflict between producer-oriented interests and the interests of environmental pressure groups. He suggests that recent emphasis placed on economic instruments stems from changes in the relative influence of the two groups. Arnold (1995) stresses the ideological and sentimental basis of a familiar criticism of corrective taxation: that they make damaging the environment simply another cost item for polluters, rather than something that is fundamentally wrong. As Helfand (1989) argues, corrective taxes fail to stigmatise pollution as command and control policies do, and therefore there is a possibility of them being considered as a "licence to pollute".

The "polluter pays principle" (PPP) is the fundamental argument used to justify the equity implications of corrective taxation since it is reasonable to require polluters to pay for even the residual damage they cause the environment if they do not have the right to pollute for free anyway. At this point lies a fundamental debate concerning property rights in the land. Do farmers have the right to use their land as they want, using for example unrestricted quantities of agrochemicals? The essence of such questions is a political one which determines the underlying assignment of property rights (Bromley and Hodge 1990). If we acknowledge farmers' property rights, then any environmentally friendly adjustment of farming requires subsidisation. The latter is accepted by the MacSharry reform of CAP (Baldock and Lowe 1996). Otherwise if we regard the environment as belonging to society as a whole, then it is legitimate to require farmers to bear the cost of polluting the environment and therefore to call for corrective taxation. Notwithstanding, the notion of property rights is not static (Anderson and Lea 1991), but rather socially constructed and continually evolving. In this light recent calls for corrective taxation by environmental groups can be seen as an effort to reassign actual property rights in land (Clunies-Ross 1993). In reality, a mixed property rights regime by way of compromise is more feasible where the right to use a resource is conditional on the levels of contamination observed or on specified input combinations. Such a regime is compatible with the notion of cross-compliance applied in the US (Poe 1997).

Therefore, although an input tax seems to be the most cost-effective policy instrument to regulate nitrate pollution, potential application appears to be problematic as a number of positive studies have revealed. Nonetheless, as this study indicates, if combined with other policies it may produce quite promising results.

References

Agriculture Committee (1997): ESA's and other Schemes under Agri-environmental Regulations, H.M.S.O, London

Anderson, G., DeBossu, A., Kuch, P. (1990): Control of Agricultural Pollution by Regulation. In: Braden, J., Lovejoy, S. (Eds.): Agriculture & Water Quality, Lynne Rienner Publishers, Colorado, 63-99

Anderson, T., Lea, D. (1991): Free Market Environmentalism. Westview Press, Oxford

Arnold, F. (1995): Economic Analysis of Environmental Policy and Regulation. John Wiley, New York, 10-17

Baldock, D., Lowe, P. (1996): The Development of European Agri-Environment Policy. In: Whitby, M. (Ed.): The European Environment and CAP Reform: Policies and Prospects for Conservation, CAB International, Wallingford, 6-25

Baumol, W., Oates, W. (1988): The Theory of Environmental Policy. 2nd Edition, Cambridge University Press, Cambridge

Beavis, B., Walker, M. (1983): Achieving Environmental Standards with Stochastic Discharges. Journal of Environmental Economics and Management 10, 103-11

Blackwood, L. (1995): Normality Transformations for Environmental Data from Compound Normal-lognormal Distributions. Environmental Monitoring and Assessment 35, 55-75

Bohm, P., Russell, C. (1985): Comparative Analysis of Alternative Policy Instruments. In: Kneese, A., Sweeney, J. (Eds.): Handbook of Natural Resource and Energy Economics, Elsevier Science Publishers, Amsterdam, 395-460

Botterweg, P., Bakken, L., Romstad, E. (1994): Nitrate leaching from agriculture soils: ecological modelling under different economic constraints. Ecological Modelling 75-76, 359-369

Braden, J., Segerson, K. (1993): Information Problems in the Design of Nonpoint-Source Pollution Policy. In: Russell, C., Shorgen, J. (Eds.): Theory, modelling, and experience in the management of nonpoint-source pollution. Kluwer Academic Publishers, Massachusetts, 1-35

Bromley, D., Hodge, I. (1990): Private property rights and presumptive policy entitlements: reconsidering the premise of rural policy. European Review of Agricultural Economics 17, 197-214

Burrell, A. (1989): The demand for Fertiliser in the United Kingdom. Journal of Agricultural Economics 40(1), 1-20

Cabe, R., Herriges, J. (1992): The Regulation of Non-Point-Source Pollution Under Imperfect and Asymmetric Information. Journal of Environmental Economics and Management 22, 134-146

Clunies-Ross, T. (1993): Taxing Nitrogen Fertilisers. The Ecologist 23(1), 13-17

Common, M. (1977): A note on the use of taxes to control pollution. Scandinavian Journal of Economics 79, 346-349

Cornes, R. (1992): Duality and Modern Economics. Cambridge University Press, Melbourne

EC (1997): Framework for Community action in the field of water policy: http://europa.eu.int/en/comm/dg11/docum/9749en.pdf

England, R. (1986): Reducing the nitrogen input on arable farms. Journal of Agricultural Economics 37(1), 13-24

Fenton, L. (1960): The Sum of Log-Normal Probability Distributions in Scatter Transmission Systems. IRE Transactions on Communications Systems, CS-8, 57-67

Field, A. (1984): Microeconomics, Norms, and Rationality. Economic Development and Cultural Change 32(4), 683-711

Giraldez, C., Fox, G. (1995): An Economic Analysis of Groundwater Contamination from Agriculture Nitrate Emissions in Southern Ontario. Canadian Journal of Agricultural Economics 43, 387-402

Griffin, R., Bromley, D. (1982): Agricultural Runoff as a Nonpoint Externality: A Theoretical Development. American Journal of Agricultural Economics 64, 547-572

Growe, N. (1997): Estimated stochastic programs with chance constraints. European Journal of Operational Research 101, 285-305

Hahn, R. (1990): The political economy of environmental regulation: Towards a unifying framework. Public Choice 65, 21-47

Halstead, J., Batie, S., Taylor, D., Heatwole, C., Diebel, P., Kramer, R. (1991): Impacts of Uncertainty on Policy Costs of Managing Nonpoint Source Groundwater Contamination. Journal of Sustainable Agriculture 1(4), 29-48

Hanley, N., Hallett, S., Moffatt, I. (1990): Research policy and review 33. Why is more notice not taken of economists' prescriptions for the control of pollution? Environment and Planning A, 22, 1421-1439

Helfand, G. (1989): Standards vs. Standards: The Incentive and Efficiency Effects of Pollution. Unpublished Ph. D. Dissertation, University of California, California

Hodge, I. (1991): Incentive Policies and the Rural Environment. Journal of Rural Studies 7(4), 373-384

Holtermann, S. (1976): Alternative Tax Systems to Correct for Externalities, and the Efficiency of Paying Compensation. Economica 43, 1-16

Huang, W., Lantin, R. (1993): A comparison of farmer's compliance costs to reduce excess nitrogen fertiliser use under alternative policy options. Review of Agricultural Economics 15(1), 51-62

Jenkinson, D., Bradbury, N., Coleman, K. (1994): How the Rothamsted Classical Experiments have been Used to Develop and Test Models for the Turnover of Carbon and Nitrogen in Soil. In: Leich, R., Johnston, A. (Eds.): Long Term Experiments in Agricultural and Ecological Sciences. CAB International, Wallingford, 128-134

Johnson, S., Adams, R., Perry, G. (1991): The On-Farm Costs of Reducing Groundwater Pollution. American Journal of Agricultural Economics 73, 1063-1073

Kall, P. (1976): Stochastic Linear Programming. Springer-Verlag, Berlin

Karagiannis, G. (1998): Environmental Sustainability and Price Support Under Production Uncertainty. In: Lekakis, J. (Ed.): Freer Trade, Sustainability, and The Primary Production Sector in the Southern EU: Unravelling the Evidence from Greece. Kluwer Academic Publishers, Dordrecht, 76-86

Kim, C., Schaible, B., Segarra, E. (1990): The Deterministic Equivalents of Chance-Constrained Programming. Journal of Agricultural Economic Research 42(2), 30-38

Larson, D., Helfand, G., House, B. (1996): Second-Best Tax Policies to Reduce Nonpoint Source Pollution. American Journal of Agricultural Economics 78, 1108-1117

MacKinnon, J., Davidson, R. (1983): Tests for model specification in the presence of alternative hypotheses. Journal of Econometrics 21, 53-70

McSweeny, W., Shortle, J. (1990): Probabilistic cost effectiveness in agricultural nonpoint pollution control. Southern Journal of Agricultural Economics 22(1), 95-104

Miles, A., Lord, E., Antony, S., Fuller, R. (1996): Spatial agricultural land use data for regional scale modelling. Aspects of Applied Biology 46, 41-48

Moxey, A., White, B. (1994): Efficient compliance with agricultural nitrate pollution standards. Journal of Agricultural Economics 45(1), 27-37

Ott, W. (1990): A Physical Explanation of the Lognormality of Pollutant Concentrations. Journal of Air and Waste Management Association 40, 1378-1383

Pan, J., Hodge, I. (1994): Land Use Permits as an Alternative to Fertiliser and Leaching Taxes for the Control of Nitrate Pollution. Journal of Agricultural Economics 45(1), 102-112

Pesaran, M., Pesaran, B. (1991): MICROFIT (Version 3.0). Oxford Univ. Press, Oxford

Poe, G. (1997): Extra-Market Values and Conflicting Agricultural Environmental Policies. Choices 3/4, 4-8

Prekopa, A. (1995): Stochastic Programming: Mathematics and its Applications. Kluwer Academic Publishers, Dordrecht

Quinn, P., Antony, S., Lord, E., Turner, S. (1996): Nitrate modelling in the United Kingdom: a Minimum Requirement (MIR) approach. Paper presented at the Inter-Celtic Hydrology and Water Resources Conference, Rennes

Rayner, A., Cooper, D. (1994): Cointegration analysis and the UK demand for nitrogen fertiliser. Applied Economics 26, 1049-1054

Schmutzler, A., Goulder, L. (1997): The Choice between Emissions Taxes and Output Taxes under Imperfect Monitoring. Journal of Environmental Economics and Management 32, 51-64

Segerson, K. (1988): Uncertainty and Incentives for Nonpoint Pollution Control. Journal of Environmental Economics and Management 15, 87- 98

Sen, A. (1977): Rational Fools: A Critique of the Behavioral Foundations of Economic Theory. Philosophy and Public Affairs 6, 317-344

Smith, J., Bradbury, N., Addiscott, T. (1996): SUNDIAL: A PC-Based System for Simulating Nitrogen Dynamics in Arable Land. Journal of Agronomy 88(1), 38-43

Stevens, B. (1988): Fiscal Implications of Effluent Charges and Input Taxes. Journal of Environmental Economics and Management 15, 285-296

Swinton, S., Clark, D. (1994): Farm-Level Evaluation of Alternative Policy Approaches to Reduce Nitrate Leaching from Midwest Agriculture. Agricultural & Resource Economics Review 23, 66-74

Vajda, S. (1972): Probabilistic Programming. Academic Press, London

Ward, N. (1998). Water Quality. In: Lowe, P., Ward, S. (Eds.): British Environmental Policy and Europe. Routlege, London, 244-263

Warrick, W., Musil, S., Artiola, J. (1996): Statistics in Pollution Science. In: Pepper, I., Gerba, C., Brusseau, M. (Eds.): Pollution Science. Academic Press, London, 95-110

Wets, B. (1983): Stochastic Programming: Solution Techniques and Approximation Schemes. In: Bachem, A., Grotschel, M., Korte, B. (Eds.): Mathematical Programming: The State of the Art. Springer Verlag, Berlin, 565-603

Wu, J., Teague, M., Mapp, H., Bernardo, D. (1995): An Empirical Analysis of the Relative Efficiency of Policy Instruments to Reduce Nitrate Water Pollution in the U.S. Southern High Plains. Canadian Journal of Agricultural Economics 43, 403-420

Xepapadeas, A. (1991): Environmental Policy under Imperfect Information: Incentives and Moral Hazard. Journal of Environmental Economics and Management 20, 113 -126

Xepapadeas, A. (1994): Controlling environmental externalities: observability and optimal policy rules. In: Dosi, C., Tomasi, T. (Eds.): Nonpoint Source Pollution Regulation: Issues and Analysis. Kluwer Academic Publishers, Dordrecht, 67-86

Xepapadeas, A. (1995): Observability and choice of instrument mix in the control of externalities. Journal of Public Economics 56, 485-498

Xu, F., Prato, T., Zhu, M. (1996): Effects of Distributions for Sediment Yields on Farm Returns in a Chance-Constrained Programming Model. Review of Agricultural Economics 18, 53-64

Zhu, M., Taylor, D., Sarin, S., Kramer, R. (1994): Chance Constrained Programming Models for Risk-Based Economic and Policy Analysis of Soil Conservation. Agricultural and Resource Economics Review 23(1), 58-65

Part 3

Evaluating policies for regional sustainability

The role of the Common Agricultural Policy in maintaining High Nature Value farming systems in Europe

Petra Hellegers

Agricultural Economics Research Institute (LEI-DLO),
P.O. Box 29703, 2502 LS The Hague, The Netherlands

1 Introduction

Human interference of European landscape by the cultivation of land for agriculture and forestry is significant for the state of landscapes and biodiversity. The so-called High Nature Value (HNV) farming systems are important in the maintenance of landscapes and biodiversity. They are often referred to as low-intensity farming systems with highly diverse habitat types (Baldock and Beaufoy 1993). They may, however, also be high-intensive farming systems with rich natural potential, like the Dutch Peatlands. Some examples of farmland with high natural values are semi-natural grasslands, breeding areas for birds, areas for migratory birds, areas with many *natural* features and the dehesas and montados which are agro-forestry systems with rotation of arable and livestock production under trees (Van Dijk 1996). Intensification of agriculture and abandonment of agricultural land are the main threats to HNV areas. This has to be avoided. This article investigates the role present and alternative Common Agricultural Policy (CAP) measures can play in maintaining farming systems responsible for the high natural value of the areas throughout the EU.

This article is based on the report of Hellegers and Godeschalk (1998). It investigates HNV farming systems in a quantitative manner, whereas more qualitative approaches are used in the recent past (Baldock and Beaufoy 1993; Beaufoy et al. 1994). This study builds upon work undertaken by Baldock et al. (1996) on marginalisation.

In section 2 some HNV farming systems in a number of study areas in the EU will be selected for further investigation. The economic viability of these farming systems is investigated in section 3. The role of present and alternative agricultural policies is discussed in section 4 and 5. An overview of the support farms in HNV areas are eligible for on the basis of agricultural policy measures is given in section 6. Future developments that might have a significant influence on HNV farming systems are described in section 7. Finally, some concluding remarks will be drawn in section 8.

2 HNV farming systems in the study areas

The selection of study areas for further investigation is based on the literature and data availability, with the aim of covering a wide range of geographical locations and most characteristic landscapes with HNV farming systems and practices in both southern and northern Europe. The Farm Accountancy Data Network (FADN) of the Commission of the European Communities (CEC) has been used for the analyses. The location of the selected study areas with a high natural value is shown in Figure 1.

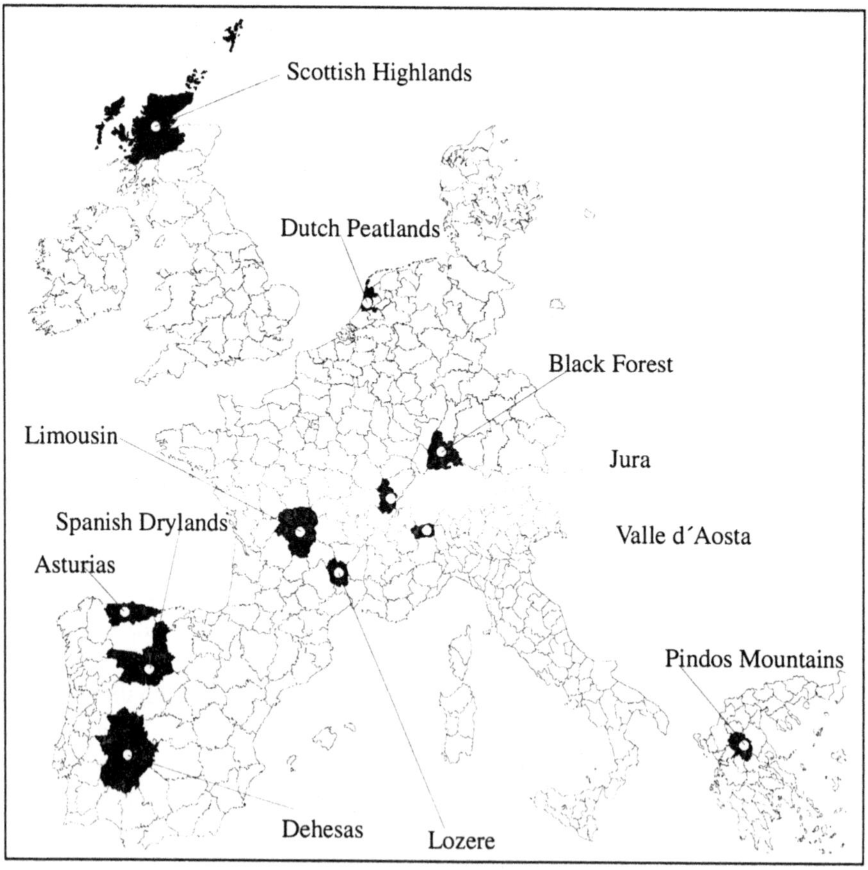

Figure 1. Location of the study areas.

According to Baldock et al. (1996) the agricultural production in extensive farming regions covered 26% of the total Utilized Agricultural Area (UAA) in EU 12[1] in 1987-91. The extensive nature of agricultural produc-

[1] EU 12: European Union from 1986 until 1995.

tion in these regions is reflected by the rather low share of 9% in the final production of EU 12. This implies that the HNV areas selected in this research, which are also rather extensive, will have only a limited share in the final production.

Specialist farms cover the largest part of the UAA in the study areas. They seem to be mainly responsible for the high natural value of the area. The share of specialist farms in the total UAA and in the total number of holdings has increased or remained constant over time in all study areas selected. The selection of the farming systems in the study areas considered to be responsible for the maintenance of the high natural value of the area is also based on the literature (Beaufoy et al. 1994) and the availability of data. In addition, attention is paid to the share of the farming types in the total area of land, since the research focuses on continuity of traditional forms of management practices on agricultural land. The farming types selected in the study areas for further investigations are: specialist dairying farms in the Black Forest, Asturias, Jura, Valle d'Aosta and Dutch Peatlands; sheep, goats and other grazing livestock farms in the Pindos Mountains, Asturias, Dehesas, Lozère and Scottish Highlands; specialist cattle-rearing and fattening farms in Limousin and Lozère and specialist cereal farms in the Spanish Drylands.

3 Viability of farms

A sound economic base is a prerequisite for a sustainable future of European cultural landscapes. This paper will focus on the economic viability of HNV farming systems. Not only the economic situation determines viability, social and regional circumstances as well as demographic and political developments are important. Whenever solutions are proposed to sustain the economic viability, this has to be done under the restriction of viability of the habitat.

In general farms are considered viable if full factor remuneration is assured. In practise farms sustain, however, their employment of factors of production for a fairly long time even if they do not fulfil this criterion. To define longer-term economic viability in this research, the development of the own financial resources has been used as a criterion. This concept is developed by Zeddies (1991).[2] On the basis of this concept farms in the study areas are divided into two groups; the viable farms and farms at risk. Of all farms selected about 70% is classified as viable and 30% is considered to be at risk.

---

[2] Farms are viable when the development of the own financial resources of the farm is positive or when the own financial resource losses are less than the depreciation relating to replacement-cost value. Farms are at risk when the own financial resource losses exceed the depreciation relating to the replacement-cost value.

Characteristics of both groups are compared, to find out why farms are viable or at risk. Viable farms did not turn out to be larger than the farms at risk. Differences in biophysical conditions between both groups are also modest, contrary to differences in intensity of farming and subsidies received. The viable farms are often the relatively more intensive farms. The share of direct subsidies in the family farm income per family work unit is higher at farms at risk compared to the viable farms. The total amount of direct subsidies is, however, higher at the viable farms. Most viable farms also receive a higher level of indirect government support, due to a higher production value.

4 Present agricultural policies in the EU

The CAP and related accompanying and structural measures can play a major role in the provision of support to HNV farming systems throughout the EU. The following measures are of interest in this context: arable and headage premiums (for beef cattle, suckler cows and sheep) as well as additional premiums on cattle where livestock densities are under 1.4 Livestock Units[3] per hectare (LU/ha) and on sheep in Less Favoured Areas (LFAs). Besides agri-environmental measures (Regulation 2078/92) and structural policies like the LFA payments might play an important role. The possibility to set quotas at a regional level may also contribute to the maintenance of HNV areas.

The maximum CAP package compensatory payments for arable crops, beef and sheep and the decrease in the production value of arable crops and beef under the 1992 CAP Reform are analysed and presented in Figure 2. For each of the four farming types the results of only one study area are presented (namely for specialist dairying farms in the Black Forest, specialist cereal farms in the Spanish Drylands, sheep, goats and other grazing livestock farms in the Dehesas and specialist cattle-rearing and fattening farms in Limousin). The results of the farming types in the other study areas show similar patterns, only the extent of the premiums varies among the study areas.

In most study areas the arable premium payments are sufficient to offset the decrease in production value. At specialist dairying farms total beef premium payments are insufficient to compensate the decrease in the production value of beef (Figure 2). Whereas at sheep, goats and other grazing livestock farms and at specialist cattle-rearing and fattening farms the total beef premium payments exceed the decrease in the production value of beef. Sheep premiums are mainly substantial at sheep, goats and other grazing livestock farms.

[3] Species and classes of livestock are converted to Livestock Units (LU) using coefficients. One dairy cow is one Livestock Unit, which is used as a reference.

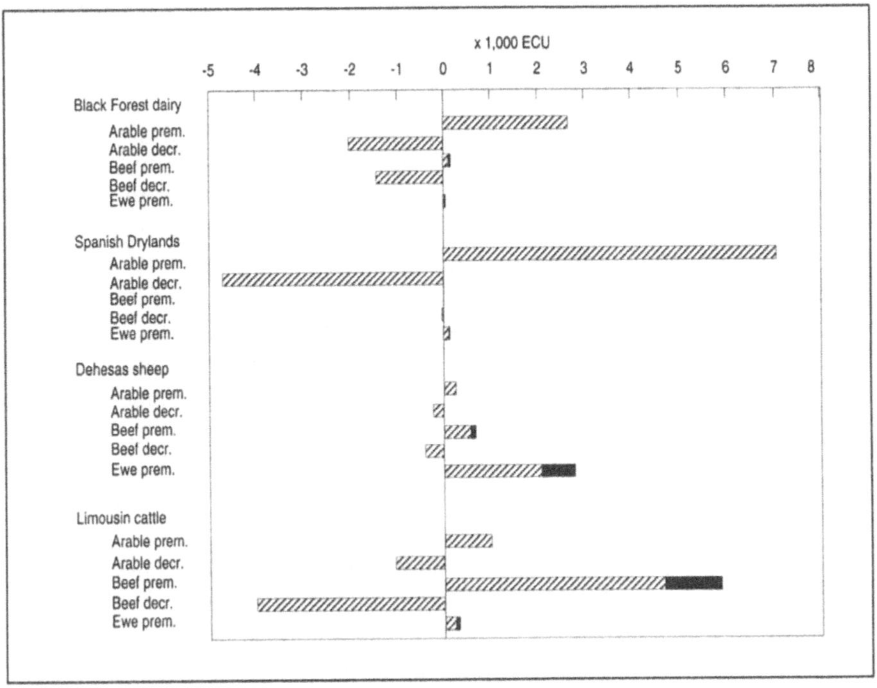

Source: FADN-CCE-DG VI/A-3; adaptation LEI-DLO.

Figure 2. Maximum CAP package compensatory payments (ECU) for arable land (first bar), beef (third bar) and sheep (fifth bar) and the decrease in production value of arable (second bar) and beef (fourth bar). The second (black) part of the third and fifth bar shows the additional beef and sheep premium (average 1990/91 – 1991/92).

Agri-environmental measures encourage farmers to introduce or continue on agricultural production methods compatible with the requirements of protection of the environment and the maintenance of the countryside and provide income support to those farmers. The measures must compensate farmers for any income losses caused by reductions in output and/or increases in costs for the part they play in improving the environment. It requires Member States to draw up programmes under which farmers are paid to farm in an environmentally friendly way. The agri-environmental schemes available in the study areas are rather diverse (de Putter 1995). With many schemes only coming into operation in 1996 it is too early to estimate the area of land affected or the extent to which schemes under the Regulation will assist the viability of farms in marginal areas or promote environmentally sensitive practices. Average compensatory allowances granted for LFA per holding, available from other sources, indicate that the level of compensatory allowances is making only a modest contribution to the viability of holdings. It is about 1,300 ECU per holding on average in EU 12 in 1994 (Brouwer and Van Berkum 1996).

5 Alternative agricultural policies in the EU

The proposals of deepening and extending the 1992 CAP Reform through further shifts from price support to direct payments, and developing a coherent rural policy to accompany this process are described in Agenda 2000. It is likely that HNV farming systems will benefit from these proposed adjustments in the CAP. These systems are often the more extensive systems, with low production value. Proposed price decreases will only have a limited impact. Besides, the farms will probably be eligible for headage premiums since they meet the livestock density requirements. Further it is likely that HNV farming systems will benefit from the increase in the budget for agri-environmental measures. Finally, Agenda 2000 also proposes to transform the support scheme of LFA into an instrument to maintain and promote low-input farming systems.

Feasible policy adjustments to maintain HNV farming systems are explored. The impact of such adjustments is shown in Figure 3, for four study areas. The assessed policy adjustments are summarised below:

- The abolition of the set-aside obligation, like proposed in Agenda 2000 does not affect a large proportion of the HNV farms and consequently the average increase in the allowances farms are eligible for is modest.
- A sensitivity analysis on the livestock density threshold, which has to be met to receive premium, is done. Two different schemes are evaluated which serve as examples. Under scheme A referred to as 'additional beef premium A', an additional beef premium of 30 ECU per animal is assessed cumulative for a threshold density of respectively 1.4, 1.0, 0.75 and 0.5 LU/ha. Under scheme B referred to as 'additional beef premium B', producers may qualify for an additional beef premium of 36 ECU per animal if they stock at a density less than 1.5 LU/ha. A further claim of 52 ECU is allowed if stocking density is less than 1.0 LU/ha. An even further claim of 85 ECU on top of the other claims is analysed for a threshold of 0.5 LU/ha. The results indicate that an additional premium for a very low density of 0.5 LU/ha is mainly interesting for sheep, goats and other grazing livestock farms and less interesting for specialist cattle-rearing and fattening farms.
- The present *rural world* supplementary premium, for which producers in all the LFAs are eligible, could be converted into a payment targeted more precisely at HNV areas. This increases the sheep premium at farming systems with sheep in HNV areas that are only partly considered as LFA, like in the Dutch Peatlands.

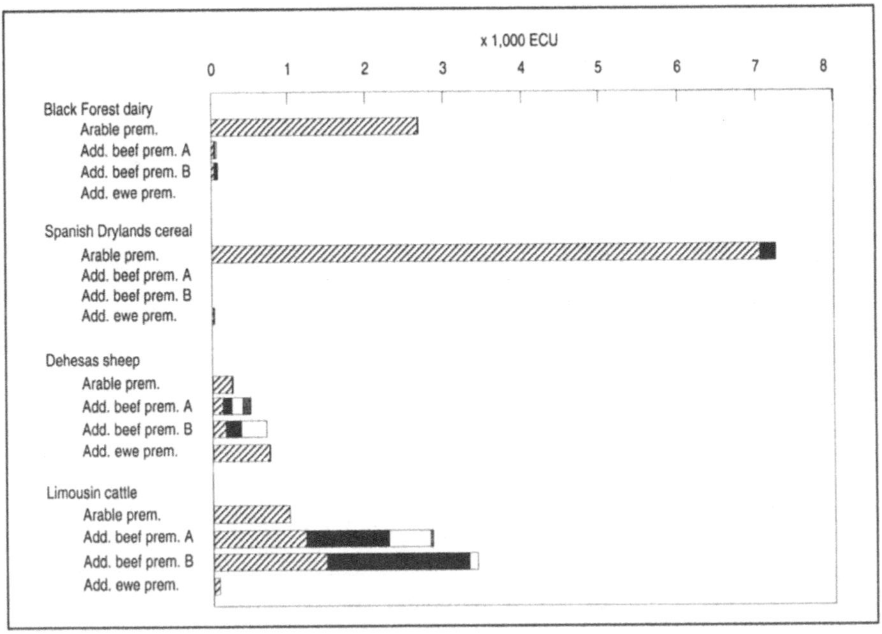

Source: FADN-CCE-DG VI/A-3; adaptation LEI-DLO.

Figure 3. Adjustments in the requirements for direct payments: arable premium if the set-aside obligation is abolished (first bar), additional beef premium A (second bar, first part; 30 ECU per animal if the threshold of 1.4 LU/ha is met, second part; 30 ECU if 1.0 LU/ha is met, third part; 30 ECU if 0.75 LU/ha is met and fourth part; 30 ECU if 0.5 LU/ha is met), additional beef premium B (third bar, first part; 36 ECU per animal if the threshold of 1.5 LU/ha is met, second part; 52 ECU if 1.0 LU/ha is met and third part; 85 ECU if 0.5 LU/ha is met) and additional ewe premiums for all HNV farms (fourth bar) (average 1990/91 – 1991/92).

Different criteria for agri-environmental measure payments are compared. Figure 4 shows the allowances farms are eligible for under various bases for payments. The basis for the agri-environmental payments is a determining factor for the level of allowances farms are eligible for. The level of the premium per unit is not differentiated by study area, in order to allow comparison. Below the advantages and disadvantages of the various bases for payments are described. Payments of 1,000 ECU per farm and of 50 ECU per hectare of Utilized Agricultural Area and per Livestock Unit as well as per hectare of forage crops and per hectare of adjusted forage crops are assessed.

- A fixed amount of payments per farm provides equal allowances for all farms, whereas Regulation 2078/92 aims to compensate farms for any income losses for the part they play in improving the environment. Since it is not likely that all farms play a similar role, this basis is not specific enough.

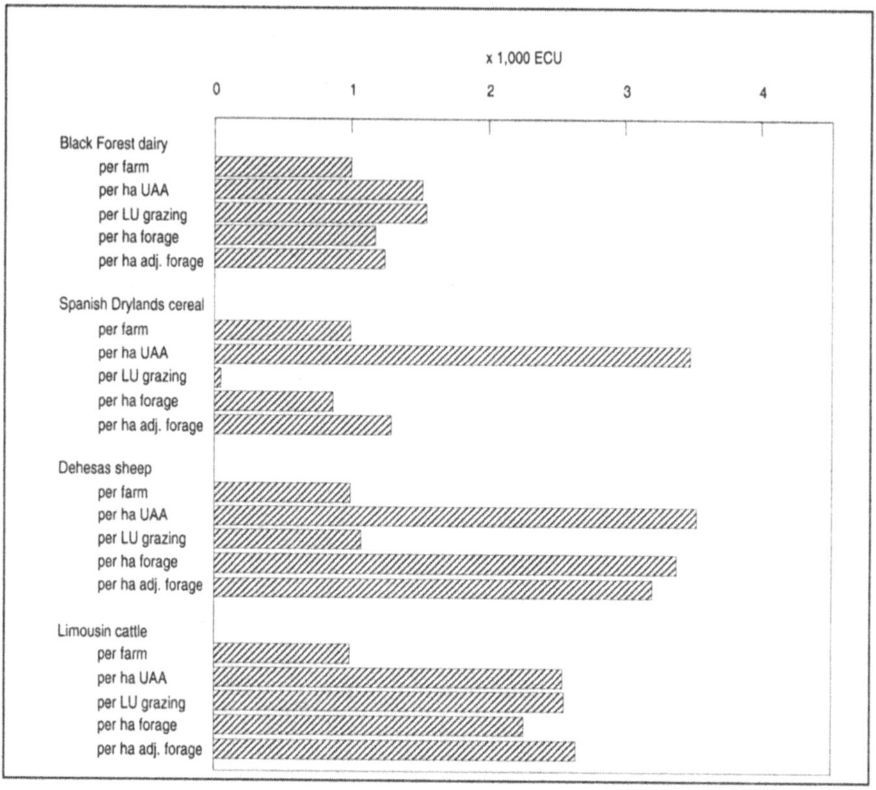

Source: FADN-CCE-DG VI/A-3; adaptation LEI-DLO.

Figure 4. Optimal use of agri-environmental payments under different bases for payments of: 1,000 ECU per farm (first bar), 50 ECU per hectare of UAA (second bar), 50 ECU per grazing Livestock Unit (third bar), 50 ECU per hectare of forage crops (fourth bar) and 50 ECU per hectare of adjusted forage (fifth bar) (average 1990/91 – 1991/92).

- An advantage of payments based on the average UAA per farm is that support is not linked to production and will not stimulate overgrazing. It provides extremely high payments to farms with a large UAA, like the specialist sheep, goats and other grazing livestock farms in the Scottish Highlands with an average UAA of 888 hectare. It is possible to introduce a maximum ceiling of payments per farm in such a case, although this is unfair towards huge co-operatives like those that exist in the former communist countries, i.e. eastern Germany.
- Payments based on the number of grazing Livestock Units per farm, can increase the production and stimulate overgrazing unless adequate ceilings are set. Payments vary largely among study areas and are extremely low at arable farms like the specialist cereal farms in the Spanish Drylands.

- An advantage of payments based on the average forage area per farm is that support is not linked to production and to other crops. Payments can be extremely high in case the forage area is large.
- Payments based on the *adjusted forage hectares*, a concept developed by Goss (1997) are also shown. It is based on the relative forage productivity. Payments based on the *adjusted forage area* are more conform to the intensity of usage compared to premiums based on the forage area.

6 Policies and economic viability

Present and alternative agricultural policies in the EU provide support to HNV farming systems. This support might increase the economic viability of farms in HNV areas. Although support received can not be fully accounted to an equal increase in savings and more positive development of the own financial resources. Nevertheless, allowances received can support farms to keep the farm viable or make the farms, which are considered to be at risk, viable again. Figure 5 summarises the support viable farms and farms at risk are maximal eligible for on the basis of present and alternative agricultural policy. The development of the own financial resources of the farm plus depreciation relating to replacement-cost value, which is used as a viability indicator in this research and the family farm income are shown in this figure. This gives an indication of the size of the support in relation to the viability indicator.[4]

Figure 5 indicates that changes in the 1992 CAP Reform make only a modest contribution to the viability of farms. Except at specialist cattle-rearing and fattening farms in Limousin, the supplementary additional beef premium provides no significant support. Agri-environmental payments could potentially be the biggest source of support in all study areas. Specialist cereal farms in the Spanish Drylands, sheep, goats and other grazing livestock farms in the Dehesas and specialist cattle-rearing and fattening farms in Limousin are eligible for considerable allowances in relation to the family farm income. Allowances are limited in relation to the family farm income at all specialist dairying farms assessed in the analysis. Mainly at specialist dairying farms considered to be at risk, other adjustments in policy are required.

There are a number of qualifications to the results of the study. The payments are calculated in a rather normative way based on structure characteristics available from FADN. The calculated allowances are the maximum amounts farms are eligible for although not always maximum amounts will be received for various reasons. Besides, there are constantly changes in the

[4] When the viability indicator is positive, farms are viable. When it is negative, farms are at risk.

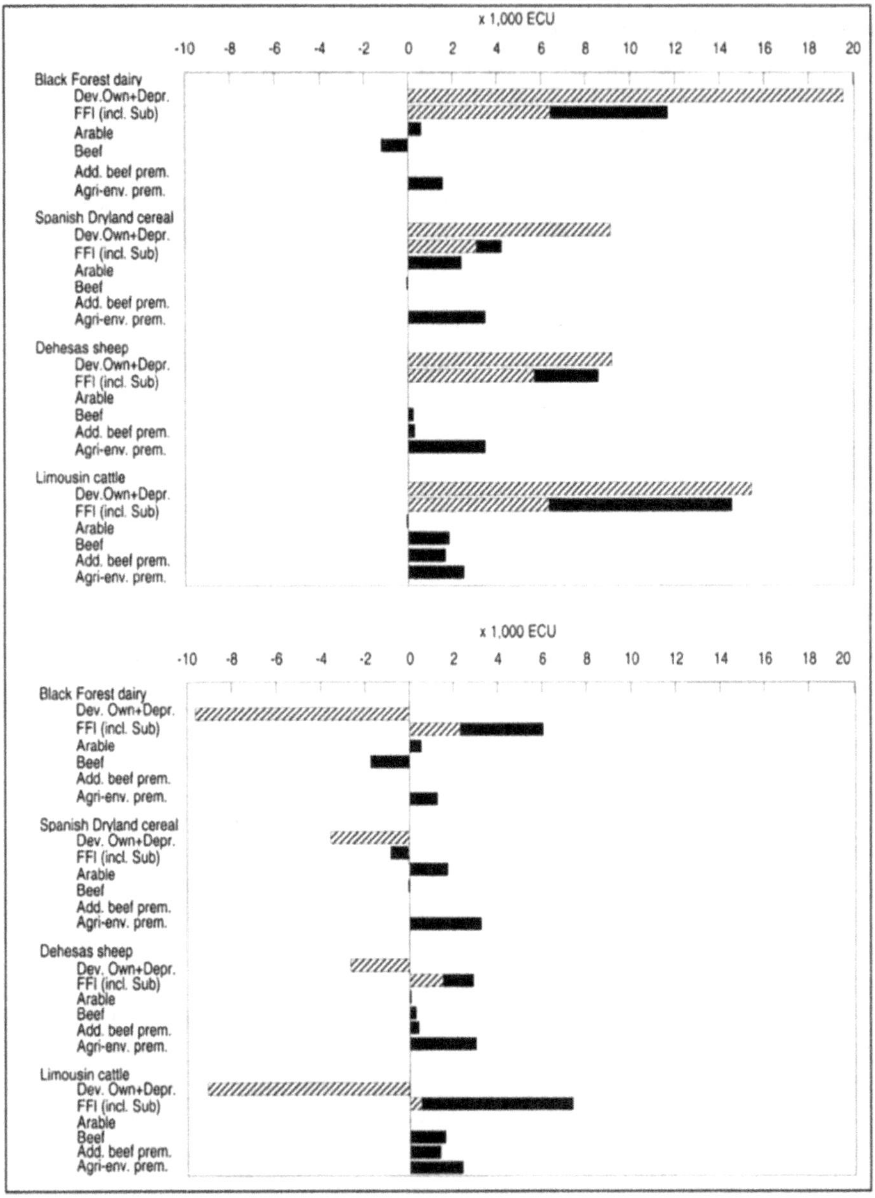

Source: FADN-CCE-DG VI/A-3; adaptation LEI-DLO.

Figure 5. Development of own financial resources plus depreciation relating to replacement-cost value (first bar) and family farm income (FFI) (second bar, including the direct subsidies, the black part) in relation to: the arable premium minus the decrease in production value (third bar), the beef premium minus the decrease in production value (fourth bar), additional beef premium B (fifth bar) and agri-environmental payments based on the UAA per farm (sixth bar) viable farms (upper part) and farms considered to be at risk (lower part) are eligible for (average 1990/91 – 1991/92).

regulations, like in the level of premiums and requirements to receive premiums. Finally, the calculations do not account for any monetary developments that were important the last few years neither for developments in the market.

7 Future developments and HNV farming systems

Future developments that might have a significant influence on HNV farming systems include the extension of the EU with the Visegrad countries and further trade liberalisation. The situation in the Visegrad countries is changing rapidly. The remaining traditional extensive agricultural systems in the Visegrad countries have very high natural values. Currently, the support for HNV farming systems is limited in the Visegrad countries, there exists some support for LFAs and organic farming. These countries are, however, gaining valuable experience in developing initiatives that aim to maintain the natural value of agricultural land. Working groups are established which develop agri-environmental programmes. It is not clear yet how the schemes will be funded. The Visegrad countries face budgetary constraints and there is no guarantee yet that the EU will provide financial assistance.

On the basis of the relatively high trade barriers which presently surround the EU and the large production potential in the Visegrad countries, it could be expected that trade liberalisation between the EU and Visegrad countries may have a considerable impact on agriculture. However, it is not likely that accession of the Visegrad countries to the EU will increase the production in the Visegrad countries drastically at once. Production in the Visegrad countries will recover gradually from the transition. Currently, these countries are not able to produce large quantities of homogeneous quality. The time path is an important aspect in this respect. The impact of the accession on the prices and production in the EU seems to be modest and consequently the accession will have only a limited impact on the HNV farming systems in the EU. An increase in the production in the Visegrad countries will probably have an impact on HNV areas in these countries. So, it is very timely to take care of the relationship between agriculture and nature conservation at HNV farming systems in the Visegrad countries. It is desirable to guide the development of agriculture in the Visegrad countries and provide incentives for agricultural practices, which are beneficial for the environment.

On the basis of the relatively high trade barriers which presently surround the EU, it could be expected that trade liberalisation between the EU and the world market will affect EU's agriculture considerably. Estimations indicate that trade liberalisation will decrease the EU production of ruminant meat and dairy products (Tyers and Anderson 1992). This may encourage extensification. On the other hand a considerable drop in ruminant meat and dairy sector prices can be a major threat to HNV farming systems. Production will be less profitable and land can be abandoned. However, this is not likely, the 1992 CAP Reform and Agenda 2000 make farmers less dependent on prices, a shift to direct payments can be observed. Appropriate policies to meet decreasing prices are important in this respect.

8 Concluding remarks

The aim of this paper was to provide insight into the role the Common Agricultural Policy (CAP) plays and might play in maintaining traditional forms of management practices at HNV farming systems in Europe.

It became clear that the 1992 CAP Reform makes only a modest contribution to the viability of farms. These changes seem to be too general to provide support on the basis of environmental achievements. Environmental conditions should be attached in order to receive premium. The total amounts of allowances farms are eligible for are limited in relation to the family farm income in most study areas. This implies that other adjustments in agricultural policy are required to maintain the HNV farming systems.

Agri-environmental payments could potentially be the biggest source of support in HNV areas. These measures seem to be very suitable to support HNV farming systems, because environmental requirements are attached to these payments. The basis of payments and the level of payments are very determining factors for the total amount of agri-environmental payments farms are eligible for. A higher level of payments can contribute considerably to the viability. Regional agri-environmental policies or policies directed towards a particular sector can also contribute to the viability of HNV farming systems.

References

Baldock, D., Beaufoy, G. (1993): Nature conservation and new directions in the EC Common Agricultural Policy. Institute for European Environmental Policy, London

Baldock, D., Beaufoy, G., Brouwer, F., Godeschalk, F. (1996): Farming at the margins, abandonment or redeployment of agricultural land in Europe. Institute for European Environmental Policy, London and Agricultural Economics Research Institute (LEI-DLO), The Hague

Beaufoy, G., Baldock, D., Clark, J. (1994): The nature of farming. Institute for European Environmental Policy, London

Brouwer, F.M., Van Berkum, S. (1996): CAP and environment in the European Union: Analysis of the effects of the CAP on the environment and assessment of existing environmental conditions in policy. Wageningen Press, Wageningen

Dijk, G. van (1996): Nature conservation and agriculture in Europe. In: Agriculture and nature conservation in Central and Eastern European countries: Proceedings of a seminar held at Dăbe, Poland, 12-14 may 1996, 31-37

Goss, S. (1997): Possible options for the better integration of environmental concerns into the various systems of support for animal products (volume I). Centre for European Agricultural Studies (CEAS Consultants Wye Ltd) and European Forum on Nature Conservation and Pastoralism (EFNCP)

Hellegers, P.J.G.J., Godeschalk, F.E. (1998): Farming in High Nature Value regions; The role of agricultural policy in maintaining HNV farming systems in Europe. Agricultural Economics Research Institute (LEI-DLO), Onderzoekverslag 165, The Hague

Putter, J. de (1995): The greening of Europe's agricultural policy; the 'agri-environmental regulation' of the MacSharry reform. Ministry of Agriculture, Nature Management and Fisheries, The Hague

Tyers, R., Anderson, K. (1992): Disarray in World Food Markets: a quantitative assessment. Cambridge University Press, Cambridge

Zeddies, J. (1991): Viability of farms. University of Hohenheim. Institute for Agricultural Economics. Report published by the Commission of the European Communities. Office for Official Publications of the European Communities, Brussels, Luxembourg

Pesticide collection programs: a proposition to prevent future contamination

Terence J. Centner and Lewell F. Gunter

The University of Georgia, 313 Conner Hall, Athens, GA 30602, USA

1 Introduction

Millions of pounds of unwanted pesticides are being stored by agricultural producers and others in barns and other buildings throughout the United States. For example, the U.S. Environmental Protection Agency (EPA) estimated that more than 13 million pounds of unwanted pesticides were located in six Great Lakes States: Illinois, Indiana, Michigan, Minnesota, Ohio, and Wisconsin (Jones 1993). Due to the environmental threat posed by these stored pesticides, governments have become concerned. The EPA adopted a federal Universal Waste Rule that partly addresses this problem (*Federal Register* 1995). State legislative and regulatory actions have also been enacted to address the disposal of unwanted pesticides. Nearly all of the individual U.S. states have become involved in collection efforts to remove unwanted pesticides from storage and to dispose of them safely (Cubbage 1996).

Unwanted pesticides consist of two categories of pesticides that are in storage. First, some agricultural producers failed to use or return pesticides whose registrations have been canceled under the federal provisions of FIFRA, the Federal Insecticide, Fungicide, and Rodenticide Act (*U.S. Code*, title 7, 1994, 1997). It is illegal to use such pesticides and thus owners may not know what to do with them. A second category consists of registered pesticides for which the possessor no longer has a use. Persons may have quantities of registered pesticides in storage for a number of reasons. A producer may have moved to a sustainable production system so no longer uses the previously purchased pesticide. Another reason may be that agricultural producers have selected new and more effective pesticides to replace pesticides they had been using, and failed to use up their stocks of older pesticides. Other producers decide to hire a pesticide contractor to apply pesticides who does not use the producers' leftover stocks of pesticides.

The existence of unwanted pesticides in barns and other agricultural buildings constitutes an unsafe situation. A natural disaster, such as a flood or tornado, could dispense the pesticides into the environment. Given the toxicity of most pesticides, disposal by a natural disaster could cause serious human injury or contamination. Another risk is that, due to human error, unwanted pesticides might be mistakenly used or applied to a crop creating health hazards for humans and the environment. Given the nature of farm barns and storage buildings, a child, person, or animal could come into contact with a pesticide and be harmed. Finally, as owners of pesticides move off a farm or die, possession of pesticides will pass to succeeding property owners. In many cases, the new owners will have little knowledge and appreciation of the toxicity of the stored pesticides.

While there are firms who specialize in the disposal of unwanted pesticides, the costs of safe disposal cause possessors to leave the pesticides in storage. This paper investigates the issue of stored unwanted pesticides through an analysis of collection efforts in different U.S. states. Collection efforts have involved voluntary producer participation so that the ways to entice owners of unwanted pesticides to take part is essential. Due to the hazardous nature of pesticides, programs have to be well planned with sufficient safety features. As pesticide owners are hesitant to dispose of their substances if costs are involved, the availability of funding is important. It is concluded that an initial targeted collection program may be employed to start removing dangerous stored pesticides, but governments should expect their programs to evolve as they gain experience and coordinate pesticide collection with other hazardous waste. Tying pesticide collection with existing hazardous waste disposal efforts, such as household collection programs, may be encouraged.

2 Regulatory authority

Pesticides in the United States are regulated by the EPA under the Federal Insecticide, Fungicide, and Rodenticide Act (*U.S. Code*, title 7, 1994, 1997). Under FIFRA, the EPA allows American states to administer pesticide disposal programs. Several state governments have enacted special laws to regulate agricultural collection programs (Table 1). Yet the programs have not removed most unwanted pesticides from storage. Moreover, persons in many areas have not had an opportunity to participate in a meaningful collection program and new unwanted pesticides continue to accumulate.

Whenever pesticides are being discarded rather than being used for their intended use, they may need to be disposed according to regulations concerning hazardous substances under the U.S. Resource Conservation and Recovery Act (*U.S. Code* 1994). Because most pesticides are hazardous, their disposal, and also state pesticide collection programs, must comply with the federal hazardous waste provisions. Hazardous wastes are defined by U.S. federal law as a solid waste with characteristics that cause them to present special dangers or potential hazards to human health or the environment (*U.S. Code* 1994). Discarded materials that are in a liquid or semisolid forms are included within the definition of solid waste. Discarded materials include materials that are abandoned or are considered inherently waste-like.

Table 1. Regulatory initiatives for the collection of agricultural pesticides.

Florida Statutes Annotated § 403.7264 (1996)
Hawaii Code Annotated § 149A-13.5 (1996)
Idaho Code § 22-3423 (1996); Idaho Administrative Procedures Act, rule 02.03.03.850 (1994)
Illinois Compiled Statutes Annotated, title 415, §§ 60/19.1 (1997)
Iowa Code Annotated §§ 455B.488, 455F.8 (1990)
Kansas Statutes Annotated § 65-3415 (1996)
Kentucky Revised Statutes Annotated § 224.10-610 (1996)
Maryland Environmental Code Annotated §§ 9-1801, 9-1802 (1996)
Michigan Compiled Laws Annotated §§ 324.8307, 324.8715, 324.8716 (1996)
Minnesota Statutes Annotated §§ 18B.065, 18B.26 (1996); Minnesota Rules, rule 1509.0020 (1997)
Montana Code Annotated §§ 80-8-111 to -213 (1995); Montana Laws, no. 42 (1997)
Nevada Revised Statutes § 586.270 (1995); Nev. Administrative Code § 586.011 (1993)
New York Department Environmental Conservation, Technical Administrative Guidance Memorandum 2006 (1993)
North Carolina General Statutes § 143-468(b) (1996); N.C. Session Laws, no. 261 (1997)
North Dakota Century Code § 19-18-04 (1995); N.D. Laws, Senate Bill 2083 (1997)
Oregon Administrative Rule 340-113-070 (1991)
Pennsylvania Code, title 7, §§ 128b.1 to .18 (1993)
South Carolina Code Regulations 27-1082 (1996)
South Dakota Codified Laws Annotated §§ 38-20A-54 to -55 (1996)
Vermont Statutes Annotated, title 6, §§ 918, 1103, 1104 (1996)
Washington Revised Code § 15.58.045 (1993); Washington Administrative Code §§ 16-228-157 to -160 (1996)
Wisconsin Administrative Code ATCP 34.01 to .09 (1992)

The EPA has prescribed regulations that espouse human and environmental safety and has adopted regulations that identify hazardous wastes. Parts 260 through 272 of the *Code of Federal Regulations* prescribe detailed regulations for the disposal of hazardous wastes. Persons discarding hazardous wastes are hazardous waste generators. Hazardous waste generators need an EPA generator identification number and must meet various requirements that provide for the safe disposal of hazardous substances.

Because there exist many persons with relatively small quantities of common hazardous waste, relaxed regulations for three universal waste products were prescribed in Part 273 of the *Code of Federal Regulations*. Pesticides, batteries, and thermostats were classified as universal wastes, and Part 273 is known as the Universal Waste Rule. Stocks of unused pesticide products collected and managed as part of a waste pesticide collection program qualify to be treated as universal wastes. With the less onerous regulatory provisions of the Universal Waste Rule, the EPA estimates annualized savings of $76 million for generators of pesticides (*Federal Register* 1995).

Under the relaxed rules of Part 273 of the *Code of Federal Regulations*, farmers taking pesticides to a collection program do not have to meet the paper work normally required of generators disposing of hazardous waste. Persons managing agricultural pesticides with a collection program qualify as handlers of universal wastes. Under Part 273, handlers are categorized as small and large quantity handlers of universal waste, and separate provisions define standards for each category. Part 273 sets forth fewer burdensome requirements for handlers, as opposed to the basic provisions for persons handling hazardous waste. The relaxed provisions concern employee training, a contingency plan, hazardous waste biennial reports, transport, storage, and manifests for each shipment of hazardous waste (*Federal Register* 1995).

3 Organizational features

Due to the hazardous nature of unwanted pesticides and the potential complications that would accompany a mishap or accident, many state collection programs mandate precautionary measures. Preregistration, appointments, site visits, on-site collections, and other safety measures are important features of a number of collection efforts. As governments gain experience with the disposal of pesticides, they may be expected to revise their programs and substitute fewer burdensome provisions to economize on costs.

Some state pesticide collection programs require the preregistration of each pesticide collected for disposal. Preregistration serves as an application procedure whereby the necessary information is made available to facilitate the orderly collection and legal disposal of unwanted pesticides. Preregistration generates information on the types of pesticides that need to be collected and the quantities of pesticides that end users would like to have collected. With this information, the state can determine what should be collected, given available financial resources. Preregistration offers an opportunity to secure additional information on the condition of containers, location of pesticides, and whether the applicant or material qualifies under the state program. Preregistration also provides information for the development of bid specifications for use in contracting for the disposal of the pesticides.

Preregistration may offer other benefits. It requires participants to examine products to determine their identity. Participants thereby may discern the usefulness of stored products and may note problems concerning the condition of older products. Moreover, the preregistration information facilitates special safety precautions for leaky containers and for scheduling how much time is needed to complete the collection.

A variation of preregistration is to schedule an appointment over the phone for the delivery of an unwanted pesticide. Iowa has adopted an appointment directive as part of its Toxic Cleanup Days for the collection of pesticides and other toxic wastes (DeWitt 1997). During a two-week period preceding the collection, persons with unwanted pesticides call and book an appointment for the delivery of their materials. Participants deliver their materials pursuant to their appointment. The appointment means participants may be met at the collection site entrance to confirm their scheduled appointment, and directed to the appropriate collection stations or locations at the site.

A few state pesticide collection programs have incorporated site visits and other safety features to help guarantee that the collection process does not entail a spill or an accident. Colorado, for its 1995 pesticide collection program, included a visit to each site to determine the weight of the pesticides, the conditions of their containers, and to tag the containers for pickup (Panter 1996). The Pennsylvania regulations allow for state officials and the contractor to physically inspect the premises, but a visit is not required (*Pennsylvania Code* 1993). This provides an opportunity to verify the preregistration application, to draw samples of unknown pesticides, and to ascertain the safety of aged pesticide containers whenever the preregistration information suggests that extra precautionary measures may be important. With the more complete information that accompanies a program with a site visit, there should be fewer possibilities for a mishap.

Another safety measure involves on-site pesticide collection. At least one state, Colorado, arranged for the physical collection of accepted preregistered pesticides from their diverse sites because it minimized the chance that an accident might occur on the way to the collection site (Panter 1996). A variation of this requirement is to make on-site collection available if needed. The Pennsylvania regulations provide that deteriorating or otherwise unsafe containers, or quantities of pesticides that are too large, too heavy, or otherwise incapable of being safely transported to a central site, shall be collected on the farm by the contractor (*Pennsylvania Code* 1993). Most pesticide collection programs, however, do not involve site collection. The major reason is the additional expenses of such programs.

A number of additional features of pesticide collection programs may contribute to their safety. First, selection of nonpermanent collection sites is most important. The site must be convenient for persons with unwanted pesticides and needs to facilitate the safe collection of hazardous wastes. Safe collection generally includes an impervious layer with a proper slope. Running water, electricity, sanitary facilities, and garbage disposal may also be important. Another safety feature is a toll-free telephone number to be used if there is a spill or problem with transportation.

The provision of new containers for the safe transport of aged or damaged containers may be part of a pesticide collection program. Some states provide for this with on-site pickup. Vermont, for its 1991 collection program, distributed heavy study plastic bags to participants requesting assistance for leaking containers (Karnatz 1991). Georgia offered drums to preregistered individuals to enable them to safely convey damaged containers to the collection site (Tolar 1996).

4 Sources of funds for disposal

U.S. states have adopted different funding sources to pay for pesticide collection efforts. As funding is a major limitation on collection programs, an explicit source of funds is critical to a successful long-term program. Four major categories of funds have provided monies for collection programs: grants, user fees, state pesticide registration fees, and state taxes on sales of pesticides. Funding methods have been implemented differently across U.S. states, with some states employing more than one type of funding as collection programs change.

Governmental grants have provided funding for many efforts. While this funding method has been helpful, reliance solely on this form of financing often is not conducive to a long-term program.

A user fee is a second funding option, and user fees mean that a disposal program does not become dependent on governmental benevolence. This may be preferred as disposal is an expense connected with private business activities. Although user fees can coerce participants to assume responsibility for their unwanted pesticides, user fees are unlikely to change purchasing decisions. Moreover, persons possessing unwanted pesticides may not participate in a collection program when there is a fee. Established pesticide programs show insignificant sums being raised from user fees. Since user fees often do not cover the costs of disposal, provisions for other sources of funds will be required.

State pesticide registration monies constitute a popular financing provision for collection programs in states with established agricultural pesticide programs. While only a portion of the registration fee is allocated to cleanup and collection programs, the monies do address the problem of unwanted pesticides.

A fourth funding possibility is a tax on pesticide products. Monies from the tax on pesticides sold are deposited into a fund to be used for enumerated purposes including collection programs.

5 Equity and efficiency considerations of funding sources

Characteristics of each funding approach may be reviewed with respect to collection incentives and the distribution of costs. A "polluter-pays" principle may be advocated to internalize negative externalities. Under this principle, a fee or charge on individuals or firms responsible for the pollution would be advocated. Fairness issues advocate the presence of a linkage between the source of disposal funds and the ownership of unwanted stored pesticides. Concern also exists in encouraging safe disposal. Analyzing funding sources, what conclusions might be made?

Using grant monies for the disposal of unwanted pesticide stocks shows that grant funding involves the use of unspecified sources of funds that are unrelated to ownership of unwanted pesticides. Reliance on one-time grants to fund pesticide disposal also raises questions about the ability to maintain a long-term disposal program.

The use of user fees to finance disposal may be more equitable due to the relation between the funds and unwanted pesticides. User fees are imposed on the owners of unwanted stocks. A user fee program may reduce future pesticide use and accumulation, since the user knows he will pay for disposal. In opposition, however, user fees provide a disincentive for participation.

The most common source of funding is the use of state pesticide registration fees. This involves a fee on the yearly registration of each pesticide with a portion of the collected monies being used for the collection of pesticides. Registration fees, imposed on pesticide manufacturers, may not create a barrier to participation, but are not very equitable. The fees come from current and future purchasers of pesticides rather than current owners of unwanted pesticides.

Pesticide tax funding for disposal act to increase cost for pesticide users in accordance with pesticide supply and demand elasticities (Gunter, Jeong and White 1996). However, as with fees, pesticide taxes are imposed on future pesticide users rather than on owners of existing unwanted stocks.

6 Evolution of collection programs

The hazardous nature of pesticide disposal means that efforts may need to be tempered with a pragmatic and cautious approach. Care must be taken to avoid accidents that would cause contamination. States in the U.S. have treated stored pesticides as a major concern and have worked hard in developing strategies to respond to this environmental issue. Yet, most states have not developed a meaningful type of permanent program. Thirty states lack statutory or administrative provisions that would establish a permanent initiative for collecting unwanted agricultural pesticides (Centner 1998b). While most U.S. states have some type of collection program, they need to move beyond their temporary efforts to adopt a permanent reliable program to remove accumulated pesticides.

The collection efforts of about one-half of the U.S. states may be classified as targeted efforts. These generally consist of programs offering a disposal option in areas with a high probability that farmers are storing unwanted pesticides. Some targeted programs are limited by the availability of funding. Targeted efforts offer an efficient start, given the limited availability of funding, and reduce potential contamination problems posed by unwanted pesticides. However, targeted programs often only involve the collection of a small percentage of unwanted pesticides. Targeted programs do not achieve a long-term solution for the disposal of unwanted pesticides because they do not address the continued generation of unwanted pesticides.

Thus, targeted programs cannot be expected to collect all of the accumulated pesticides. Governments wanting to remove a majority of unwanted pesticides from storage need to institute a permanent program that provides for the disposal of both accumulated pesticides already in storage and pesticides currently being relegated to storage because possessors no longer have a use for them.

Several states have recognized the need for a long-term solution, and two basic approaches may be discerned. The first approach is an agricultural program with a long-term apparatus for program funding and the safe disposal of unwanted agricultural pesticides. A second approach is to adopt a household program to handle modest quantities of unwanted pesticides from farmers. When administrative and infrastructures are in place, both of these long-term approaches lend themselves to reducing collection costs.

As costs for the disposal of unwanted pesticide have varied considerably, recent programs showing that modest costs are possible deserve attention. By reducing administrative costs, as occurs under an appointment system, costs for the disposal under an agricultural pesticide collection program might be approximately $1.50 to $3 per pound. The new U.S. Universal Waste Rule, with its relaxed requirements concerning pesticide collections, suggests that lower collection costs might be possible. It is estimated that with experience and the adoption of a household hazardous waste program, they can move to a relaxed program where costs would be about $1 per pound (Centner and Gunter 1997).

Despite the long-term solution adopted, the program will need to employ efforts to garner producer participation. Many agricultural producers remain distrustful of participating in governmental programs due to a fear that their storage of pesticides is illegal. Beginning efforts, including targeted programs for agricultural producers, offer an opportunity for a government to establish sincerity and the lack of adverse legal consequences. Targeted programs also give the government experience in meeting the regulatory requirements that govern the disposal of hazardous waste. After successfully conducting targeted collections, a government can move to a permanent collection facility. The knowhow, expertise, and infrastructure of an existing household collection effort may provide a superior means to dispose of pesticides with other hazardous wastes.

7 Evaluating the efficacy of state efforts

Regulatory efforts and reported U.S. state collections of unwanted pesticides may be measured to advance some thoughts about efficacy. Four criteria may be selected: an agricultural collection initiative, permanent funding for the agricultural initiative, comparison of amounts collected to expenditures for new pesticides, and reported state hazardous materials programs accepting agricultural pesticides (Centner 1998a). Summaries of these criteria for U.S. states with the most successful programs are set forth in Table 2.

The existence of a written agricultural collection initiative provides an important institution to support addressing this environmental issue. U.S. states with regulatory provisions have been noted in Table 1. States with an agricultural initiative are assigned two points, otherwise zero, and this score is used to calculate the predicted efficacy of a state's collection efforts.

Table 2. Efficacy scores for superior U.S. state's pesticide collection efforts.

State	Agricultural Initiative	Permanent Funding	Collection to Expenditures*	Reported State Household Program	Predicted Efficacy
Connecticut			3	2	5
Florida	2		1	2	5
Hawaii	2	2	1		5
Illinois	2	2	1		5
Iowa	2		2	2	6
Kentucky	2		3		5
Maryland	2		2	2	6
Massachusetts			3	2	5
Michigan	2	2	2	2	8
Minnesota	2	2	2		6
Mississippi	2	2	2		6
Montana	2	2	2		6
Nevada	2	2	3		7
North Carolina	2	2	3		7
North Dakota	2	2	2		6
Pennsylvania	2	2	3		7
South Dakota	2	2	2		6
Vermont	2	2	3		7
Washington	2		3		5
Wisconsin	2		3		5

*Reported by Centner and Gunter.

Second, an important need of a state program is a provision to provide a foundation for a permanent program. As less than 15% of existing accumulated pesticides may be removed in a given collection effort, a few collections servicing a given area may not remove most quantities of stored pesticides (Spitzmueller 1995). Only through a continuing permanent program can a majority of accumulated unwanted pesticides be removed from storage and disposed of safely. The permanency of the agricultural collection initiatives may be evaluated by determining which programs have long-term or permanent funding. Such funding is provided by whenever a state requires that part of the pesticide registration fee be used for a collection program or when a tax on pesticides sold provides funds for collection efforts. States are assigned two points for having a funding provision, otherwise a score of zero was assigned.

A third efficacy measure may evaluate the success of existing state efforts in collecting unwanted pesticides. One aspect of this measure consists of the quantities of pesticides collected. A second aspect concerns the amounts of pesticides being used in each state. The comparison of amounts collected in each state to expenditures for new pesticides provides for a rating of states that evaluates efficacy. A comparison of amounts collected in each state to expenditures for new pesticides provides for a rating of states in Table 2. Three points were assigned to states with the highest collection-to-expenditure ratio. States with medium and low collection to expenditure ratios were assigned two and one points, respectively. States that did not report any collected pesticides were assigned zero points.

A fourth efficacy criterion is the existence of a state hazardous materials collection program that has reported positive results in collecting agricultural pesticides. A state with a program is assigned two points.

The addition of the points relegated to each efficacy criterion is summarized in the last column of Table 2 as a predicted efficacy score. Although under a given criterion significant differences may exist between state programs, an evaluation may perform an insightful interpretation of regulatory institutions. The evaluation may predict the success of a state in responding to the environmental problem of stored unwanted pesticides. Collection efforts in the states of Michigan, Nevada, North Carolina, Pennsylvania, and Vermont might be studied to gather guidance on how to develop a superior response for eliminating stored agricultural pesticides (Centner 1998a).

8 Concluding comments

American state governments have instituted pesticide collection programs due to the risks inherent in the storage of unwanted pesticides. Because pesticides are dangerous, and their storage is often in old barns and agricultural structures that may not be very secure, some type of governmental oversight is appropriate to help eliminate situations that constitute a threat to human health and the environment. The continued storage of unwanted pesticides creates unnecessary risks of harm and possibilities for environmental damage.

The evaluation of the existence of an agricultural collection program, permanent funding for such a program, and state hazardous waste collection provisions offer ideas for developing better responses to eliminate sources of potential contamination. The research involves the development of an environmental response for a problem. Temporary and targeted governmental efforts are shown to constitute good starting points. However, once established, temporary programs may not be sufficient to meaningfully address an environmental problem. A program may need to evolve to meet additional challenges.

For pesticides, collection programs need to evolve to garner enough producer participation to meaningfully remove most unwanted pesticides. This requires a permanent solution for unwanted pesticides being generated. Moreover, pesticide collection might be better coordinated with the collection of other hazardous waste.

While the lack of funding has precluded many governments from engaging in greater pesticide collection efforts, the inquiry should focus on whether an area can afford not to act due to the risks to water, land, and air associated with accumulated pesticides. Given the rather modest costs required to fund a pesticide collection program and to coordinate the collection of pesticides with household hazardous waste, additional regulatory efforts should be encouraged. More research is needed on the costs inflicted on society by pollution. Legislative bodies that fail to direct appropriate efforts to address an environmental problem may be remiss in failing to provide for the future safety of their citizens and their natural resources.

References

Centner, T.J. (1998a): Disposing of Pesticides as Hazardous Waste: State Pesticide Collection Programs. Stanford Environmental Law Journal 17, 353-395

Centner, T.J. (1998b): Unwanted Agricultural Pesticides: State Disposal Programs. Journal of Environmental Quality 27, 736-742

Centner, T.J., Gunter, L.F. (1997): Financing the Disposal of Unwanted Agricultural Pesticides. University of Georgia Agricultural Economics Faculty Series 97-06, Athens

Code of Federal Regulations (1996): Title 40, parts 260-273

Cubbage, C.P. (1996): State Agricultural Pesticide Collections Survey. Michigan Department of Agriculture, Lansing

DeWitt, R.D. (1997): Household Hazardous Materials Toxic Cleanup Days. Iowa Department of Natural Resources, Des Moines IA, 1-36

Federal Register (1995): Volume 60, pp. 25492-25539

Gunter, L.F., Jeong, K.H. and White, F.C. (1996): Multiple Policy Goals in a Trade Model with Explicit Factor Markets. American Journal of Agricultural Economics 78: 313-330

Jones, M. (1993): Agricultural Clean Sweep: Waste Pesticide Removals 1988-1992. U.S. Environmental Protection Agency, Region 5, Chicago

Karnatz, A. (1991): Obsolete Pesticide Disposal Project. Vermont Department of Agriculture, Food & Markets, Montpelier

Panter, K.L. (1996): Northern Colorado Front Range Pesticide Recovery Program, Project Final Report. Colorado State University Cooperative Extension, Lakewood

Pennsylvania Code (1993): Title 7, section 128b.6(a)(1)

Spitzmueller, J. (1995): 1994 Report of Waste Pesticide Collection in Minnesota. Minnesota Department of Agriculture, St. Paul

Tolar, B.R. (1996): Summary Report: 'Georgia Clean Day 95'. Georgia Department of Agriculture, Atlanta

United States Code (1994): Title 7, §§ 136-136y (1988 & Supp. 1997); Title 42, sections 6921B6939

Nature conservation in urban landscapes. Implementation and acceptance issues

Georg Kneer

Department of Ecological Economics and Environmental Sociology,
UFZ Centre for Environmental Research, Permoserstr. 15, D-04318 Leipzig, Germany

1 Introduction

So far, nature conservation and landscape protection have only played a subordinate role in environmental sociology. Bearing in mind the potential for conflict inherent in this field, this is astonishing. How nature and the landscape can best be used is the subject of intense social debate. Since different groups of users compete to avail themselves of nature and the landscape, nature conservation and landscape protection schemes often clash with various users' interests. One important task of sociological research is to analyse the use of nature and the landscape as a major area of social conflict. Sociological analysis thus complements the general conservation debate mainly involving ecologists and legal experts, and which in recent years has been joined by economists.

The following considerations provide a sociological analysis of the implementation of conservation and landscape protection measures. To this end a theoretical framework is developed which combines questions of implementation and acceptance (I). The regulation of "impact and compensation" (*Eingriffs- und Ausgleichsregel*) will be used as an example of the application and development of this approach (II).

2 Theoretical framework

Merely drawing up and adopting a political action programme are by themselves no guarantee of success. Instead, the effectiveness of a political programme depends on the specific conditions and forms of its application. Awareness of this marks the starting point of what is known as "implementation research".[1] The term implementation indicates the enforcement or translation into practice of a binding political programme (Mayntz 1980). It should be added that the term "implementation" is not uniformly applied.

[1] The difference between the programme goals and the programme effects are addressed by another branch of research known as "evaluation research" or "impact research". These effect analyses consider the effects of programmes without more closely analysing the implementation of the programmes. This "enforcement blindness of evaluation studies" (Bussmann 1993: 263) is probably one of the reasons why implementation research flourished in the mid-1970s.

We can distinguish between a narrow and a broad approach. A narrow understanding defines implementation as the actual enforcement or performance of an individual *measure*, and thus solely refers to the final phase of the administrative action. A broader understanding (and one on which this paper is based) regards implementation as the implementation of a political programme, and thus includes all the administrative processes, especially decisions concerning the selection of the measure, the legal form of the measure chosen, and whether the measure is to be used in concrete individual cases.

The implementation of a political programme is a specific phase of the policy cycle which follows the phase of programme formulation. To be more precise, a political action programme must be developed, drawn up, adopted and then introduced before implementation takes place. However, these phases of the policy cycle can only be isolated in analytical terms; in practice they are closely interrelated and partly overlap. Political programmes consist of laws, statutory regulations, and administrative guidelines.[2] They contain (more or less precise) information about the initial situations, goals, the institutions to be commissioned with implementation, and the intended target groups, as well as information about the means and instruments to be used to achieve the goals.

Programmes can never contain enough detail to cover all aspects of their implementation and application. Therefore numerous decisions concerning concrete, context-specific schemes and individual cases still have to be taken during the implementation process. The enforcement of a programme always requires decisions, while programme formulation and implementation are different parts of a sequential decision cycle. Developing a programme means taking programming decisions, i.e. choosing and specifying the framework and the general direction of the programme. Programme formulation is, in other words, the development and adoption of decision premises for future decisions (Luhmann 1994). By contrast, programme implementation involves programmed decisions, i.e. interpretation, translation and specification. This two-step model of policy decision-making holds true for all political spheres. The field of environmental and conservation policy is especially characterised by grey legal concepts and decisions that are left to the discretion of the actors in the implementation process (Braun 1997). The fact that political programmes need to be expressed in more detail is by no means merely due to the scale of the matter, i.e. the complexity of the subject to be regulated. The social and time dimension also play a part. Political programmes are thus kept general – and frequently ambigu-

---

[2] Hucke (1996: 61; my own translation) points out that "procedural requirements and recommendations for limits drawn up by private institutions also [develop] such a high degree of environmental policy commitment that they too must be ascribed to environmental policy programmes".

ous – precisely because greater acceptance und support (form diverse groups of actors) can then be hoped for. Moreover, the programmatic establishment of first of all the decision premises allows the greater flexibility of implementation practice over time – the concrete implementation of the programmes can always be adapted of changing requirements without the programmes themselves having to be amended.

The two steps of the decision-making process can be observed in all types of programmes. Distinguishing between final and conditional programmes is common practice (Becker 1989: 454-457). Final programmes indicate goals and purposes and sometimes establish priorities between competing goals. Conditional programmes have the form "if A – then B"; i.e. if a certain condition is fulfilled, a certain measure must be taken. Conditional programmes can be divided into search programmes, choice programmes and work programmes. Search programmes encompass decisions on relevant and best measures, choice programmes on best measures, and work programmes require decisions on enforcement. On the whole, the scope for decision lessens from final programmes via search and choice programmes to working programmes (Becker 1989: 459).

Besides differentiating between final and conditional programmes, there are other aspects that can serve to classify political programmes. These chiefly include typologies orientated towards instruments and programme outcomes. Instruments are often grouped into planning, regulatory, economic and information instruments.[3] Following the proposal of Lowi (1964: 125ff.), programme outcomes can be divided into distributive, regulative and redistributive policies. Distributive policies share out money or services without imposing supplementary costs on specific groups. Regulative policies directly charge the target groups with the costs. Redistributive policies take the money from the 'losers' and give it to the 'winners'.

The above considerations concentrate on the characteristics of political programmes. However, this is not the only factor determining the implementation phase. The characteristics of the implementation field are equally important. The implementation field is formed a) by the actors or groups of actors involved, and b) by the relations between the actors or groups of actors. What actors or groups of actors are involved in the implementation field depends on the specific policy or programme type. Usually there are

[3] When classifying political and state action in terms of instruments, it should be borne in mind that almost every political programme makes use of a variety of control instruments and media. Regulatory programmes, for example, work not only with bans and regulations (i.e. with the control medium 'the law') but also with the medium of money, for violations are punished by a fine. In contrast to economic programmes which in turn also contain regulatory elements, regulatory programmes uses bans and regulations primarily. Classification is thus oriented towards the *dominating medium* control. For more on the various classification approaches (cf. König and Dose 1993).

four different kinds of actors in the field of environmental and nature conservation policy, namely the administration, the target group, interest groups and the courts. The target group is the group of actors directly affected by the administrative instructions and regulations. The interest groups are the actors who are only indirectly concerned. These include residents in the vicinity of nuclear power stations, motorways and incineration plants, or environmental and conservation groups. These examples show that the group of interested actors itself consists of different people and groups. Moreover, the administration, the target group and the courts are not monolithic units either. Although this distinction between four actor groups is also a simplification, it still helps to explain the programme implementation.

It should be pointed out that the administration is not solely responsible for carrying out the programme. Enforcement is determined by the actions and behaviour of all four groups. Both the target group and the interest groups try to influence the decisions of the public administration in 'bargaining' or negotiation processes. Administrative decisions are usually prepared in negotiations with actors who are directly or indirectly involved, and mutual arrangements or agreements are used instead of unilateral administrative orders. Current research into the state and administration in particular has shown that the activity of public authorities is not or at least not solely orientated towards the model of sovereign acting, but rather towards a model of cooperation.[4] That the enforcement of a programme often takes the form of a negotiation process can partly be explained by the fact that each of the four groups of actors involved hopes to benefit. From the administration's viewpoint, negotiations ensure or increase the effectiveness of decisions and reduce the risk of failure in later stages of the implementation process. Moreover, negotiations support flexible learning and adaptation strategies (Schneider 1996: 47). Finally, bargaining helps to avoid or reduce expensive, time-consuming court proceedings. However, it cannot be claimed that the implementation authorities always want to avoid a legal examination. In actual fact, if the target groups and interest groups go to court, this is actually to the advantage of the administration. Taking legal actions results in the responsibility for the passing of unpopular measures being shifted to another group of actors, namely the courts; moreover a legal

[4] The (by no means new) observation of negotiation and bargaining processes between the administration and the parties involved has had a sustained effect on the discussion of the state and administration over the past few years. A large number of newly emerging definitions ranging from 'negotiating administration' via 'inter-organisational networks' to the 'cooperative state' document the current interest in the negotiation process. Braun's assessment (1997: 29) that the model of the negotiating, cooperative state currently represents the central control-theory paradigm which unites such differing approaches as interest group theory, implementation research and system theory is probably no exaggeration.

ruling enables the faster, smoother enforcement of the subsequent implementation processes (cf. Dammann 1997: 49-50).

From the point of view of the target groups, negotiations help to decrease or to weaken regulations. One of the reasons interest groups use negotiations is to compensate for or at least reduce their disadvantages. These considerations explain the interests of the three groups in cooperative negotiations.[5] Readiness to enter into negotiations is no guarantee of a commonly agreed outcome; after all, the negotiations may fail. This often results in a fourth actor being dragged into the dispute – the courts. In principle the implementation actors can lodge an appeal. In concrete bargaining processes they cite their right to take legal action in order to strengthen their position. Dammann (1997: 54) correctly describes the discussions between administration, target group and interest groups as "multilateral negotiations in the shadow of justice".

In this context another concept needs to be clarified. Cooperative action by the administration is not the same as informal action. Cooperative action is often expressly intended, i.e. legally programmed, and therefore formally regulated.[6] Participation by those directly or indirectly involved in numerous approval procedures is explicitly invited. Furthermore, the legislator recommends or commits the administration to attend preliminary negotiations – negotiations that take place before the actual procedure gets underway.[7] Formal regulations, instructions, and institutional structures in general make up the multilateral negotiations between the different actors. However, they do not determine the actions of the actors involved. Institutional structures enable negotiation processes, yet also reduce the freedom of ac-

---

[5] The actors' interests – and thus the forms of cooperation – depend not least on whether proceedings are pending (irrespective of by whom they were initiated) (cf. Hucke and Ullmann 1980, Lübbe-Wolff 1992).

[6] Bohne (1984) for example incorrectly subsumes cooperative action by the administration under informal action by the administration; Dose (1994) also fails to systematically distinguish between the two terms, even though he expressly refers to cooperative law and thus legally programmed cooperation. By contrast, I conscientiously draw a distinction between the two: cooperative action by the administration means every form of action by the administration which is not unilateral or sovereign, especially accords between the administration and the actors of society in the form of preliminary negotiations, arrangements and formal agreements (cf. Bulling 1989). By contrast, informal action by the administration refers to action by the administration which is not strictly legally determined. In addition to formal components, action by the administration always includes informal components, too, as nothing can ever be completely determined by legal regulations. Informal action by the administration is thus not necessarily illegal, but merely not expressly laid down (cf. Schulze-Fielitz 1992).

[7] One example is the Ninth Directive on the Implementation of the German Pollution Control Act (*Bundesimmissionsschutzgesetz*) dated 18 February 1977 in the version published on 29 May 1992, which obliges the approval authority to enter into preliminary negotiations.

tion of the actors involved by encouraging, hindering or excluding specific options. Whether and how the actors make use of the given scope depends on their power, interests, strategies and value orientation.

The fact that the implementation process takes the form of a negotiation process or depends on cooperative discussions is one reason why the programme results cannot be accurately predicted. The implementation of the programme is not a mechanical or technical process which transforms inputs into exactly predictable outputs. Programme enforcement is instead more of a social process. The change of interest and power constellations as well as the actors' options to take actions and make choices lead to uncertainty and unpredictability. Consequently the actual results are often unintended effects (Hasse 1997). In this context, *enforcement deficits* should be mentioned. An enforcement deficit means that the goals of the programme have not been fully achieved, i.e. discrepancies exist between the results intended and those actually realised. In the field of environmental and conservation policy in particular, the term enforcement deficit has had a meteoric career. Enforcement deficits can be observed in almost all fields. However, closer examination reveals that the term enforcement deficit is often overworked. The programme goals are expressed in relatively general, unspecific terms, so that the implementation actors have more or less broad scope for decisions. If legal regulations are not interpreted strictly enough in ecological terms, or if the regulations themselves are too weak, this does not necessarily indicate the existence of an enforcement deficit;[8] this is only the case when the action actually taken differs from that planned. As policy programmes consist of valid laws, regulations and administrative rules, enforcement deficits indicate illegal programme implementation (Schomerus 1987: 20).

The enforcement of the programme is often organised in a bargaining or negotiating process. Cooperative procedures help to achieve or ensure acceptance for the administrative decisions. Acceptance means agreement. The questions of implementation and acceptance are closely linked. Programme enforcement uses multilateral negotiations in order to examine the readiness for acceptance, to eliminate any obstacles to acceptance, and to produce and ensure acceptance. If public authorities do not manage to secure acceptance, they will provoke protest, conflict and legal action. This is why a sociological approach which analyses the implementation of political programmes has to address the successful or unsuccessful procedure of acceptance "production". The change of direction towards the control-theory paradigm of the cooperative state marks the overcoming of the selective

[8] Conceptions which diagnose any deviation from an ecologically desirable action as enforcement deficits – such as that of Hucke (1996: 61), who describes the "disregard of regulation scope and action instances" as an implementation deficit – are dubious.

consideration of programme enforcement merely from the viewpoint of the government, to which implementation research initially tended (cf. Mayntz 1980: 237). The linkage of implementation and acceptance questions in the text also contradicts the dominance of the "top-down viewpoint"; questions of creating acceptance and safeguarding cannot solely be explained from the legislater's viewpoint, as the actions by all implementation actors must be systematically taken into account.

3 Carrying out the impact regulation

Nature conservation and landscape protection policy in Germany chiefly uses planning instruments as well as command and control instruments. Economic incentives and information instruments are used too, but less than the other instruments. Examples of planning instruments as well as command and control instruments include landscape planning, the creation of nature reserves and species protection (Mitschang 1994). The impact regulation is a mixture between a command and control instrument and an economic instrument. Economic programmes include conservation contracting and incentive programmes by the German *Länder* (federal states). Recommendations, warnings and appeals by the nature conservation authorities are examples of information instruments. The use of these instruments in the sphere of nature conservation and landscape protection does not essentially differ from instrument usage in the sphere of environmental policy where planning, command and control instruments predominate as well.[9]

The impact regulation is a relatively new instrument of nature conservation and landscape protection which is embodied in the 1976 German Federal Nature Conservation Act (*Bundesnaturschutzgesetz, BNatSchG*).[10] The regulations it contains were extended and modified by §§ 8a–c of the German Federal Nature Conservation Act in 1993. §§ 8a-c integrates the impact regulation into urban planning. The main amendment is that the impact regulation is brought forward to development planning in order to simplify, reduce and accelerate planning and project enforcement. It should be stressed that in the sphere of nature conservation and landscape protection

[9] Closer examination does in fact reveal differences between environmental protection and nature conservation. Our own survey on local government environmental protection in German towns and cities with more than 200,000 inhabitants revealed that less importance is attached to the predominant role of planning and regulative instruments in conservation than in environmental protection (cf. Ring et al. 1998).

[10] Although the impact regulation follows on from § 20 of the 1935 German Reich Nature Conservation Act (RNG), it goes much further. The old regulation provided for the involvement of the competent conservation authorities in all planning or measures which could result in major changes to the open landscape. By contrast, the impact regulation does not stop at their involvement, but also specifies a material decision programme (cf. Gassner 1996: 175).

the German Federal government can only provide a legal framework. Framework legislation means that the German government can only pass laws which need to be carried out and can be carried out. The German Constitutional Court long gave the federal legislator the opportunity to enact complete regulation concerning the content of *individual parts* of legislative material. The Basic Law Amendment Act dated 27. October 1994 defines framework legislation competence more rigidly, only allowing detailed or complete regulation in substantiated exceptions. As far as the impact regulation is concerned, above all the environment impact assessment clause in § 8 of the German Federal Nature Conservation Act could be problematic as, according to Freytag and Iven (1997: 127), this is a detailed regulation which is outside the competence of the German government. Specific legislation is laid down by the various German *Länder*, all of which have now adopted the impact regulation and formulated it in concrete terms.

The impact regulation is the fundamental area protection norm of the German Federal Nature Conservation Act (Bizer 1997: 80). In contrast to specific area protection like nature reserves, the impact regulation is aimed at area protection in general. The goal of the act is to prevent negative changes to nature or the landscape. This does not imply that nature and landscape must not change anymore. Instead, the legislator's interest is to preserve the overall potential of nature and the landscape (Mitschang 1994: 211). Although impacts which harm nature or exploit the landscape are not illegal, they must be compensated by those using nature and the landscape. The impact regulation is therefore orientated towards the "polluter-pays-principle" (Heidtmann 1993: 69).

The impact regulation stipulates that all projects which may harm nature and the landscape must be examined. § 8 of the German Federal Nature Conservation Act and the corresponding legislation of the German *Länder* specify the procedure. Firstly, the facts of impact are to be defined.[11] Avoidable impairment is forbidden,[12] while unavoidable impairment must

[11] In line with the framework legislation competence, the Nature Conservation Act merely makes an extremely general definition of the circumstances constituting impact. The *Länder* reserve the right to a more detailed definition of impact, including the possibility to specify standardised projects which regularly meet these conditions (positive list). Projects which do not meet these conditions can be placed on a negative list. Under Hamburg's Nature Conservation Act, for example, flood protection schemes do not represent impact. It should be added that a national exemption is made for land use in agriculture, forestry and fishery. According to § 8 of the German Federal Nature Conservation Act, proper land use for agriculture, forestry and fishery does not constitute impact. Everyday activities concerning the primary economic sector are thus excluded from the impact regulation; however, this is by no means the case for the extraordinary or far-reaching forms or agriculture, forestry and fishery such as the conversion of grassland, orchards and wetlands into arable land (cf. Gassner 1996: 184-185).

[12] The term 'avoidance' (as well as all other terms in the relevant legal wording) is of

be compensated (entailing the elimination of all lasting damage after completion). If impairment cannot be avoided or compensated, the situation must be carefully weighed up. If nature and landscape interests are given priority, the impact must be forbidden. The German Federal Nature Conservation Act contains no further regulations in cases in which nature and landscape interests are not given priority. § 8 of the German Federal Nature Conservation Act enables the German *Länder* to lay down additional regulations, an option which all the German *Länder* have exercised. Besides natural substitutes such as landscape greening, the *Länder* have also developed financial compensation schemes.[13] The regulations of the impact regulation have a precise sequence: avoidance takes priority over compensation, while compensation is preferred to substitution measures.

The above explanations have already touched upon the question of programme classification. Some further considerations need to be added. The impact regulation can be described as a graded conditional programme. Although the impact regulation is aimed at specific results, it contains some 'if – then conditions' such as: if the impact is avoidable, it is forbidden; if there are unavoidable impairments, they must be compensated; if impairments cannot be avoided or compensated and nature and landscape interests have priority, impact must be forbidden, etc. The implementation authorities have to examine whether the conditions specified in the programme exist. When using the impact regulation it has to be decided whether impacts exist, whether there are unavoidable impairments, whether the interests of nature and the landscape have priority and so on. Other decisions concerning relevant measures are required, such as decisions about the type and extent of compensation or substitute measures. To this extent, the impact regulation can be classified as a conditional search programme.

A programme classification also has to describe the steering instruments and the programme results. With regard to the steering instruments, the impact regulation mainly uses command instruments; with the compensation charge, the impact regulation contains an additional economic element.[14] As far as programme results are concerned, the impact regulation can be described as a regulative programme. The target group actors have to pay the

---

course a legal term. In terms of ecological science any impact is avoidable, for any project can simply be abandoned. From a legal angle, 'avoidable impairment' means an unnecessary (environmental) impairment which in terms of type and scale would not have arisen had an alternative, less ecologically harmful type of impact been accepted (cf. Schmidt and Müller 1995: 155).

[13] Strictly speaking we ought to refer to a *replacement charge*, since 'compensation payment' does not (contrary to what it may suggest) serve the compensation of the impact, but rather its replacement, i.e. the general aim of conservation and landscape management.

[14] From an economic angle, the incentive and control effect stemming from the compensation charge are judged as limited (cf. Hartje 1994: 337-341; Bizer 1997: 82-87).

costs of compensation or substitute measures without any redistribution between two or more groups. Frequently in policy research it is claimed that especially the enforcement of redistributive policies leads to conflicts. The example of the impact regulation shows that the implementation of regulative policies too can be controversial.

In addition to the programme features, the actors and actor relations are also important for a sociological approach. The nature conservation authorities are just one of a number of authorities involved in implementing the impact regulation. This is because the impact regulation is not an independent decision instrument.[15] There is no specific administrative procedure for the impact regulation; instead it is tied to other approval procedures. The specific authority which is responsible for approving the project has to carry out the impact regulation, too. Although the responsible authority has to take into account the view of the nature protection authority, the former's decision may deviate from the latter's viewpoint.

Those who carry out the project are known as the *target group*. According to § 8 of the German Federal Nature Conservation Act and the legislation regulating its implementation at the level of the Land, the party responsible for impact is subject to certain material and legal obligations, such as avoidance and compensation. When these obligations are formulated for the specific case concerned and then implemented, communicative contact regularly takes place throughout this process between the admininistration and the target group. In addition to the target group's application and the subsequent decision taken by the responsible authority, there are numerous other instances of communication serving areas such as stock-taking and information procurement, and thus ultimately the immediate preparation of the decision. In particular whenever complex impacts are planned, communication is not restricted to isolated contacts but takes the form of a continual process. From the target group's viewpoint, these contacts and communicative negotiations provide an opportunity to swing the final decision in its favour. Although the obligations of the intervention rule (such as the avoidance or compensation obligation) must be observed and are not in themselves open to discussion, as indicated above the authorities still enjoy a certain degree of flexibility as the legal requirements and other regulative guidelines do not specify in detail how compensation or replacement is to take place. Empirical studies also show that the target groups try to exert an

---

[15] To be more accurate, the impact regulation comprises a non-independent instrument from a procedural viewpoint, but it is in fact an independent material regulatory programme. "This means that a project which according to a specific legal regulation requires approval and results in an impact should be judged using both the material standards of this specific regulation as well as those of the conservation legislation impact regulation. This results in the cumulative examination of the circumstances of approval and impact." (Ramsauer 1997: 420-421).

influence on the authorities in informal negotiations and bargaining processes. The arguments most frequently presented are the prospects of job creation and boosting the region's economic attractiveness (cf. Burmeister 1988: 155).

The *interest groups* comprise both individual and collective actors. Individual actors, such as residents, or the neighbours of airports and federal highways etc., can join up to form collective actors such as citizens' action groups. Under § 29 of the German Federal Nature Conservation Act, direct involvement in the implementation of nature conservation regulations is limited to "acknowledged" nature protection associations. In the context of the impact regulation, this possibility is limited to participation in the planning procedures (*Planfeststellungsverfahren*).

The participation rights of the acknowledged conservation associations include the opportunity to make a statement and to inspect the expert's reports. The law also stipulates that the associations must be informed in good time of the location, type and scope of impact, so that they have sufficient opportunity to formulate and submit a (usually written) statement on the project from the angle of conservation. Furthermore, the associations must be allowed to examine the relevant experts' reports. The right of participation is legally inforceable. Legal action can be taken to ensure the participation of conservation associations in proceedings already underway, while substantive decisions resulting from proceedings from which associations were excluded can be contested for this reason alone. There is no right to representative legal action (i.e. a right on the part of conservation associations to force cases to be examined) at federal level. Nevertheless, twelve of the sixteen Länder have permitted various forms of conservation-related representative action, although the actual scope of rights to take legal actions varies from state to state (cf. Diefenbach 1997: 574).

As pointed out, the acknowledged nature protection associations are the only interested actors which are directly involved in the carrying out of the impact regulation. The other interested actors can only sway the other actors in the field of implementation by means of direct or indirect action, for example by influencing the political arena. Direct influences include informal contacts, discussions and petitions; indirect influences include the distribution of leaflets and demonstrations.

More extensive possibilities of participation and involvement can arise for the interest groups from the fact that the implementation of the impact regulation (as seen above) is linked to other procedures, some of which also make provision for a certain degree of involvement. Nevertheless, it should not be overlooked that the scope of participation and involvement differ considerably for the target and interest groups. Moreover, the two groups of actors have different rights of action. If the competent authority goes beyond the legal demands of nature conservation and landscape maintenance, or if the applicator believes it has done so, he may seek remedy by way of legal protection. If, however, the impact permitted does not take full account of these demands, no legal remedy is possible, even if it is demonstrated beyond all doubt that there is still room for manoeuvre within the requirements of conservation (cf. Jarass 1997: 427). The interest group's limited or non-existent scope to take action is therefore also one of the main reasons why insufficient action is taken against enforcement deficits in the area of nature and landscape protection (cf. Lübbe-Wolff 1993).[16]

Enforcement deficits can be classified in three different basic types. Firstly, the impact regulation is applied too late or even not at all to some impacts. In other words, some impacts are actually started before they are examined for compliance with conservation regulations (cf. Schomerus 1987: 29). This can lead to circumstances which are often difficult to rectify later, and against the authorities do not always take action. Secondly, procedural faults can occur, such as the failure of the responsible authorities to properly observe the requirements of the permission procedure. Thirdly, enforcement deficits may also arise after the decision process and the planning of compensation measures has been completed. Many cases are known in which the legally binding compensation or substitution measures specified are implemented inadequately (or even not at all) owing to the failure of proper checks to be carried out; there have been other cases in which medium- and long-term compensation measures have not been maintained, and in which the compensatory payments received have been retained or not used for nature conservation purposes (cf. Heidtmann 1993: 74, Schomerus 1987: 27-31). According to information from BUND (Friends of the Earth Germany), losses amounting to millions of Deutschmarks are incurred every year. In the state of Hessen alone, losses over the past few years are said to total some DM 400 million (BUND 1996: 27). The lasting improvement of enforcement needs legal measures which in addition to the obligation of compensatory and substitution measures also stipulate an obligation to check their effectiveness. The first steps in this direction are contained in the planned amendment of the Bavarian Conservation Act, under which compensation measures are in future to be inspected by neutral, sworn experts.

[16] In my opinion, it makes sense to distinguish between the causes of enforcement deficits and the reasons for inadequate action against enforcement deficits. In addition to the complexitiy of relevant normative regulations and the resulting uncertainties of the regulating authorities, the causes of enforcement deficits are in particular inner-administrative shortcomings such as the authorities' insufficient personnel, funds, competence and organisation.

4 Summary

To sum up, four different actor groups are involved in carrying out the impact regulation: the administration, the target group, the interest group and the courts. Both the target groups and the interest groups try to exert an influence on the public administration during bargaining and negotiation processes; moreover, the decisions of the responsible authorities can be examined by the courts. The target group and the interest group have very different possibilities of participation and involvement, and their rights to take legal action are also fundamentally different. The insufficient participation of the interest groups, especially their limited possibilities of taking legal action, are probably a major reason for the currently poor state of enforcement (cf. Lübbe-Wolff 1993). The lasting improvement of enforcement can thus not be solely achieved by administrative reform; instead fundamental changes must be made to the environmental legislation in force. Above all, broadening the possibilities of involvement on the part of nature protection associations must be considered. It is to be welcomed that efforts have lately been made in this respect; the draft for a codification of an environmental law, which the Independent Expert Commission for the Preparation of an Environmental Law Code (*Unabhängige Sachverständigenkommission zum Umweltgesetzbuch*) has submitted to the German Federal Ministery of the Environment, also makes provision for steps in precisely this direction (cf. Lübbe-Wolff 1998).

References

Becker, B. (1989): Öffentliche Verwaltung. Lehrbuch für Wissenschaft und Praxis. Schulz, Percha

Bizer, K. (1997): Marktanaloge Instrumente im Natur- und Landschaftsschutz. Eine ökonomische Analyse des deutschen Naturschutzrechts. Analytica, Berlin

Bohne, E. (1984): Informales Verwaltungs- und Regierungshandeln als Instrument des Umweltschutzes. Verwaltungsarchiv 75, 343-373

Braun, D. (1997): Die politische Steuerung der Wissenschaft. Ein Beitrag zum 'kooperativen Staat'. Campus, Frankfurt/M., New York

Bulling, M. (1989): Kooperatives Verwaltungshandeln (Vorverhandlungen, Arrangements, Agreements und Verträge) in der Verwaltungspraxis. Die Öffentliche Verwaltung 42, 277-289

BUND (1996): Ausgleichsabgabe: 400 Millionen Defizit. Naturschutz und Landschaftsplanung 28, 27

Bussmann, W. (1993): Was haben Vollzugsstudien der Verwaltungspraxis gebracht? Schweizerisches Jahrbuch für Politische Wissenschaft 33, 261-275

Burmeister, J.H. (1988): Der Schutz von Natur und Landschaft vor Zerstörung. Eine juristische und rechtstatsächliche Untersuchung. Werner, Düsseldorf

Dammann, K. (1997): Vollzugsdefizite oder Vollzugsfehler? Juristische Risiken bei Umweltschutz- und Technikkonflikten. In: Hiller, P., Krücken, G. (Eds.): Risiko und Regulierung. Soziologische Beiträge zu Technikkontrolle und präventiver Umweltpolitik. Suhrkamp, Frankfurt/M., 39-69

Diefenbach, W. (1997): Klagemöglichkeiten der Naturschutzverbände auf dem Gebiet der Verkehrswegsplanung nach der Rechtsprechung des Bundesverwaltungsgerichts. Natur und Recht 19, 573-576

Dose, N. (1994): Kooperatives Recht. Defizite einer steuerungstheoretischen Forschung zum kooperativen Verwaltungshandeln. Die Verwaltung 27, 91-110

Freytag, C., Iven, K. (1997): Anforderungen und Konsequenzen der neuen Rahmengesetzgebungskompetenz des Bundes für das Bundesnaturschutzrecht. Natur und Recht 19, 121-128

Gassner, E. (1996): Bundesnaturschutzgesetz (BNatSchG), Kommentar, München

Hartje, V.J. (1994): Naturschutzabgaben. Eine ökonomische Bewertung ihres Einsatzes nach dem Bundesnaturschutzgesetz. In: Mackscheidt, K., Ewringmann D., Gawel, E. (Eds.): Umweltpolitik mit hoheitlichen Zwangsabgaben? Duncker & Humblot, Berlin, 331-347

Hasse, R. (1997): Nicht-intendierte Effekte kooperativer Risikoregulierung bei der Implementation des Gentechnikgesetzes. In: Hiller, P., Krücken, G. (Eds.): Risiko und Regulierung. Soziologische Beiträge zu Technikkontrolle und präventiver Umweltpolitik. Suhrkamp, Frankfurt/M., 70-89

Heidtmann, E. (1993): Landschaftsplanung und Eingriffsregelung, die wesentlichen Planungsinstrumente des Naturschutzes und der Landschaftspflege. Eine Einschätzung 15 Jahre nach Einführung des neueren Naturschutzrechts aus Sicht der Verwaltung. Natur und Recht 15, 68-75

Hucke, J. (1996): Die Implementation umweltpolitischer Programme – Strukturen und Erfolgsbedingungen. In: Gawel, E. (Ed.): Institutionelle Probleme der Umweltpolitik, Sonderheft der Zeitschrift für angewandte Umweltforschung. Analytica, Berlin, 59-72

Hucke, J., Ullmann, A.A. (1980): Konfliktregelung zwischen Industriebetrieb und Vollzugsbehörde bei der Durchsetzung regulativer Politik. In: Mayntz, R. (Ed.): Implementation politischer Programme. Empirische Forschungsberichte. Athenäum, Königstein/Ts., 105-126

Jarass, H.D. (1997): Die Beteiligung von Naturschutzverbänden an der Änderung von Planfeststellungsbeschlüssen und an Plangenehmigungen. Natur und Recht 19, 426-432

König, K., Dose, N. (1993): Klassifikationsansätze zum staatlichen Handeln. In: König, K., Dose, N. (Eds.): Instrumente und Formen staatlichen Handelns. Nomos, Baden-Baden, 3-150

Lowi, T.J. (1964): At the Pleasure of the Mayor. Patronage and Power in New York City, 1898-1958. Sage, London

Luhmann, N. (1994): Politische Planung. Aufsätze zur Soziologie von Politik und Verwaltung, 4. Auflage, Westdeutscher Verlag, Opladen

Lübbe-Wolff, G. (1992): Das Kooperationsprinzip im Umweltrecht – Rechtsgrundsatz oder Deckmantel des Vollzugsdefizits. In: Benz, A., Seibel, W. (Eds.): Zwischen Kooperation und Korruption. Abweichendes Verhalten in der Verwaltung. Nomos, Baden-Baden, 209-232

Lübbe-Wolff, G. (1993): Vollzugsprobleme in der Umweltverwaltung. Natur und Recht 15, 217-229

Lübbe-Wolff, G. (1998): Anforderungen an das Umweltgesetzbuch – Zum UGB-Entwurf der Unabhängigen Sachverständigenkommission. Zeitschrift für Angewandte Umweltforschung 11, 43-62

Mayntz, R. (1980): Die Implementation politischer Programme. Theoretische Überlegungen zu einem neuen Forschungsgebiet. In: Mayntz, R. (Ed.): Implementation politischer Programme. Empirische Forschungsberichte. Athenäum, Königstein/Ts., 236-249

Mitschang, S. (1994): Die Aufgaben und Instrumente des Naturschutzes und der Landschaftspflege nach dem neuesten Stand des Bundes- und Landesrechts. Umwelt- und Planungsrecht 16, 206-215

Ramsauer, U. (1997): Die Bedeutung der naturschutzrechtlichen Eingriffsregelung für die Planfeststellung am Beispiel der Transrapid-Planung. Natur und Recht 19, 419-426

Ring, I., Frank, K., Kneer, G. (1998): Incentives for nature conservation in urban landscapes, UFZ-Discussion Papers 4/1998, Leipzig

Schmidt, R., Müller, H. (1995): Einführung in das Umweltrecht. Beck, München

Schneider, J.-P. (1996): Kooperative Verwaltungsverfahren. Problemebenen der Kooperation in multilateralen Interessenstrukturen, aufgezeigt am Beispiel von Nachvollziehender Amtsermittlung, Vorhaben- und Erschließungsplan sowie Konfliktmittlung. Verwaltungsarchiv 87, 38-67

Schomerus, T. (1987): Defizite im Naturschutzrecht. Nomos, Baden-Baden

Schulze-Fielitz, H. (1992): Informales oder illegales Verwaltungshandeln? In: Benz, A., Seibel, W. (Eds.): Zwischen Kooperation und Korruption. Abweichendes Verhalten in der Verwaltung. Nomos, Baden-Baden, 233-253

Local Agenda 21 as an intergovernmental approach to sustainable development: a promising new strategy?

Sandra Greiner

Institut für Finanzwissenschaft, Universität Hamburg,
Von-Melle-Park 5, D-20146 Hamburg, Germany

1 Introduction

'Sustainable development' usually refers to the definition given in the Brundtland Report, which identifies it with actions taken to meet present needs without compromising the ability of future generations to meet their own needs. Despite the simplicity of this definition, the concept is beset by tremendous implementation difficulties, mainly due to its high level of complexity and aggregation. Since sustainability is the cumulative result of all individual activities, no particular individual, firm or government can be held responsible for its implementation. How progress in sustainability can be achieved in spite of this interdependence and individual disincentives to act for the common good is the main issue discussed in this paper. Based on the economic assumption of rational, self-interested individuals, it focuses on the incentive-compatibility of action taken at different levels of government by asking how incentives can be enhanced by institutional arrangements.

Local Agenda 21 marks the first time that the necessity for the lowest governmental level to be involved in an area of global concern has been claimed. Although at first glance counterintuitive, the paper argues for the rationality of this initiative in view of the good prospects which local government has in taking advantage of private interests. Since the issue of sustainability itself has both local and global dimensions (for although global environmental problems are just the cumulative effect of the vast amount of individual action, there are some macroeconomic parameters which greatly affect local action, such as terms of trade, exchange rates, energy prices, etc.), potential problem-solving institutions must also extend to these levels. This paper provides a conceptual outline of how complementary action favouring sustainable development can be taken by both central and local government.

2 The orthodox view: why nobody cares about sustainable development

Despite extensive scientific findings and growing concern about global environmental problems all over the world, actions taken to solve these problems as defined by the term 'sustainable development' are trailing behind. As has frequently been stated, a wide gap persists between awareness of the problems involved and (individual) action. This assessment comes as no surprise in traditional economic analysis, as the theory of public goods predicts that without state intervention, sustainable development is very unlikely.

The concept of sustainability covers not only the protection of the environment and natural resources, but also aspects of intergenerational and intragenerational equity, such as the necessity of redistribution between North and South (Agenda 21, preamble).[1] In view of their nature, these issues can be classified as public goods. Purely public goods as opposed to private goods are defined by two conditions. Firstly, it is impossible to exclude anyone from their consumption, irrespective of their own contribution (non-excludability principle); and secondly, consumption is not rival, meaning that one person consuming the good does not impair anyone else's ability to consume exactly the same amount and/or quality of the same good (principle of non-rival consumption) (Musgrave and Musgrave 1980: 55-57). A classic example of a purely public good is the lighthouse. A sailor being safely guided to the harbor by the light issuing from a lighthouse does not curtail the light provided for other sailors. Moreover, excluding some group of sailors from seeing the lighthouse is very difficult. However, as non-excludability and non-rival consumption need not necessarily go together, we have the following four possible combinations (see Figure 1):

EXCLUSION / CONSUMPTION	Feasible	Infeasible
Rival	1	2
Non-rival	3	4

Source: Musgrave and Musgrave (1980: 57).

Figure 1. Categories of private and public goods.

[1] Improving living conditions in the developing countries and environmental goals, long considered to be in strict opposition to each other, have now been reconciled within the concept of sustainable development. Since poverty in the developing countries is seen as one of the major causes of environmental destruction, e.g. deforestation, distributional measures have now become an indispensable factor of long-term environmental policy. However, discussing whether this new positive view of the relationship between social development and environmental improvements is actually more appropriate than earlier antagonistic views arguing that more environmental damage results from higher consumption if welfare in the developing countries is increased would go beyond the scope of this paper.

Whereas the first quadrant represents the case of a clear-cut private good, quadrants 2-4 represent different cases of public good.

Looking at the three issues of sustainability mentioned above, these can be classified under the public-good categories 2 and 4: If a desired distributional situation is politically defined (such as in Agenda 21, which explicitly quantifies the North-South transfers required), once implemented it can be considered a purely public good (Nowotny 1991: 29-30).[2] No-one can be excluded from benefiting from the situation, nor does anyone's utility derived from a situation of "intragenerational equity" reduce anyone else's ability to benefit. As for environmental protection and intergenerational equity, at least the condition of non-excludability holds.[3] They are, however, rival in consumption, since using natural resources in any form clearly implies changing their amount and/or composition. For example, preserving a certain stock of natural resources clearly reduces the opportunities available to those seeking to exploit it.

In economic theory, the non-excludability of goods gives rise to what is known as the 'prisoners' dilemma, a social dilemma situation with uncooperative behaviour being the dominant strategy for every individual. Since no-one can be excluded from consuming the public good even if they have made no contribution or payment, adopting a free-rider position maximises individual utility. As a result, in a world of rational and self-interested individuals, none of the public good will be provided. Hence the existence of a public good makes a case for government intervention in the market economy (Musgrave and Musgrave 1980: 54-62). This dilemma has often been stated by environmental economists for global environmental problems such as the greenhouse effect (Hanley et al. 1997: 37ff.; Krumm 1996: 6ff.).

3 Sustainable development: a case for central authority?

In addition to the dilemma surrounding general public goods, the global dimensions of sustainability further complicate its provision. Because of these dimensions, co-operative behaviour and contributions to the common good will be of no consequence if nobody follows suit. Positive effects can only be achieved on the basis of large-scale cooperation.

The theory of fiscal federalism takes these relations into account. To boost efficiency, the theory argues for a link between the public good's dimensions and the governmental level responsible for its provision (Kirsch

---

[2] The implementation of intragenerational equity can be seen as the provision of a variety of goods such as foreign aid and other forms of support.

[3] The difficult question of what is meant by 'intergenerational equity' will not be examined in detail here. Instead, it is argued that as a minimum, intergenerational equity requires the preservation of all essential non-substitutable natural resources, so that for the most part it can be presented under the goal of environmental protection.

1984: 118-119). According to Olson's principle of fiscal equivalence, the responsible level of government should coincide with the range and scope of the public good's effects on welfare (Olson 1969). In other words, in order to prevent inefficiencies on an institutional basis, individuals belonging to the collective which benefits from the public good should also belong to the collective which finances and decides upon the quantity and quality of the good. Public goods with a narrow range of welfare impact such as a public swimming pool should therefore be financed and decided upon at a local level, whereas far-reaching public goods can only be efficiently provided at a higher level such as regional or state government, or in international co-operation.

Hence, it is apparent from an economic viewpoint that the appropriate level for the provision of the global public goods commonly understood by the term sustainability can only be the global level (Zimmermann 1995: 222ff.). However, given the situation that at the global level the provision of public goods depends on voluntary agreements between sovereign states, the economic proposals face serious implementation difficulties. In the absence of a global authority, all international treaties must be formulated such that each contracting party's benefits from the agreement outweigh its losses (Kirchgäßner 1995: 38). If the provision of the public good itself does not lead to a beneficial situation for every single party, this could be achieved by the winners providing financial recompense for the other parties' losses. As Coase argued in 1960, an efficient allocation can thus be agreed even without state authority (Mueller 1991: 314).

Given the situation that the industrialised countries consume almost 80% of the world energy production and 75% of natural resources while only accounting for 20% of the world population, it is at the very least doubtful that a strict global regime of environmental and developmental obligations will be in every party's interest. In the case of the industrialised countries in particular, it is not apparent that the benefits of such agreements will outweigh their losses arising if, for instance, emissions of greenhouse gases have to be cut back to a sustainable level. With the prevailing distribution of resource consumption, these countries will face much higher compliance costs than developing countries.[4] In this case, the compensation alternative suggested by Coase is unworkable because this would mean developing countries compensating the industrialised countries for reducing their emissions.

---

[4] It is unclear whether the industrialised countries would also benefit more from international agreements on, for example, climate protection than the developing countries. On the one hand, they are said to be more aware of the problem because environmental interests correlate positively with economic well-being. On the other hand, however, they are less vulnerable to the adverse effects of climate change because they have more resources to be invested in adaptation strategies.

Notwithstanding the considerable progress that has been made in the past, these distributional effects are a constant problem in international environmental policy and may limit the scope of voluntary agreements (Heister 1997: 21; Görrisen 1993: 126 and 138ff.). There are reasons to assume that these agreements will lag behind what is considered sustainable:

> "The global-warming problem is, indeed, besieged by roadblocks that do not motivate nations to act. Until the major polluters can be convinced that global warming represents a real threat, I would anticipate that progress on a protocol to the Convention of Climate Change, which would mandate explicit CO_2 emission reductions, will be very slow. This progress hinges on a demonstration that benefits associated with curbing GHGs (greenhouse gas emissions) outweigh the associated costs." (Sandler 1997: 106).

4 Decentralised authority: a promising approach to global problems?

From the viewpoint of orthodox fiscal federalism, chapter 28 of Agenda 21 seems completely paradoxical. This chapter, which calls for local authorities to undertake a consultative process with their citizens and to adopt a Local Agenda 21 in their community (Agenda 21, paragraph 28.3), obviously violates the efficiency conditions discussed above. Furthermore, if national governments are considered too small and too weak to deal with global problems, how can local government be expected to do a better job?

It is widely accepted that local governments are better placed regarding their knowledge of the local situation and their citizens' preferences. Since community leaders are far more responsive to local needs than any federal or state government could possibly be, they can also find more suitable and thus more cost-efficient ways of achieving environmental goals (Butler and Macey 1996: 64). However, the question remains of what incentives local governments have to combat international environmental and developmental problems if their own (costly) contribution will have no noticeable effect on the global situation? Although it could be argued that the provision of global public goods would also have positive side-effects for local goods (reducing the amount of waste, for example, would serve both local and global interests), this incentive alone does not appear strong enough; if it were, such projects would in all likelihood already have been realised by local authorities. In the case of public goods with large amounts of spillover, even strong decentralisation-advocates would therefore argue for a central authority (Zimmermann and Kahlenborn 1994: 189).

5 Reconsidering sustainability: the relativity of the public-good assumption

On the basis of the arguments considered so far, the prospects of the huge environmental and developmental global challenges being successfully tackled appear rather poor. Assuming rational actors, neither the global nor the local level can be expected to take appropriate and/or sufficient action due to the lack of incentives. If social dilemmas persist at all levels of government which prevent the provision of the public good, there is little hope that the problems will actually be solved on the basis of idealism and goodwill alone. Is there any way out of this dilemma?

We will certainly not be able to come up with an easy answer if we continue with the simplified public-good model. Although the reduction of the view to the problem of public goods is helpful to understand the basic conflicts, we will have to adopt a more complex perspective for problem-solving strategies. In this context, the assumption of strict separation between private and public goods must be abandoned. Instead, we will operate with the more realistic assumption of mixed goods which have aspects of both private *and* public good. In between the two polar cases of purely private and purely public goods, the limits between private and public goods become fluid depending upon the level of externalities.[5] With a greater level of externalities, the degree of a good's public-ness rises. On the other hand, with only few externalities involved, a public good can turn into a "practically private" good (Bonus 1980: 50-51).

When we introduce the concept of externalities, we are no longer interested in the collective phenomenon "sustainability" as a delimited public good. Instead, we examine it in a more decomposed form and shed light on the uncountable and highly heterogeneous individual activities which in their aggregate form constitute sustainability. Sustainable development is regarded as the sum of positive externalities which private actions (meaning individual actions taken in order to meet private demands) exert upon the global situation. Therefore, unlike the undifferentiated view taken above, the key role will be given to individual reasons for sustainable or unsustainable behaviour. Taking a different tack and attempting to circumvent the dilemmas of public goods, the challenge will be to find strategies which turn sustainability into "practically private" goods.

---

[5] Externalities arise when the actions of one agent directly affect the environment of another agent. These can either be positive or negative (Varian 1992: 432).

6 Privatising sustainability: the example of the Fifty-Fifty Project

In order to study private stakes in the subject, the viewpoint must be reduced to the level of small-scale individual action. Instead of the highly abstract and comprehensive global view, we will therefore consider the strongly limited decentralised options for acting in favour of the global good. As an example, the "Fifty-Fifty Project" aimed at the more rational use of natural resources in schools will be examined in detail. As an individual project, the example illustrated below has a very limited impact upon the global situation. However, we feel that small-scale action of this type can make a vital contribution to the common good if copycat and snowball effects are taken into account. In terms of its exploitation of private interests, the Fifty-Fifty Project is a very instructive example. Therefore, rather than considering it a significant contribution to the high demands of Local Agenda 21, the example serves to illustrate the principles involved.

6.1 Fifty-fifty and private interests

In 1994, the Department of the Environment in Hamburg initiated the Fifty-Fifty Project as a model experiment designed to reduce water and energy consumption at 24 schools. Under the project, financial savings from saving energy and water are shared equally: half the savings are allocated to the resource-saving school, while the other half is assigned to the Department of Youth and Education, which funds the school's use of resources. The idea behind the concept is to reward the responsible actors (students, teachers and superintendents) for their efforts. Concentrating only on the potential for resource-savings via behavioural changes as opposed to technological measures, the Fifty-Fifty Project gives priority to the incentive system and can therefore be considered an economic approach to environmental problems (Umweltbehörde Hamburg 1996).

Since its initiation in 1994, the Fifty-Fifty Project has steadily advanced. Whereas at the beginning only a small group of pilot schools was included in the project, it has now been opened up to any Hamburg schools interested in participating. In 1994-97, the schools involved recorded considerable savings, as summarised in Figure 2 below. In total, the financial savings during the first three years of the project amounted to DM1.87 million, while a total of 5,762 tons of CO_2 and 30,941 m^3 of water were saved (Burchardt 1998).

For the purpose of our investigation it will be instructive to study the private good and externality components in this particular case. Looking at the private gains, there are at least two winning parties which profit directly from their participation in the Fifty-Fifty Project: Both the participating schools and the Department of Youth and Education gained DM936,000

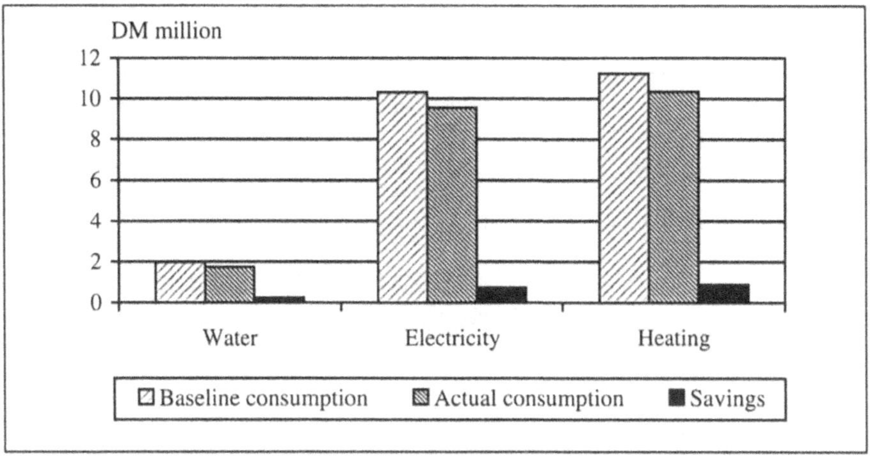

Source: Burchardt (1998), own calculations.

Figure 2. Cost-savings in DM million 1994-97 in all participating schools.

from successful resource-saving, far outweighing the efforts undertaken by the schools' members (switching off lights, etc.) and the administrative costs of the Department of Youth and Education.

The Department of the Environment can be identified as a second-glance winner of the project. Although it had to bear the costs of initiating the project, it also benefited from a considerable gain in prestige since the Fifty-Fifty Project has come to be widely recognised as a good example of decentralised resource-saving approaches. Weighing up these gains and losses, the Fifty-Fifty Project can on balance also be regarded as a very favourable project for the Department of the Environment and its members. After all, the overall costs of the project are relatively low, merely comprising administrative costs, making it much cheaper than projects requiring investment in new technology. Apart from the external study by the private engineering office IBEK (Bremen), whose proposals included the idea for the Fifty-Fifty Project, it was elaborated solely by the staff of the Department of the Environment. Moreover, if we assume that the primary aim of the Department is to take high-profile, publicly lauded action for environmental protection, the Fifty-Fifty Project scores relatively well since public awareness of the project is high – as is the boost to the Department's reputation.

The project losers are the power and water suppliers, chiefly Hamburg's power and gas utilities (HEW and Hamburger Gaswerke GmbH), which incurred a loss in turnover of DM1.64 million.

The following Table 1 sums up the private gains and losses of this example of Local Agenda 21 policy.

Table 1. Private gains and losses of the Fifty-Fifty Project.

	Private gains	Private losses
Department of Youth and Education	DM936,000 (1994-97)	Administrative costs
Department of the Environment	Gains in reputation	Administrative costs
Participating schools	DM936,000 (1994-97), gains in reputation	Efforts undertaken to save resources
HEW, Hamburger Gaswerke	None	DM1.64 million in turnover (1994-97)

Source: Burchardt (1998), own presentation.

These private gains and losses have private good character: they are rival in consumption and the non-excludability principle holds. Although the actual purpose for initiating the project was to make a contribution to the global public good, in view of the far clearer private advantages, meeting the global challenges was instead a positive side-effect of the project. The Department of the Environment's ingenuity assembled this winning coalition in which all the actors immediately involved in the Fifty-Fifty Project can each be considered to benefit, while the individual costs arising were externalised to third parties[6] not involved in setting up the project. By pursuing this dual course of global and individual benefits, the Fifty-Fifty Project turned out to be a rather successful and very dynamic project alternative.

6.2 Fifty-fifty and network effects

Besides the aspects of private good and its positive externalities upon sustainability, the Fifty-Fifty Project offers yet another relevant aspect to be studied in connection with the Local Agenda 21 process – the positive example set to others. After the first schools had successfully joined the project, other institutions in Hamburg learned from their example and began to work out their own Fifty-Fifty-Systems. In March 1998, the University of Hamburg officially decided to participate in the project and is now starting implementation. Furthermore, the city council's Departments of Commerce and of Urban Development (which are located in the same building) have also joined in. The Fifty-Fifty Project's influence is by no means limited to

[6] As far as HEW is concerned, the externalisation of costs has been relatively easy. With a high percentage of state-ownership at the time the Fifty-Fifty Project was initiated, HEW was according to its statutes obliged to promote energy-saving measures, despite this being contrary to its commercial interests. The conditions were favourable since the project initiators did not have to overcome opposition from the losing parties.

institutions in Hamburg, for with inquiries from local authorities as far away as Japan, the project's reputation has now acquired an international dimension. Thanks to the widespread demand for advice, the Department of Youth and Education has recently set up a sub-department comprising six officials solely in charge of the Fifty-Fifty Project.

For economic analysis, these effects can best be analysed within the framework of network externalities. By classical definition, network externalities are positive changes in utility that one consumer exerts upon other consumers of the same product. However, these are not reflected in market prices, meaning that the consumer is not rewarded to an extent matching his impact on others. Positive network effects are consequently not taken into consideration in his purchase decision (Steyer 1997: 206). Network effects can be direct (e.g. in a telephone network, where each user directly profits from each additional user because his communication possibilities increase); they can also be indirect. An example of the latter is the production of operating systems: The more consumers who use the same standard, the greater the variety of programmes will become and the faster prices will fall (Tirole 1993: 405).

In the case of the Fifty-Fifty Project, both direct and indirect network effects arise. Direct network effects accrue to the Department of the Environment in terms of prestige. With every additional institution implementing the Fifty-Fifty Project, awareness of its achievements is enhanced and even extends beyond the boundaries of Hamburg.[7] Indirect network effects are reflected in the lessons learned from different Fifty-Fifty Projects. The more institutions who participate, the more detailed knowledge will be acquired to further refine the concept. Aggregating the experience and creativity of all institutions will enable the flexible, efficient application of the concept to be improved and solutions to be found for future problems.

As can be observed from the examples, positive network effects require the existence of a common interest in the innovation.

7 Lessons to be learned from the Fifty-Fifty Project

Given the paramount issues of Agenda 21, the Fifty-Fifty Project appears rather insignificant. Even in relation to overall energy consumption in the City of Hamburg, the level of savings is almost negligible, accounting for merely about 0.013% (Burchardt 1998, Umweltbehörde Hamburg 1997: 182-183, own calculations). Furthermore, the concept of sustainability goes far beyond the simple claim of saving resources and requires the simultaneous consideration of economic, ecological and social aspects in a participa-

[7] This example is rather specific, as network effects are not reciprocal but only accrue to one party. The Department of the Environment can be distinguished as a consumer and the imitating bureaucracies as producers of network effects.

tory approach. Although the Fifty-Fifty Project obviously lacks social and/or developmental side-effects, the high degree of public participation can be considered an advantage. Seen in this light, although the project can by no means serve as a representative of the Local Agenda 21 process, it is a good example which highlights some general mechanisms and produces further insights into what might be relevant for the process as a whole.

The formation of winning coalitions and the exploitation of network effects are of course general driving forces which can lend momentum to Local Agenda 21 activities. Understanding how to identify and bring together such winning coalitions where private interests coincide with contributing to the global public good makes it easier to meet local sustainability goals. What part of Local Agenda 21 policies actually adheres to this principle is hard to determine since they have long become so manifold that a complete inventory is impossible. In a world of selfish and rational individuals as suggested in economic theory in general and in this paper in particular it can, however, be assumed that these projects will turn out to be the most successful in terms of substantive progress. Briefly outlined and following the propositions of public-choice theory,[8] the subsequent correlations between private utility and commitment to Agenda 21 activities could play a decisive role in this context: For community leaders, the reasons for supporting the Local Agenda 21 goals would be to improve their chances in upcoming elections and to gain prestige either within or outside their community. However, this mechanism can only work with knowledge of and a positive demand for Local Agenda 21 on behalf of the local electorate. As for administrative officials, gaining prestige is also important. As in the Fifty-Fifty Project example, ideal projects are low-budgeted and help to fulfill their official administrative goals in a way that is obvious to the public. Within bureaucracy, once a new field of activity has been adopted, it will usually tend to persist and develop its own momentum since the officials in charge have an interest in enlarging their budget and their range of competence as assumed by public-choice theory (Lane 1993: 58-64). The continuation of the projects will therefore be most likely.

Other important actors include environmental and developmental NGOs (non-governmental organisations), which will engage in Agenda 21 activities if these fit into their profile and can be communicated well to their constituencies. The private interest of businesses in participating lies in marketable projects or in improving public relations if deemed necessary. Com-

---

[8] Basically, the public-choice theory applies the economic assumption of rational and self-interested individuals to the political and the administrative sphere. As originally suggested by Anthony Downs, the public-choice literature has developed around the assumption that "parties formulate policies in order to win elections, rather than win elections in order to formulate policies" (Mueller 1993: 179).

bining these private interests in strategic alliances will promote the effectiveness of Local Agenda 21.

Network effects seem to have played a considerable role in the Agenda 21 process. One indication of this is the dynamic rate at which local government in Germany has become involved in Agenda 21 activities: Whereas in spring 1996 only 17% of the 157 German city councils questioned by the German Institute for Urban Development (DIFU) had decided to set up their own Agenda 21 (Rösler 1996: 48-49), the number has grown rapidly ever since. When the survey was repeated in the following year, the number had risen to 36% in 1996, with another 56 councils preparing the corresponding decision (Rösler 1998: 19). Besides the absolute increase in number, there has also been an increase in the speed with which new councils are joining in. Obviously, the growing number of local authorities already involved in the Agenda process makes joining more attractive for those councils which have not yet decided to do so.

Without going into detail, the reasons for positive network effects could from the viewpoint of individual rationality be as follows: For community leaders, supporting Agenda 21 will become more rewarding and offer more opportunities to enhance their prestige if there is wider knowledge of its existence and more attention is paid to it – which is certainly the case if the network of participating local authorities expands. This is also true for administrative officials and NGOs. Also, as in the case of the Fifty-Fifty Project, the catalytic effect of best practices can be considered to generally apply to the projects.

8 Local Agenda 21 – a second-glance success

Notwithstanding the various topics that have not been addressed in this paper, we suggest that network effects and private sustainability gains are two aspects of Local Agenda 21 which can considerably help to promote sustainability. Therefore, the re-delegation of responsibility for the global public good to the local level is appealing, despite being counterintuitive at first glance. Then again, these effects existed of course long before Agenda 21 was established. In Germany in particular, Local Agenda 21 itself has often been criticised for not providing any tangible change apart from giving a new name to activities related to regional sustainability already performed by local authorities. Private gains could have been exploited previously. The integrated, interdisciplinary and participatory approach advocated by Local Agenda 21 has been known and put into practice in urban development planning for the past 20 to 25 years (Bundesministerium für Raumordnung, Bauwesen und Städtebau 1996: 21). Many local authority officials will feel like the head of the Department of the Environment of Iserlohn, who stated that what is now claimed under the banner of Local

Agenda 21 reminded him of the highly complex urban development programmes of the 1970s and the urban marketing projects of the 1980s which had left him skeptical towards the feasibility and viability of such programmes (Ahrens 1996: 75). Because of the already existing programmes, some German communities even rejected the initiation of a Local Agenda 21 process (Rösler 1996: 47-49).

Returning to the initial question of whether or not Local Agenda 21 turns out to be a promising new strategy, it is not enough to simply point out the effects outlined above. We also have to ask whether it can promote the utilisation of these effects *beyond* what was already possible.

Here we argue that setting up Local Agenda 21 gives tremendous support to network effects and private gains. Although the global decision has no legal power and Agenda 21 remains a declaration of goodwill, in view of these effects it does, however, have significant impact on the local situation.

First of all, Local Agenda 21 represents an external standard with which local authorities all over the world ought to comply. This will raise positive network effects beyond those applying in the past since the potential for the exploitation of network effects has been enlarged to the maximum extent possible. Moreover, with Local Agenda 21, network effects are further enhanced by the institutionalised interchange of ideas and co-operation, for example under the International Council of Local Environmental Initiatives (ICLEI) set up to support local authorities worldwide in their Agenda 21 activities. Institution-building and the setting of central standards are forms of governmental intervention also advocated by economic theory in order to promote the exploitation of network effects and to correct market failure and inefficiencies (Röver 1996: 429).

As for the potentials of private sustainability gains, these are also expanded by Agenda 21 with respect to immaterial motivation. The high priority that has been attributed to the sustainability issue on behalf of the global level is of great symbolic value and thus creates new incentives e.g. for community leaders and officials. By re-evaluating the significance of the subject, their chances of gaining prestige via the adoption of sustainability policies are raised. Moreover, in view of the international attention paid to the subject, involvement in fields of global concern becomes more attractive to locally operating NGOs, which are especially dependent on concerted action because very often their activities for the global public good only make sense if they are not working alone.

As a third aspect not considered so far, one might also ask how the Local Agenda initiatives affect global decision-making in the long-run. By means of successful international campaigns presented to the United Nations such as the Cities for Climate Protection Program initiated by ICLEI (ICLEI 1997), local authority networks have become a new actor in international conferences. By demonstrating how progress in sustainability can be achieved without excessive economic sacrifices in local government all over the world (possibly even creating net gains for participating communities through positive side-effects), they are bound to weaken the dominant role of so-called national interest-positions from within.

9 Conclusion

This paper suggests that although the issue of sustainability is so huge that no subordinate governmental level could have an incentive to tackle the global problems involved or even hope to have a significant impact on its own, assigning responsibility to local government within a given framework is a promising strategy. The external creation of standards and institutions can provoke considerable changes within local authorities and can put to work private interest-based mechanisms. Hence, even without strict reduction targets or coercive strategies on behalf of the global level, additional momentum can be gained at the local level via central action.

The challenge facing local governments and administrative officials in charge of the Local Agenda 21 process (who are usually based in environmental departments) is to identify and set up strategic alliances. With regard to the projects' viability, these should not depend upon state subsidies but should be profitable for the participating parties. As in the Fifty-Fifty Project, the responsible administration should limit itself to bearing the costs for initiation. A great variety of possible partnerships could be considered as forms of co-operation. Besides the public-public partnership as in the case of the Fifty-Fifty Project, public-private partnerships and co-operation with the third sector (non-profit organisations) would also be feasible. Moreover, the co-operation partners do not necessarily have to be located within the area concerned, for the universal character of Local Agenda 21 means partners from outside can also be involved. One far-reaching alternative would be the consideration of co-operation with partners in developing countries within joint implementation and compensation projects (Michaelowa 1997: 131-134).

Besides making use of private interests, this paper argues for the vital role of concerted action being taken by central and decentral authorities. Central commitments and institution-building can significantly influence local initiatives. Conversely, the growing number of Local Agenda 21 initiatives will also affect decision-making at international conferences on sustainable development. Just how interaction benefits can be further increased, e.g. by more precise central standards and also via various forms of global compensation payments for local efforts, remains to be examined.

References

Ahrens, P.P. (1996): Das Beispiel der Stadt Iserlohn. In: DIFU (Ed.): Lokale Agenda 21: Dokumentation eines Erfahrungsaustauschs. Berlin, 73-78

Bonus, H. (1980): Öffentliche Güter und der Öffentlichkeitsgrad von Gütern. Zeitschrift für die gesamte Staatswissenschaft (JITE) 136, 50-81

Bundesministerium für Raumordnung, Bauwesen und Städtebau (Ed.) (1996): Lokale Agenda 21. Bonn

Bundesministerium für Umwelt, Naturschutz und Reaktorsicherheit (1992): Konferenz der Vereinten Nationen für Umwelt und Entwicklung im Juni 1992 in Rio de Janeiro – Dokumente – Agenda 21. Bonn

Burchardt, R. (1998): Das Energiesparprojekt "fifty-fity". Unpublished paper to be received from: Umweltbehörde Hamburg, Fachamt für Energie u. Immissionsschutz, Stromreferat 165

Butler, H.N., Macey, J.R. (1996): Using Federalism to improve Environmental Policy. The AEI Press, Washington DC

Görrisen, T. (1993): Grenzüberschreitende Umweltprobleme in der internationalen Politik. Nomos Verlagsgesellschaft, Baden-Baden

Hanley, N., Shogren, J., White, B. (1997): Environmental Economics in Theory and Practice. Macmillan Press Ltd, Houndsmills Basingstoke

Heister, J. (1997): Der internationale CO_2-Vertrag: Strategien zur Stabilisierung multilateraler Kooperation zwischen souveränen Staaten. J.C.B. Mohr (Paul Siebeck), Tübingen

ICLEI (Ed.) (1997): Local Government Implementation of Climate Protection – Report to the United Nations. ICLEI-Canada

Kirchgäßner, G. (1995): Internationale Umweltprobleme und die Problematik internationaler öffentlicher Güter. Zeitschrift für angewandte Umweltforschung 8(1), 34-44

Kirsch, G. (1984): Fiscal Federalism. WiSt 3, 118-124

Krumm, R. (1996): Internationale Umweltpolitik – Eine Analyse aus umweltökonomischer Sicht. Springer, Berlin Heidelberg New York

Lane, J.E. (1993): The Public Sector. London and others

Michaelowa, A. (1997): Klimapolitik und Hamburgs lokale Agenda 21 – ein globaler Ansatz. In: Eine Welt Netzwerk Hamburg e.V, Jochen Menzel (Eds.): Rio – Hamburg und zurück. Konkret Literatur Verlag, Hamburg

Mueller, D.C. (1991): Constitutional Rights. Journal of Law, Economics, and Organization 7(2), 313-333

Mueller, D.C. (1993): Public Choice II. Cambridge University Press, Cambridge

Musgrave, R., Musgrave, P. (1980): Public Finance in Theory and Practice. 3rd Edition. McGraw-Hill Kogakusha Ltd., Tokyo and others

Nowotny, E. (1991): Der öffentliche Sektor – Einführung in die Finanzwissenschaft. 2nd Edition. Springer, Berlin Heidelberg New York

Olson, M. (1969): The Principle of "Fiscal Equivalence": The Division of Responsabilities among different Levels of Government. The American Economic Review 59, 479-487

Rösler, C. (1996): Stand der Umsetzung der Lokalen Agenda 21 in deutschen Städten. Erste Ergebnisse der Difu-Umfrage. In: DIFU (Ed.): Lokale Agenda 21: Dokumentation eines Erfahrungsaustauschs. Berlin, 45-55

Rösler, C. (1998): Deutsche Städte auf dem Weg zur Lokalen Agenda 21. Ergebnisse der 2. Umfrage. In: DIFU (Ed.): Städte auf dem Weg zur Lokalen Agenda 21. Dokumentation des 2. Erfahrungsaustauschs. Berlin, 17-26

Röver, A. (1996): Marktversagen aufgrund von Netzwerkexternalitäten. WiSt 8, 427-429

Sandler, T. (1997): Global Challenges: An approach to environmental, political, and economic problems. Cambridge University Press, Cambridge

Steyer, R. (1997): Netzexternalitäten. WiSt 4, 206-210

Tirole, J. (1993): The Theory of Industrial Organization. 6th Printing, The MIT-Press, Cambridge MA

Umweltbehörde Hamburg (Ed.) (1996): Fifty-fifty. Hamburg

Umweltbehörde Hamburg (Ed.) (1997): Umweltatlas Hamburg 1997. Hamburg

Varian, H. (1992): Microeconomic Analysis. 3rd Edition. W.W.Norton & Company Inc., New York London

Zimmermann, H. (1995): Umweltföderalismus im globalen Maßstab. In: Zimmermann, K., Hansmeyer, K.-H., Henrichsmeyer, W. (Eds.): Umwelt und Umweltpolitik in Europa: Zwischen Vielfalt und Uniformität. Europa Union Verlag, Bonn

Zimmermann, H., Kahlenborn, W. (1994): Umweltföderalismus. Ed. Sigma, Berlin

Outlook

Perspectives for economic research into sustainable policies

Kilian Bizer

SOFIA – Sonderforschung Institutionenanalyse, Fachhochschule Darmstadt, Haardtring 100, D-64295 Darmstadt, Germany

1 Introduction

Sustainability is a highly controversial concept when it comes to policy recommendations. While widespread agreement is possible on the necessity of the sustainable utilisation of environmental resources, there is no consensus on what a sustainable policy actually is. Although any environmental policy issue could illustrate this point, a look back at the general discussion of the possibility of sustainable policies once started by an article of Ludwig et al. (1993) in *Science* and taken up in a special issue of *Ecological Applications* will best illuminate the difficulties. It reveals that researchers are rather ambiguous over whether the concept of sustainability yields policy recommendations or not. With respect to resource management, Ludwig et al. (1993) hold that uncertainty is the crucial issue to be addressed and that it necessarily leads to overexploitation. The reason why Ludwig et al. are so frustrated by natural resource management is exemplified by the California sardine and the Peruvian anchoveta (see Ludwig et al. 1993: 17). The California sardine was overexploited despite warnings from the California Division of Fish and Game. The fishing industry countered these warnings with scientific statements which claimed that a pelagic species[1] could not possibly be overexploited. There is as yet no consensus. The Peruvian anchoveta became a major source of fish meal for cattle feed once the Pacific sardine collapsed. The yields decreased rapidly from 10 million metric tons to zero within just a few years. General agreement on the causes of collapse has not been reached.

In their follow-up article in *Ecological Applications*, Hilborn and Ludwig (1993: 550) conclude that ecological research will never bring about results with sufficient certainty to serve policy-makers as a primary tool for decision making. Although their critics agree on the role of uncertainty, they stress it as something which ecological research must address (Lee 1993: 563; Costanza 1993: 580).

[1] Pelagic species live in the upper waters of the open sea, as opposed to benthic species, which live at the bottom of the sea.

This article is structured around three basic questions. Firstly, why is sustainability still a controversial issue and what follows from the controversy methodologically? Secondly, what can modern economics contribute to the development of sustainable policies? And thirdly, which interdisciplinary paths appear promising?

The first question will be addressed by briefly summarising the analysis of a cultural theorist (Roe 1996), who basically claims that researchers are culturally bound in their view of sustainability (section 2). We will then conclude some methodological implications from this claim (section 3). In this article it is suggested that a major contribution of economics lies in providing a behavioural model to predict outcomes under a given set of incentives and institutions (section 4). If this is what economics can do, its role within interdisciplinary research entails links to both the social and the natural sciences (section 5).

2 Competing interpretations of sustainability

The dispute in *Ecological Application* shows that sustainability is also a highly controversial issue within academia, where competing views prevail concerning the management of natural resources. These views are of a fundamental nature, i.e. they are held by individuals as a general belief largely independent of the immediate situation.

As individual beliefs depend on the culture, interpretations of sustainability vary according to cultural beliefs about nature and its management (Roe 1996). Cultural beliefs are transmitted to individuals by upbringing, and they are moulded by the specific education, peers, parents etc. Yet although individuals belong to a culture, they are also capable of changing it. An incentive to change culturally transmitted beliefs occurs if the actual world differs from that stipulated. Such differences surprise individuals, and if they are frequently or fundamentally surprised, they will change their view in order to avoid surprises.[2]

The article by Ludwig et al. was recognised by their critics as a fundamental change of view by the authors. Ludwig et al. originally viewed resources as manageable and nature as a system which is tolerant up to certain thresholds but reacts perversely beyond such levels. But apparently their stipulated world differed substantially from the actual world in many cases they reviewed. Roe (1996) concludes that Ludwig et al. (1993) changed their view because they searched for clear boundaries in ecosystems and never found them. By changing their view, Ludwig et al. (1993) shift their hopes from the management of ecosystems as the supply side of natural

[2] In the terms of social psychology, individuals reduce dissonance between their own views and the world as it is experienced (Festinger 1957).

functions to the demand side, i.e. the demand of nature by society. In other words, they believe that social systems can be more easily managed than natural systems.

The shift in their fundamental view drew attention because generally natural scientists are trained to understand nature as something which responds according to systematic characteristics. The approach of natural scientists is to categorise, to identify components and links as the causes and effects of changes. Underlying their analysis is the view that nature is a system, i.e. an ecosystem, and researchers are schooled to detect the driving forces of its phenomena. Of course, the natural sciences do not hold the belief that any change of an ecosystem could be predicted. But their research aims to develop appropriate models in order to achieve or to support a given state of an ecosystem. On the basis of such research, they give warnings to reduce resource utilisation or to leave certain areas to themselves. In this sense, natural scientists hold the general belief that ecosystems are predictable and can be intentionally influenced. This belief is part of the tacit dimension of their knowledge (Polanyi 1966), just as social scientists basically believe that society can be influenced by norms and incentives etc. Again, this does not mean that social scientists believe that social systems can actually be managed in all circumstances. But they are trained to ask the questions which direct them towards manageability.

Thus, the doubts of Ludwig et al. (1993) present a serious challenge to a fundamental belief of their discipline. The challenge increases as they place their hopes in the management of social systems about which their discipline has nothing to offer. For social scientists do not hold beliefs about nature which stem from their discipline any more than natural scientists hold beliefs about social systems founded in their disciplinary training. As sustainability involves ecological as well as social and economic criteria, interdisciplinary research is confronted with the explicit disciplinary beliefs each researcher holds as well as those beliefs which are not specific to the discipline. These beliefs will clash when researchers attempt to define sustainability. To bring about a constructive interdisciplinary and cross-cultural discussion, academic actors should defend their views by making their fundamental beliefs transparent as well as presenting the evidence in support of their view.

Sustainability, therefore, should not be understood as a final set of goals which should be achieved, but instead as a continuous interdisciplinary attempt to interpret evidence in the light of cultural beliefs about the manageability of natural and social systems. The best way to promote interdisciplinarity is to defend one's own view, and the best way to defend one's view is to insist that evidence matters, always, whatever the view (see with this argument Roe 1996: 12 referring to Wildavsky 1995: 15).

3 Methodological pluralism

Aside from understanding sustainability as a concept requiring interdisciplinary research, it also calls for methodological pluralism in the academic disciplines concerned. Methodological pluralism functions as a form of sensitivity analysis by revealing how strongly results depend on a given scientific approach. It also serves as a way of managing uncertainty.

Managing uncertainty is seen as a crucial element in research into sustainability (Norgaard 1989, Funtowicz and Ravetz 1994). The carrying capacities of ecosystems are not well known and the changes of ecosystems are often unpredictable (Köhn 1998). Often, these uncertainties give rise to vague policy goals which in turn lead to equally vague policy instruments (Bizer 1999). As sustainability is meant to bring about "a balance between three interrelated systems – the economy, social systems and ecological systems" (*O'Hara, Shandas* and *Vazquez* in this volume), vague policies are only desirable if the systems remain resilient or take a turn for the better.

Methodological pluralism, to put it simply, means little more than being open to different methodological approaches and accepting different results as mirrored images of uncertainty. Before turning to some of the practical implications, it should be emphasised that such pluralism entails a somewhat modest research programme: There is no discipline which is able to give ultimate answers on sustainability, and there is no research project, however extensive, which can yield a precise recipe for sustainable policy. For this reason, many contributions in this volume stress the importance of implementing dialogues and supporting consensual strategies among stakeholders.

In this context, one of the crucial questions asked by *O'Hara* et al. (in this volume) is "who evaluates the trade-offs?", and they point out that selecting measures is already part of evaluating viable development paths. Discourse processes, then, are an invitation to participants to express their concerns as well as their priorities and allow individuals to respond in an integrated way instead of only as consumers or producers regardless of their other "going concerns" (Commons 1934).

The general issue of stakeholder approaches is to represent interests of the relevant groups. If interests are strong, they will be well represented; if they are weak they might not justify participation and the group will be neglected. In many cases this mechanism serves as a selecting process of "true" and "false" interests. But in those cases where many individuals have only little interest, their costs of organisation might not be overcome by the expected results, or in other words, transaction costs will prevent them from participating. Then, interests are not well represented and the results of the stakeholder process will be biased. Unfortunately, environmental problems often affect large groups with high organisational costs.

A practical solution could be to compensate certain groups for participating. Such compensation must come from the state or a dominant interest group which is interested in reaching a consensus for a given project. But compensation may be seen as a veiled buy-out of citizen initiatives or environmental groups. Instead of receiving funds directly, environmental groups have frequently been reimbursed for the expenses incurred in drawing up technical reports supporting their choice (see the Alcoa Agreement in Gebers et al. 1999, also WZB 1994).

If a private group such as a company reimburses environmental groups, it will choose the group according to its interests. But if the state engages in reimbursement, some criteria must be developed to decide whose interests are legitimate (including to what extent) and are therefore worthy of financial support, and whose interests are not. Such an assessment can be designed using traditional cost-benefit analysis.

Stakeholder processes are one way of depicting group interests in public decision-making. The accompanying research aid provides information on the consequences of decisions. As the consequences are uncertain, it appears reasonable to take various methodological approaches to illustrate the dependence of outcomes on the underlying assumptions and methodological limitations.

4 Economics as a science of behaviour

Normative economics is concerned with identifying the best outcome and its characteristics. In the context of sustainability, normative economics is concerned with describing why sustainability is a necessary condition for the development of a society. Apart from the continuing discussion of what the characteristics of a "best" solution concerning sustainability are, in this section some concepts are introduced which allow a broader perspective on the analysis of human behaviour in economics. It will start by outlining the behavioural model of standard economics. Then, three concepts will be discussed which connect economics to two of its sister disciplines, sociology and psychology.

Economists base their work on the assumption that all societal action must be explained by observing individuals. This *methodological individualism* has one obvious advantage – it examines the individual interests behind social forces. Whereas sociological research may take a group or a movement as the driving entity, economists inevitably ask what the interests of the individual group members are and analyse them in terms of individual benefits and costs, i.e. relative prices (Lindenberg and Frey 1993).

Over the years, the classic behavioural model of economics has frequently been criticised. Among the deficiencies detected early on was the absence of a preference theory. Economists restricted their analysis to behaviour, and they explained behaviour by assuming rational choice on the basis of basically unknown preferences (see Figure 1). These unknown preferences were only revealed by actual decisions. But as rationality in itself makes no sense to the individual without being related to motives, knowledge of preferences plays a major role in predicting behaviour (Sen 1993, Lewin 1996). Revealed preference theory also fails whenever individuals have good reasons to keep true preferences private and tell public lies. This is the case, for example, if individuals are asked about their share in financing public goods or if revealing true preferences will lead to persecution (Kuran 1995).

The standard behavioural model of economics is based upon the assumption that individuals behave rationally. It is assumed that individuals have a given set of preferences which for any given set of choices allow the most desirable one to be identified. Depending on restrictions such as budgetary constraints etc., the individual chooses the best alternative.

In order to conduct interdisciplinary research, which besides ecology includes other disciplines of the social sciences as well as law, this should be understood as a working hypothesis. Individual behaviour may well depend on complex institutional settings, it may be habitual rather than rational, and it can be based on frames or cognitive limits. In a rational model, such behaviour may appear as anomalous or irrational behaviour, although interdisciplinary institutional analysis might be able to explain it by showing how social frameworks affect individual decisions.

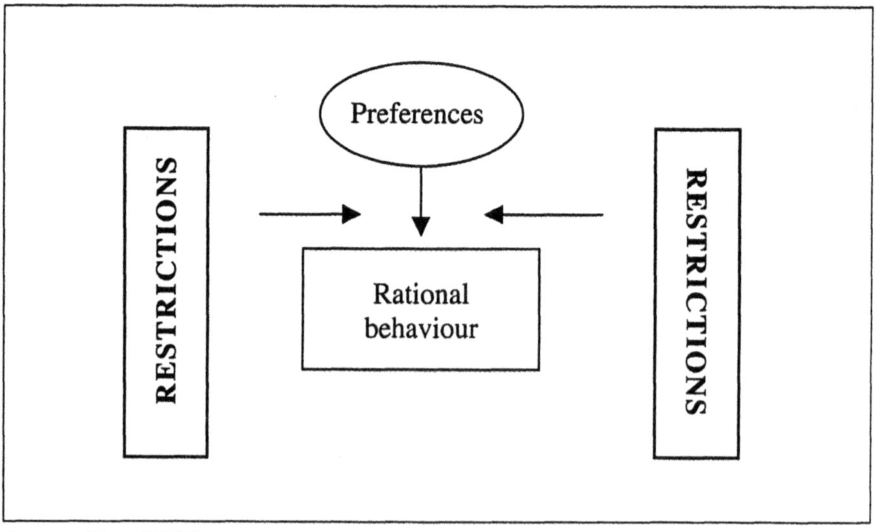

Source: Bizer (1998).

Figure 1. Standard model of rational behaviour.

Modern economics inspired by institutional, psychological or sociological analysis is about to take the various aspects of human behaviour into account again which were previously neglected. In order to suggest some cornerstones of a behavioural model for interdisciplinary research, three important modifications of the standard economic model will be discussed: cognitive limits, endogenous preferences and institutions.

4.1 Cognitive limits

Cognitive limits are frameworks of decision-making based on specific opinions, beliefs or knowledge. As far as knowledge is concerned, cognitive limits can be translated into bounded rationality as described by Simon (1955). Then, individuals take into account that information is costly and turn to satisficing needs instead of maximising utility. In a framework of purely rational individuals, decisions bounded by cognitive limits appear "irrational", "anomalous" or "biased".

An example of cognitive limits is described by Friedman (1998: 934) in which individuals are confronted with three face-down cards in an experiment. In a game called "Monty Hall's Three Doors" they know that two cards are non-winning cards; the other one wins. They have to pick one card, then the game host *turns over a non-winning card* and gives them the chance to switch to the remaining card. Most of the roughly 100 subjects stuck to their initial choice. Only about a third of the subjects switched (Friedman 1998: 935), even though this is the rational decision. As the initial probability of winning is 1/3 for the first choice, that leaves an initial probability of 2/3 for the remaining two cards. And as the host *always* turns over a non-winning card, the probability of the last card being the winning card rises to 2/3.

In the experiment subjects had to repeat the game ten times. Up to the seventh time the rate of switching increased from about ten to forty percent, only to steadily decrease to 30 percent by the tenth time. On average 28.7 per cent switched in the first run. In a second run the individuals were exposed to specific modifications. These included measures of learning enhancement such as a track record of their decisions or the overall statistical results of forty individuals. Such measures increased rationality. In the second run the switching rate rose to 46.0 percent. Nevertheless, a majority still remained irrational.

In fact, the example reveals that individuals are not as capable of identifying dominant strategies as researchers want them to be. Many of them might actually simplify the experiment by applying Bayesian posterior probabilities to the remaining two cards, i.e. they take the revealment of a blank by the host as a change of probability to 1/2 for each of the two remaining cards (Friedman 1998: 936).

Individuals have insufficient statistical knowledge, and even if they are helped to enhance their process of decision-making they cannot adapt to it effortlessly, i.e. at no cost or within short periods. But it is not only the lack of specific knowledge which causes cognitive limits. Sometimes the existence of specific knowledge or beliefs has the same effect. Take the example of physicians being asked:

> "if a test to detect a disease, whose prevalence is 1/1,000, has a false positive rate of 5 percent, what is the chance that a person found to have a positive rate actually has the disease, assuming you know nothing about the person's symptoms?" (Boudon 1996: 130).

More than half of the physicians answered that the subject is ill with a probability of p = .95. Only 18 percent of the physicians answered correctly by saying that the answer is p = .02.[3] In his analysis of the case Boudon reconstructs the systematic "false" answers to the professional understanding of "test" among physicians and the unspecified denominator of "rate". The question leaves open whether false positive refers to "true positive" or "true negative". Most of the physicians related it to "true positive" because they associate "test" with something which holds a minimal validity; otherwise it would not be a test. Consequently, the majority of physicians expected a probability of nearly 1.[4]

The latter example illustrates that a belief connected with a specific form of knowledge may constitute a cognitive limit. It also shows that such limitations may be acquired by education or profession and may take the form of explicit beliefs ("a test has minimal viability") much more than simple information deficits. Boudon, similar to Friedman in the previous context, recommends that research should look for good reasons for apparently biased choices in order to explain anomalies. While Friedman implicitly views anomalies normatively as something individuals will and should overcome, Boudon suggests explaining such behaviour because "the criteria which make a set of reasons good are hard to define absolutely and should rather be defined relatively" (Boudon 1996: 148).

4.2 Endogenous preferences

In the standard economic model, preferences are given exogenously and do not change over time. Taking preferences as given and assuming rational

---

[3] "[T]he correct argument is: T [number of persons positive for 100,000 people] = M [number of people ill] + 5% (not M) = 100 + 5% (99,900) = 5,095. Hence, Pr (M/T) = 100/5,095 = 0.02." Boudon (1996: 131).

[4] "T (number of persons positive for 100,000 people) = M (number of people ill) + 5% M = 100 + 5% (100) = 105. Hence it is readily drawn: Pr (M/T) = 100/105 = .95." Boudon (1996: 131).

behaviour, individuals become computational machines or "rational fools" (Sen 1977).

Preferences are understood as "reasons for behaviour, that is, attributes of individuals that (along with their beliefs and capacities) account for the actions they take in a given situation." (Bowles 1998: 78). Preferences are institutionally transmitted, cognitively mediated and depend on the individual's social and cultural context. Preferences include emotions as well as norms which the individual has internalised. In contrast to Figure 1, Figure 2 shows that institutions influence preferences and individual behaviour.

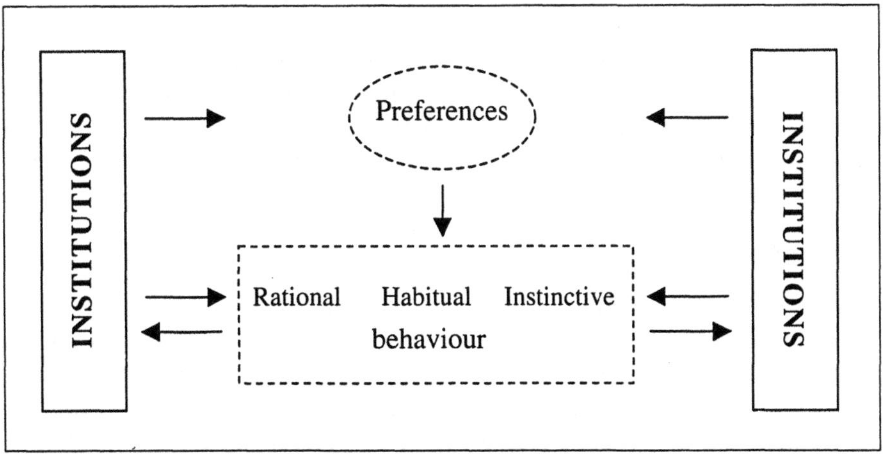

Source: Bizer (1998).

Figure 2. Interdependence of institutions and individual preferences and behaviour.

In the standard behavioural model, the regulation of markets must satisfy the condition of setting the correct incentives in order to induce the required behaviour. If preferences are endogenous, such regulation can alter behaviour by changing preferences and might lead to adverse effects. Frey and Oberholzer-Gee (1997) termed this the "crowding out of intrinsic motivation" and presented evidence from siting two repositories to store nuclear waste in Switzerland.

In order to demonstrate a crowding out of intrinsic motivation, a sample of inhabitants of two sites selected for the repositories were asked about their acceptance. The questioning took place shortly before an actual referendum on the same topic, and the questionnaire was designed as a self-contained referendum: 50.8 percent voted in favour, and 44.9 percent against the nuclear waste repository (for details, see Frey and Oberholzer-Gee 1997: 749).

When the respondents were asked whether they would accept the repository if the Swiss Parliament offered compensation, the level of acceptance dropped to 24.6 percent. The actual amount of fictitious compensation ranged from more than US $2,000 to $8,700 and had no significant effect on the result.

Frey and Oberholzer-Gee (1997) conclude that monetary compensation can destroy altruistic values. This limits the applicability of price incentives, at least in those areas where intrinsic motivation exists, and suggests that policy research should generally attempt to explore preferences. For the behavioural model of economics, "crowding out" is an important extension as many policy issues such as environmental, health, public safety suggest that altruistic and possibly intrinsic preferences are prevalent.

The design of policy instruments should, in conclusion, reflect that preferences can be endogenous, i.e. the design of the instrument influences preferences and thereby behaviour. Although Frey and Oberholzer-Gee (1997) review a case of compensation paid to individuals, negative price incentives such as charges could have a symmetric effect.

4.3 Institutions

It was shown that cognitive limits are a characteristic of human decision-making processes, and that cognitive limits include more than just computational limitations. It was also demonstrated that the assumption of exogenous preferences – which in itself, so to speak, forms a cognitive limitation of economists – should be relaxed in certain circumstances and preference endogeneity should be allowed. These modifications of the standard behavioural model of economics enable questions to be asked about the origin of preferences, a question standard economics has entirely neglected.

In an attempt to grasp an answer, Figure 2 suggests that preferences are influenced by institutions. The "old" institutionalists (Commons 1934, Dewey 1922) perceived institutions as something with both societal and individual dimensions. An individual institution could be a personally adopted habit, for example eating an apple around its equator first, or a group-specific routine, such as wearing buggy trousers, or a culture, for instance quoting your sources in an academic environment. Institutions, according to this approach, are not simply organisations, but rules which govern thought, behaviour and the interaction of human beings.

The fundamental influence of institutions stems from learning. Individuals learn behaviour from peers and parents. But not all learning takes place in a conscious process. Most of it is performed subconsciously and transmitted culturally. Cultural learning provides individuals with categories and concepts as well as with interpretations of phenomena beyond the immediate experience of the individual (Denzau and North 1994: 15). Also, all attempts to reconcile habitual and rational behaviour are based on the fact that behaviour is learned:

> "Habits form part of our cognitive abilities. Cognitive frameworks are learned and emulated within institutional structures. The individual relies on the acquisition of such cognitive habits, before reason, communication, choice or action are possible." (Hodgson 1998: 180).

Rational behaviour is a specific part of habitual behaviour. Individuals learn to think consciously in means-ends frameworks, and they learn to apply rational frameworks according to optimisation rules or according to satisficing rules. Yet the acquisition of behavioural rules never starts on a *tabula rasa*. The human mind is shaped by genetic, environmental and cultural influences long before rationality and intelligence begin to work (Plotkin 1994: 163).

Therefore, whenever the design of policy instruments and the prediction of behaviour are concerned, the learning of individuals must be included. Interest focuses on what kind of institutions hinder or inspire individuals to learn, what kind of learning is induced by a specific institution, and how all this affects the outcome under a certain policy instrument.

Within the standard approach of economics, one could be tempted to think that behaviour is adjusted as the restrictions are changed. Such fine tuning of incentives brings about the desired behaviour if (a) individuals perceive the changes as such, (b) they can adjust their behaviour effortlessly (absence of transaction cost), and (c) if such changes of behaviour do not clash with preferences.

In section 4.1, the game "Monty Hall's Three Doors" demonstrated that cognitive limits can have a strong influence on behaviour. It was also discussed that academic training can make it difficult to comprehend a situation (Boudon's physicians). In the context of institutions and regulation as a specific form of institutions, this should be explored more deeply.

Sustainability requires regulation. And regulation occurs if the state attempts to interfere with the behaviour of individuals. Such interference can take many forms. The most prominent regulative instruments are command-and-control and economic incentives. Voluntary approaches are also a means of changing behaviour, although they might not directly qualify as regulation.

On the assumption that the state should always interfere in the least possible way without endangering the overall goals, the general policy should be to give the relevant agents the chance to voluntarily comply. Of course, there is little reason to expect great and substantial changes from voluntary approaches. But there can be no doubt that voluntary agreements, for example, can serve as a supplementary instrument within a general command-and-control or economic incentives framework (Bizer 1999). The important feature of all voluntary approaches is that they potentially do not result in a "crowding out" of intrinsic motivation. And, theoretically speaking, they might even be capable of "crowding in" motivation. Such a "crowding in" is not empirically established. And it appears only reasonable that it takes more than voluntary approaches to induce individuals to adopt norms such as civic duty etc.[5]

However, a general regulative framework which allows for voluntary approaches but ensures compliance is "responsive regulation" (Ayres and Braithwaite 1992). This approach responds to the specific conditions of the individuals concerned. It is not naive in assuming goodwill but offers consensual strategies as initial alternatives before resorting to stricter measures if this goodwill should fail. Such an approach gives clear rules to the relevant agents. It builds an institution itself while respecting the institutional setting of the agents. In other words, the framework of responsive regulation allows the regulated individual to be perceived as an institutionally and culturally embedded actor while securing the policy goals.[6]

In conclusion, the design of sustainable policies should take into account that individuals frequently act under cognitive limits or with ethical intentions. Policy approaches which simply assume rational behaviour are liable to crowd out intrinsic motivations and may actually worsen the situation. But if the design of sustainable policies takes preferences into account, allows for cognitive limits, and develops appropriate institutions, its effects might easily go beyond what could be done by strict command-and-control policies.

5 From ecological to socio-ecological approaches

Before a sustainable policy is designed, the basic ecological functions must be known to which the social system should respond. The standard approach of economics was to demand an environmental goal, and then to design policy instruments which would afford the least resources. The design of cost-effective instruments is still a major issue in environmental economics, and cost-effectiveness is the crucial advantage economic instruments have over command-and-control policies or voluntary approaches.

The critical point of cost-effectiveness is that it implies a limited perspective. Policy instruments affect decisions in more ways than one. If mul-

[5] In Nicomachean Ethics (1103b: 3-7), Aristotle holds that the difference between a good and a bad constitution is whether it is capable of bringing virtue to the citizens. A little later (1103b: 22-25) he points out the importance of education.

[6] Ayres and Braithwaite (1992) quote many positive examples of responsive regulation from Australia. But if responsive regulation is just a cover for deregulation, as Steinzor (1998) points out for the United States EPA, it harbours more risks than chances.

tiple goals exist, they frequently offset each other. Say there is an environmental goal such as an emission level of 1,000 tons of SO_2 per annum. Another goal is not to disturb the economy by shifting costs onto it. And finally, there is a regional goal to support industry despite their emissions. A tax on SO_2 would be cost-efficient. A spatially differentiated command-and-control approach would do the most damage to the economy if enforcement were strict. And a voluntary approach would perhaps not help the goal to be attained, but would not disturb the economy (Bizer 1999). In this context, the criterion of cost-effectiveness is of little help. Despite the fact that of the policies described cost-effectiveness is only achieved with the tax, the weighing-up of trade-offs remains an open issue just as in open discourse processes. This issue of making good decisions in multi-criteria contexts is addressed by *Rauschmeyer* (in this volume), who concludes that neither cost-benefit analysis, nor open discourses, nor any other normative judgement can substantiate final decision-making. He suggests applying multicriteria analysis instead as a decision aid where it can help alternative decisions to be found.

But there is not only the problem that cost-effectiveness will not be the only argument for or against a specific approach. In addition, the interface between ecology and economics is inadequately represented by simply assuming that there is an emission level of a certain substance which is sustainable. The difficulties are usually addressed under the concepts of *critical loads, safe minimum standards, carrying capacities* or *levels of resilience.* These concepts do not result in specific amounts of emissions as required by traditional environmental economics. Frequently, the underlying ecological systems require extensive modelling to reflect the major links of the system. It is a traditional strength of ecological economics to maintain close links with the natural sciences, especially ecology, and to reflect the specific conditions of the ecosystem. Most of the articles in this volume take up issues along these lines. *Frank* and *Ring* (in this volume), for example, develop a model for optimum biotope establishment with a given amount of subsidies. *Hellegers* (in this volume) analyses the effects of Common Agricultural Policy on High Nature Value farming, and concludes that subsidies should be redirected by including environmental conditions. And *Schmieman* and *Van Ierland* (in this volume) present a dynamic analysis of acidification and tropospheric ozone taking into account the cumulative environmental effects of SO_2, NO_x and VOC.

Section 4 dealt with economics as a science of behaviour. Implicitly, a position of *understanding* the motives of behaviour was taken. This is clearly outside mainstream economics where preferences are still dealt with as something exogenously given. *Understanding* human behaviour can be based on "an introspective survey of the operation of those motives by which men are mainly influenced in their economic activities" (Keynes

1890: 173 quoted in Lewin 1996: 1298). Although this understanding of human behaviour is the primary cause of broadening the behavioural model, it should be emphasised that in many instances the predictive power compared to the standard economic model of behaviour would be enhanced. This is at least true for those cases where endogenous preference changes are prevalent or where institutions influence behaviour in a systematic and non-rational way. It is also true where cognitive limits frame decisions.

If indeed the behavioural model suggested brought about additional predictive power, it could be successfully defended within the discipline of economics. In order to do so, the model must not be correct in terms of the underlying assumptions, but it must produce good results (Friedman 1953). But Friedman's notion of a good model represents very much what is frequently criticised as "misplaced concreteness" (Daly and Cobb 1990: 36) which describes an abstraction which is not reflected by its own limits. Taking this approach, one may very well be able to describe time series of the past by abstracting the model. But it does not follow that the model will be able to predict the future. In order to predict, the relevant parameters must be included, and these are determined by heuristics, by understanding the actual causes of behaviour. If these are neglected, the prediction of the model will eventually fail. Understanding human behaviour prevents such "misplaced concreteness", even though it does not prevent errors concerning causes and effects.

To understand behavioural causes, standard economics must be supplemented by the findings of disciplines which carry an understanding of the dependence of individuals on their societal context as well as the relationship between individual preferences and behaviour. In this respect, economics can greatly profit from both sociology and psychology (Hodgson 1998, Frey 1997, Lewin 1996, Sen 1977).

Social phenomena, such as the environmental movements in Europe during the 1980s, are of distinct relevance to an ecologically sound policy. But research addressing such phenomena is still largely unconnected to environmental economics and ecological economics. Currently, sustainability is discussed at many political levels. Perhaps the most interesting is Local Agenda 21, which has induced many local round tables where industry, environmental and social groups as well as the local administration discuss and coordinate local initiatives. While it is uncertain what the outcome will be, Local Agenda certainly has an influence on building common values among the parties concerned as well as improving mutual information flows.

Another aspect not yet fully included in ecological economics is the law and its influence on building a basis for communication, information and bargaining. Interdisciplinary work between economics and the law should play a major role as many issues of implementation rest on the possibilities determined by law. And whatever the environmental problem, the underlying institutional setting must be analysed in legal terms. In this volume, an analysis of the legal framework is given by *Centner* and *Gunter*, who study pesticide collection programmes in the United States, and by *Kneer*, who takes a sociological perspective on the existing body of nature protection law in Germany and finds a severe enforcement deficit which could be lowered by increasing the participation rights of environmental groups. Such approaches need to be further developed with an interdisciplinary emphasis.

6 Outlook

*Inter*disciplinary research is much more scarce than *intra*disciplinary research. But interdisciplinary research is also much more costly in many respects: it takes more communication of basic concepts, a great willingness to understand and to explain, and enormous efforts in designing a common research agenda. Therefore research should be welcomed which can contribute a solution without requiring interdisciplinary efforts. An example of such a contribution is *Greiner* (in this volume) who shows in the context of Local Agenda 21 that an appropriate institutional framework can induce agents to act as if climate control were among their goals. Disciplinary boundaries are frequently perceived as obstacles. Yet *Greiner's* article shows that they serve as a helpful institution: they frame our minds. Of course, it is taking disciplinary boundaries too far if we overlook a solution for the sake of rigorous analysis within our field. This is what Daly and Cobb (1990: 164) criticise when they attempt to reintroduce the *homo oeconomicus* to his community. Policy advice guided exclusively by standard economics will fail to perceive that individuals might act upon their beliefs rather than on a narrow cost-benefit analysis.

Research into sustainable policies usually raises questions which can only be answered in an interdisciplinary context. Unfortunately, within the academic community, interdisciplinarity is still less rewarded than disciplinary research. While it makes perfect sense that one should be competent in one's discipline before entering interdisciplinary projects, the art of designing relevant policy advice on sustainability only begins when disciplinary boundaries are crossed.

The apparent limits to sustainable development are twofold: first and foremost, we do not know the ecological thresholds or resilience of ecosystems, and regardless of the doubts dumped on the issue by Ludwig et al. (1993), ecological research must aim to know (Costanza 1993). Secondly, even in cases where we do know, or to put it more carefully, where knowledge prevails over uncertainty for some time, the political system is unable to overcome the resistance of interest groups. This is the case, for example, with issues of intra- and intergenerative distribution, as well as with many environmental problems. Research in economics must take up these issues in conjunction with the other social sciences. To do so,

> "[e]conomics must be more than ecological. It must be socio-ecological. That is, not only must the biophysical bases of economic activity be understood, but so must the sociological and political. Economic activity involves the transformation of physical materials and energy, but this occurs through the medium of socio-economic structures, the understanding of which is equally important to economic analysis." (Jacobs 1996: 14).

References

Aristotele (1985): Nicomachische Ethik, hrsg. von Günther Bien, Felix Meiner Verlag, Hamburg

Ayres, I., Braithwaite, J. (1992): Responsive Regulation, Transcending the Deregulation Debate. Oxford University Press, New York, Oxford

Bizer, K. (1998): Institutionen, Individuen und Responsives Recht. SOFIA–Discussion papers No. 98-3, Sonderforschung Institutionenanalyse (SOFIA) Darmstadt

Bizer, K. (1999): Voluntary agreements: cost-effective or a smoke screen for failure? Environmental Economics and Policy Studies, forthcoming

Boudon, R. (1996): The 'Cognitivist Model'. A Generalized Rational-Choice Model. Rationality and Society 8(2), 123-150

Bowles, S. (1998): Endogenous Preferences: The Cultural Consequences of Markets and other Economic Institutions. Journal of Economic Literature 36 (March 1998), 75-111

Commons, J.R. (1934): Institutional economics: Its place in political economy. Macmillan, New York

Costanza, R. (1993): Developing ecological research that is relevant for achieving sustainability. Ecological Applications 3, 579-81

Daly, H.E., Cobb, J.B. Jr. (1990): For the common good. Green print, London

Denzau, A.T., North, D.C. (1994): Shared Mental Models: Ideologies and Institutions. Kyklos 47, 3-31

Dewey, J. (1922): Human Nature and Conduct. An Introduction to Social Psychology. Random House, New York

Festinger, L. (1957): A theory of cognitive dissonance. Stanford University Press, Stanford

Frey, B. (1997): Not Just for the Money. Edward Elgar, Cheltenham UK

Frey, B., Oberholzer-Gee, F. (1997): The Cost of Price Incentives: An Empirical Analysis of Motivation Crowding Out. American Economic Review 87(4), 746-755

Friedman, M. (1953): Essays in Positive Economics. The University of Chicago Press, Chicago

Friedman, D. (1998): Monty Hall's Three Doors: Construction and Deconstruction of a Choice Anomaly. American Economic Review 88(4), 933-946

Funtowicz, S.O., Ravetz, J.R. (1994): The worth of a songbird: ecological economics as a post-normal science. Ecological Economics 10, 197-207

Gebers, B., Biekart, J.W., Bizer, K. et al. (1999): New Instruments for Sustainability – The New Contribution of Voluntary Agreements to Environmental Policy. Cameron and May, London

Hodgson, G.M. (1998): The Approach of Institutional Economics. Journal of Economic Literature 36 (March 1998), 166-192

Hilborn, R., Ludwig, D. (1993): The Limits of Applied Ecological Research. Ecological Applications 3, 550-552

Jacobs, M. (1996): What is Socio-Ecological Economics? Ecological Economics Bulletin 1, 2 (April)

Keynes, J.N. (1917) [1890]: The scope and method of political economy. Macmillan, London

Köhn, J. (1998): An approach to Baltic Sea Sustainability. Ecological Economics 27, 13-28

Kuran, T. (1995): Private Truths, Public Lies: The Social Consequences of Preference Falsification. Harvard University Press, Cambridge, MA

Lee, K. (1993): Greed, Scale Mismatch, and Learning. Ecological Applications 3, 560-564

Lewin, S.B. (1996): Economics and Psychology: Lessons For Our Own Day From the Early Twentieth Century. Journal of Economic Literature 34, 1293-1323

Lindenberg, S., Frey, B.S. (1993): Alternatives, Frames, and Relative Prices: A Broader View of Rational Choice Theory. Acta Sociologica 36, 191-205

Ludwig, D., Hilborn, R., Walters, C. (1993): Uncertainty, Resource Exploitation, and Conservation: Lessons from History. Science 260, 17-36

Norgaard, R.B. (1989): The case for methodological pluralism. Ecological Economics 1, 37-57

Plotkin, H.C. (1994): Darwin machines and the nature of knowledge: Concerning adaptations, instinct, and the evolution of intelligence. Penguin, Harmondsworth

Polanyi, M. (1966): The tacit dimension. Doubleday & Co., Garden City, N.Y.

Roe, E.M. (1996): Sustainable development and cultural theory. International Journal of Sustainable Development and World Ecology 3, 1-14

Sen, A. (1977): Rational Fools: A Critique of the Behavioural Foundations of Economic Theory. Journal of Philosophy and Public Affairs 6(4), 317-44

Sen, A. (1993): Internal Consistency of Choice. Econometrica 61(3), 495-521

Simon, H. (1955): A Behavioral Model of Rational Choice. Quarterly Journal of Economics 69(1), 99-118

Steinzor, R.I. (1998): Reinventing Environmental Regulation: The Dangerous Journey From Command To Self-Control. Harvard Environmental Law Review 22, 103-202

Wildavsky, A. (1995): But it is true? A Citizen's Guide to Environmental Health and Safety Issues. Harvard University Press, Cambridge, MA

WZB (1994): Der Neusser Kompromiß. WZB-Mitteilungen 63 (März 1994), 22-26

Contributions to Economics

Hagen Bobzin
Indivisibilities
1998. ISBN 3-7908-1123-8

Helmut Wagner (Ed.)
Current Issues in Monetary Economics
1998. ISBN 3-7908-1127-0

Peter Michaelis/Frank Stähler (Eds.)
Recent Policy Issues in Environmental and Resource Economics
1998. ISBN 3-7908-1137-8

Jessica de Wolff
The Political Economy of Fiscal Decisions
1998. ISBN 3-7908-1130-0

Georg Bol/Gholamreza Nakhaeizadeh/
Karl-Heinz Vollmer (Eds.)
Risk Measurements, Econometrics and Neural Networks
1998. ISBN 3-7908-1152-1

Joachim Winter
Investment and Exit Decisions at the Plant Level
1998. ISBN 3-7908-1154-8

Bernd Meyer
Intertemporal Asset Pricing
1999. ISBN 3-7908-1159-9

Uwe Walz
Dynamics of Regional Integration
1999. ISBN 3-7908-1185-8

Michael Carlberg
European Monetary Union
1999. ISBN 3-7908-1191-2

Giovanni Galizzi/Luciano Venturini (Eds.)
Vertical Relationships and Coordination in the Food System
1999. ISBN 3-7908-1192-0

Gustav A. Horn/Wolfgang Scheremet/
Rudolf Zwiener
Wages and the Euro
1999. ISBN 3-7908-1199-8

Dirk Willer
The Development of Equity Capital Markets in Transition Economies
1999. ISBN 3-7908-1198-X

Karl Matthias Weber
Innovation Diffusion and Political Control of Energy Technologies
1999. ISBN 3-7908-1205-6

Heike Link et al.
The Costs of Road Infrastructure and Congestion in Europe
1999. ISBN 3-7908-1201-3

Simon Duindam
Military Conscription
1999. ISBN 3-7908-1203-X

Bruno Jeitziner
Political Economy of the Swiss National Bank
1999. ISBN 3-7908-1209-9

GPSR Compliance

The European Union's (EU) General Product Safety Regulation (GPSR) is a set of rules that requires consumer products to be safe and our obligations to ensure this.

If you have any concerns about our products, you can contact us on ProductSafety@springernature.com

In case Publisher is established outside the EU, the EU authorized representative is:

Springer Nature Customer Service Center GmbH
Europaplatz 3
69115 Heidelberg, Germany

Batch number: 10725973

Printed by Printforce, the Netherlands